# Visual Object Tracking from Correlation Filter to Deep Learning

Weiwei Xing • Weibin Liu • Jun Wang •
Shunli Zhang • Lihui Wang • Yuxiang Yang •
Bowen Song

# Visual Object Tracking from Correlation Filter to Deep Learning

Weiwei Xing ⓘ
School of Software Engineering
Beijing Jiaotong University
Beijing, China

Weibin Liu ⓘ
Institute of Information Science
Beijing Jiaotong University
Beijing, China

Jun Wang ⓘ
College of Electronic Information
Engineering
Hebei University
Baoding, Hebei, China

Shunli Zhang ⓘ
School of Software Engineering
Beijing Jiaotong University
Beijing, China

Lihui Wang
Department of Information
and Communication
Army Academy of Armored Forces
Academy
Beijing, China

Yuxiang Yang ⓘ
School of Software Engineering
Beijing Jiaotong University
Beijing, China

Bowen Song
School of Software Engineering
Beijing Jiaotong University
Beijing, China

ISBN 978-981-16-6244-7        ISBN 978-981-16-6242-3   (eBook)
https://doi.org/10.1007/978-981-16-6242-3

This Springer imprint is published by the registered company Springer Nature Singapore Pte Ltd.
The registered company address is: 152 Beach Road, #21-01/04 Gateway East, Singapore 189721,
Singapore

# Preface

This book introduces some representative trackers through practical algorithm analysis and experimental evaluations. This book is intended for professionals and researchers interested in visual object tracking, and also can be used as a reference book by students. Readers will get comprehensive knowledge of tracking and can learn state-of-the-art methods through this content. In general, this book is organized as follows:

Chapter 1 introduces the wide application, existing challenges, and basic concepts in visual object tracking. Chapter 2 introduces some algorithm foundations from correlation filter basics, typical deep learning model, and performance evaluation. Chapter 3 presents the correlation filter-based visual object tracking. Chapter 4 mainly introduces correlation filter with deep feature for visual object tracking. Chapter 5 introduces deep learning-based visual object tracking. Finally, Chap. 6 summarizes our work and points out the potential future research directions for visual object tracking in appearance model construction and update.

Beijing, China                                                                                            Weiwei Xing
June 2021

# Acknowledgements

First of all, we would like to thank every one of the collaborators who worked tirelessly together and contributed to producing this monograph. We would also like to thank the organizers of visual tracking benchmarks for providing large-scale datasets to evaluate the trackers comprehensively. We would highly appreciate the help and assistance of the current and graduated students in our research group during the production of this book. In particular, we wish to thank Mr. Xinjie Wang, Mr. Menglei Jin, and Mr. Jiayi Yin for their time and efforts in providing materials and reviewing for revising the entire book and Mr. Hui Wang, Ms. Huaqing Hao, Mr. Yanhao Cheng, Ms. Yuxin Wang, and Mr. Yang Pei for improving the individual chapters of this monograph. We also want to especially thank the editor of Springer, Jing Dou, for her patience, support, guidance, and editorial assistance in the course of the preparation of this work. Part of the content in this book is based on the work supported by the National Natural Science Foundation of China under Nos. 61876018 and 61976017 and the Beijing Natural Science Foundation under No. 4212025.

This monograph, especially those proposed object tracking algorithms in Chaps. 3–5, is mainly prepared based on the following research papers of our group. We would like to give a special acknowledgement to all the authors for their contributions and to the related publishing organizations for their permission to use these materials. The referenced papers are as follows:

1. Jin, M.L., Liu, W.B., Xing, W.W.: A robust visual tracker based on DCF algorithm. International Journal of Software Engineering and Knowledge Engineering, 29(11n12):1819–1834 (2019)
2. Jin, M.L., Liu, W.B., Xing, W.W.: A robust Correlation Filter based tracker with rich representation and a relocation component. KSII Transactions on Internet and Information Systems, 13(10): 5161–5178 (2019)
3. Wang, J., Liu, W.B., Xing, W.W., Zhang, S.L.: Visual object tracking with multi-scale superpixels and color-feature guided Kernelized Correlation Filters. Signal Processing: Image Communication, 63: 44–62 (2018)

4. Yang, Y.X, Xing, W.W., Zhang, S.L.., et al.: Visual tracking with long-short term based Correlation Filter. IEEE Access, 8, 20257–20269 (2020)
5. Wang, J., Liu, W.B., Xing, W.W.: Discriminative context-aware Correlation Filter network for visual tracking. In: Intelligent Systems and Applications. Advances in Intelligent Systems and Computing, 1250, pp.724–736 (2020)
6. Wang, J., Liu, W.B., Xing, W.W., Wang, L.Q., Zhang, S.L.: Attention shake siamese network with auxiliary relocation branch for visual object tracking. Neurocomputing, 400, 53–72 (2020)
7. Yang, Y.X, Xing, W.W., Zhang, S.L., et al.: A learning frequency-aware feature siamese network for real-time visual tracking. Electronics, 9(5):854 (2020)
8. Song, B.W., Lu, W., Xing, W.W., Xiang, W.: Real-time object tracking based on improved adversarial learning. In: IEEE International Conference on Systems, Man, and Cybernetics (SMC), pp. 3576–3581 (2020)
9. Yang, Y.X, Xing, W.W., Wang, D.D., Zhang, S.L., et al.: AEVRNet: Adaptive exploration network with variance reduced optimization for visual tracking. Neurocomputing, 449, 48–60 (2021)

# Contents

# About the Authors

**Weiwei Xing** received the B.S. degree in Computer Science and Technology and the Ph.D. degree in Signal and Information Processing from the Beijing Jiaotong University, Beijing, China, in 2001 and 2006, respectively. She was a visiting scholar at the University of Pennsylvania, PA, USA, during 2011–2012. She is currently a professor at the School of Software Engineering, Beijing Jiaotong University and leads the research group on Intelligent Computing and Big Data. Her research interests include visual object tracking, computer vision, pattern recognition, and deep learning.

**Weibin Liu** received the Ph.D. degree in Signal and Information Processing from the Institute of Information Science at Beijing Jiaotong University, China, in 2001. During 2001–2005, he was a researcher in the Information Technology Division at Fujitsu Research and Development Center Co., LTD. Since 2005, he has been with the Institute of Information Science at Beijing Jiaotong University, where currently he is a professor in Digital Media Research Group. He was also a visiting researcher in the Center for Human Modeling and Simulation at University of Pennsylvania, PA, USA, during 2009–2010. His research interests include computer vision, computer graphics, image processing, virtual human and virtual environment, and pattern recognition.

**Jun Wang** received the M.S. degree in Pattern Recognition and Intelligent Systems from the Hebei University, China, in 2015. He received the Ph.D. degree in Signal and Information Processing from the Institute of Information Science at Beijing Jiaotong University, China, in 2020. He was also a visiting researcher in Visual Object Tracking at the University of Central Florida, USA, during 2018–2019. Currently, he is an associate professor at the College of Electronic Information Engineering, Hebei University. His research interests include image processing, computer vision, visual object tracking, and pattern recognition.

**Shunli Zhang** received the B.S. and M.S. degrees in Electronics and Information Engineering from the Shandong University, Jinan, China, in 2008 and 2011, respectively, and the Ph.D. degree in Signal and Information Processing from the Tsinghua University in 2016. He was a visiting scholar at the Carnegie Mellon University, Pittsburgh, from 2018 to 2019. He is currently a faculty member at the School of Software Engineering, Beijing Jiaotong University. His research interests include pattern recognition, computer vision, and image processing.

**Lihui Wang** received the Ph.D. degree in Signal and Information Processing from the Beijing Jiaotong University, Beijing, China, in 2011. She is currently a lecturer in the Department of Information and Communication, Army Academy of Armored Forces. Her main research interests include computer application, big data analysis, and three-dimensional reconstruction.

**Yuxiang Yang** received the B.S. degree in Computer Science and Technology from the Northeastern University of China, Liaoning, China, in 2014. He is currently pursuing the Ph.D. degree with the School of Software Engineering, Beijing Jiaotong University. His research interests include image processing, deep learning, reinforcement learning, and object tracking.

**Bowen Song** received the B.S. degree in Computer Science and Technology from the School of Computer Science and Technology, Heilongjiang University, China, in 2018. She received the M.S.E. degree in Software Engineering from the School of Software Engineering, Beijing Jiaotong University, China, in 2021. Her research interests include visual tracking and deep learning.

# Chapter 1
# Introduction

Visual tracking is a rapidly evolving field of computer vision that has been attracting increasing attention in the vision community. One reason is that visual tracking offers many challenges as a scientific problem. Moreover, it is a part of many high-level problems of computer vision, such as motion analysis, event detection, and activity understanding. In this chapter, we give a detailed introduction to visual tracking which includes basic components of tracking algorithms, difficulties in tracking, datasets used to evaluate trackers, and evaluation metrics.

## 1.1  Motivation and Challenge

How to make computers have vision and analyze the information in videos has always been a desire of human. In recent years, Artificial Intelligence (AI) gradually applied in various industries, along with the continuous improvement of machine learning and deep learning research [1], such as automatic driving [2], speech recognition [3], face recognition [4], VR games [5], etc. Visual object tracking, which provides the trajectory characteristics for behavior analysis by predicting the state of the object in the video, is one of the important components in Computer Vision (CV). It has been widely applied in intelligent monitoring [6], human-computer interaction [7], automatic driving [8, 9], virtual reality [10, 11], crime projections [12], surgical navigation [13], aerospace [14, 15] and so on.

Figure 1.1 shows some common application scenarios for visual object tracking. In smart traffic, visual object tracking can judge whether there is a violation by monitoring the tracking the vehicles, such as illegal U-turn, speeding, etc. In human-computer interaction, computers can determine the instructions of the person and make corresponding actions without pressing the buttons, by tracking and calculating the states of human body parts, such as hands, legs, head, eyes, etc. In automatic driving, visual object tracking can perceive the change and motion of

© The Author(s), under exclusive license to Springer Nature Singapore Pte Ltd. 2021
W. Xing et al., *Visual Object Tracking from Correlation Filter to Deep Learning*,
https://doi.org/10.1007/978-981-16-6242-3_1

| Intelligent monitoring | Human-computer interaction | Autopilot | Virtual reality |
| Crime prediction | Surgical navigation | Missile navigation | Military reconnaissance |

**Fig. 1.1** Some applications of visual object tracking

the objects around the vehicle to provide a certain reference for vehicle computer. In virtual reality, visual object tracking combined with object segmentation algorithm can calculate the location and shape of the objects. For example, in the application of virtual changing, the shape of cloth can be automatically adjusted to make it more suitable for the outline of the human body. In crime prediction, monitoring and tracking the sudden aggregation and dispersion of people or other objects in video could predict the abnormal and possible emergencies and help the police find out illegal crimes and improve the social environment. In surgery navigation, the success rate of surgery can be improved by tracking the position and posture of the scalpel and probe. Visual object tracking also has important applications in military fields. In missile navigation and military reconnaissance, the objects are often moving and the cameras on the missiles are also jittering, visual object tracking can be used to determine the position of the object and adjust the attitude of the missile to improve the guidance accuracy.

Several countries and institutions have established major projects around visual object tracking. In the early 1997s of American, Project Video Surveillance And Monitoring (VSAM) was co-founded by Carnegie Mellon University and the David Sarno Research Center, with the funding from the Defense Advanced Research Projects Agency (DARPA) [16]. This project aims to track people and cars in complex environments continuously with multiply video sensors, and develops visual surveillance systems. DARPA then funded project Human Identification at a Distance (HID) in 2000, which is led by University of Maryland [17]. The Framework 5 on EU information technologies also created Annotated Digital Video for Surveillance and Optimized Retrieval (ADVISOR) project in 1999 which used to manage the urban traffic systems and analyse pedestrian behaviour. At the same time, Hiroshima University in Japan hosted the Cooperative Distributed Vision Project (CDVP) project of intelligent monitoring from 1996 to 1999, in order to build community-oriented monitoring systems. The Institute of Automation, the Chinese Academy of Science and Technology also presided over the Visual Surveillance Star (VStar) project for urban traffic monitoring and management.

In addition to the visual object tracking based projects, many top publications and conferences in the world also continue to promote the progress and innovation of visual object tracking algorithms. Visual object tracking, which is the basic research direction of video processing, occupies a certain proportion in the top journals and conferences in Computer Vision (CV) every year. The top conferences of visual object tracking direction are mainly IEEE International Conference on Computer Vision (ICCV), IEEE Conference on Computer Vision and Pattern Recognition (CVPR), European Conference on Computer Vision (ECCV) and International Joint Conference on Artificial Intelligence (IJCAI), etc. While, the top journals are mainly IEEE Transactions on Pattern Analysis and Machine Intelligence (TPAMI), IEEE Transactions on Signal Processing (TSP), IEEE Transactions on Image Processing (TIP) and IEEE Transactions on Multimedia (TMM), etc. It can be seen that the research of visual object tracking is of great theoretical value and extensive application background.

With the continuous progress of science and technology, the demand of people for visual object tracking is also increasing. The objects to be tracked changes from rigid objects to non-grid objects. The background of video is from simple to complex, such as occlusion, motion blur and some other complex situations. Besides, the demand for tracking time also grows. The essence of visual object tracking is an online learning problem with the small size of non-annotated samples: How to construct a robust representation model, fast motion model and effective update model is the mainly challenge in visual object tracking. In addition, tracking tasks are more and more close to the real life. There are multiple tracking challenges in one sequence. Thus, how to design a universal tracing algorithm which could deal with the multiple challenges in one sequence is one of the key problems in the research of visual object tracking. Wu et al. [18] divided the challenges existing in visual object tracking into 11 categories. The details of the 11 challenges are as follows:

**Illumination Variation, IV**  IV refers to the situation in which the illumination of the object region changes significantly as the video plays, as shown in Fig. 1.2. This situation could lead to a sharp change in color and gray based features of the object. Thus, the color or gray feature based appearance model could not represent the object well and lead to the tracking failure.

**Scale Variation, SV**  SV refers to the situation in which the ratio of the bounding box in the initial frame to the bounding box in current frame exceeds a specific

**Fig. 1.2** Example of illumination variation

**Fig. 1.3**  Example of scale variation

**Fig. 1.4**  Example of occlusion

**Fig. 1.5**  Example of deformation

**Fig. 1.6**  Example of motion blur

threshold $ts > 1$, usually, $ts$ is set to be 2, as shown in Fig. 1.3. The scale change of the object will lead to the change of the number of pixels, which is a great challenge to construct the appearance model. Some tracking methods could find the center of the object, but fail to estimate the size. These methods may show a high accuracy score but a low success rate.

**Occlusion, OCC**  OCC refers to the situation in which the object is partially or completely occluded as the video plays, as shown in Fig. 1.4. The occlusion challenge will change the statistical and structural features of the object, which brings challenges to the tracking methods. Thus, how to re-detect and continue to track the object when occlusion occurs is one of the main problems that the tracking methods should be solved.

**Deformation, DEF**  DEF refers to the situation in which the shape of the object change significantly compared to the initial frame. This challenge is primarily aimed at non-rigid objects, as shown in Fig. 1.5. Although deformation challenge does not change the statistical features of the object, such as gray histograms, it changes the target structural characteristics. This makes it difficult to determine the boundary of the objects, and the bounding box may not cover the object properly.

**Motion Blur, MB**  MB refers to the situation that the object image is blurred due to the movement of the object or the shake of camera, as shown in Fig. 1.6. The

**Fig. 1.7**  Example of fast motion

**Fig. 1.8**  Example of in-plane rotation

**Fig. 1.9**  Example of out-of-plane rotation

blurring of the object image not only loses the detail information of the object, but also changes the structure information of the object and makes the boundary of the object become blurred. These makes boundary information changes. Thus, MB makes the trackers difficult to locate the boundary of the object and determine the object size accurately.

**Fast Motion, FM**   FM refers to the situation that the distance of the objects between two adjacent frames is over a certain threshold $tm$. Generally, $tm$ is set to be 20, $tm = 20$, as shown in Fig. 1.7. Although FM does not change the appearance of the object itself, it requires a higher search ability of the motion model. Usually, trackers assume that the motion of the object is smooth, which means the change of the object state follows the Gaussian distribution. Gaussian distribution based motion model could reduce the number of candidate samples and speed up the running time, but limits the search ability of the trackers. These make the trackers lose the objects, and result in tracking failure.

**In-Plane Rotation, IPR**   TPR refers to the rotation of the object in image plane when the video plays, as shown in Fig. 1.8. IPR can be regarded as a rotation movement of the whole pixels of the object centered at a certain position. It does not introduce new information and new pixels of the objects, but requires higher rotation invariance of appearance model.

**Out-of-Plane Rotation, OPR**   OPR refers to the rotation of the object out of the image plane when the video plays, as shown in Fig. 1.9. OPR brings the change of the object appearance and puts forward higher requirements for the update ability of tracking methods and adaptability of appearance model.

**Fig. 1.10**  Example of out-of-view

**Fig. 1.11**  Example of background clutters

**Fig. 1.12**  Example of low resolution

**Out-of-View, OV**  OV refers to the situation that the object appears at the boundary of the frame and some parts of the object jump out of this frame, as shown in Fig. 1.10. Similar to occlusion, some information of the object is lost under OV challenge. Since the object is located at the boundary of the frame, when the object moves out of frame, some background information is also lost, which increases the difficulty of some context based trackers. This challenge also affects the estimation of the size and center of the object, as well as the extraction of context information around the object.

**Background Clutters, BC**  BC refers to the situation that there are some similar objects around the object to be tracked. These objects and objects to be tracked are similar in color and shape, which may mislead the tracking algorithm, as shown in Fig. 1.11. BC challenges the discrimination ability of the appearance model. Some trackers with a weak discriminative appearance model may tend to track the wrong object and ignore the real object to be tracked, especially when the objects are close to each other or even overlaps.

**Low Resolution, LR**  LR refers to the case that the number of the pixels in object bounding box does not exceed a certain threshold $tr$. Usually, $tr$ is set to be 400 pixels, as shown in Fig. 1.12. The lack of pixels of the object makes the construction of the appearance model difficult, and the loss of detail information limits the discriminant ability of the appearance model.

It is worth noting that the 11 challenges described above do not appear alone. Usually, there exist multiple tracking challenges at the same time in one video sequence. The videos which are obtained from real life and contain multiple challenges in the complex scenes in visual object tracking. Thus, how to design a tracking algorithm with good tracking effect for every challenge is still a problem to be solved in visual object tracking.

## 1.2   Basic Concepts and Features

Visual object tracking is a classic research direction in the field of computer vision. In 1982, Man et al. [19] constructed the framework of computer vision and demonstrated that the Fourier transform of spatial frequency sensitive data can derive the retinal receptive field geometry. That is, we can detect edges and contours by Laplace or the second derivative method to find zero intersection in image intensity gradient. The excitatory and inhibitory receptive fields can be constructed by Difference Of two Gaussians (DOG) function. Visual systems can use two-dimensional convolutions and Gaussian filters as operators to optimize the bandwidth of the optical distribution. It provides the theoretical basis for computer vision and visual object tracking. In 2014, Arnold W. M. Smeulders et al. [20] gave a specific definition of visual object tracking in TPAMI, one of the top journals in computer vision fields. That is "tracking is the analysis of video sequences for the purpose of establishing the location of the target over a sequence of frames (time), starting from the bounding box given in the first frame."

Arnold W. M. Smeulders et al. [20] not only gave the definition of the visual object tracking, but also summarized the principle and process of some existing visual object tracking algorithms. The visual object tracking is divided into five parts: object area, appearance model, motion model, tracking algorithm and update model. General video object tracking ideas and processes are shown in Fig. 1.13. At the beginning of tracking, the object region that needs to be tracked should be selected. Then, the appearance model is constructed based on the object image, and the motion model is constructed according to the relationship of the object states between two adjacent frames. Tracking algorithms, which are based on different principles, such as similarity matching and optimization, calculate the state of the object in current frame through appearance model and motion model. Update model is used to update the appearance model and motion model of the object, in order to make the appearance and motion model adapt to the change of shape and appearance change of the object, caused by deformation and occlusion of the object. The position and state of the object in each frame could be predicted through iteration. In the five parts in Fig. 1.13, the object area refers to the image of the object that needs to be tracked. Normally, the object area is constructed by a bounding box. Such as NCC tracker [21]. Some object areas are constructed in an elliptical

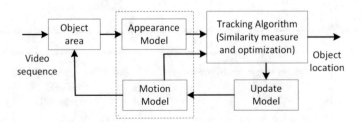

**Fig. 1.13**  Basic ideas of visual object tracking

way, such as MST tracker [22]. The appearance model mainly extracts the feature representation of the object image. According to the features extracted from objects, the appearance model can be divided into two dimension image array [21, 23], one dimension histogram [24–26], and the feature vector [27–29]. The motion model is to model the motion pattern of the object. Usually, it is assumed that the motion of the object in the video is smooth. That is the center of the object in the next frame is around the center of the object in current frame. Therefore, the motion model is mainly based on the Gaussian distribution [30, 31]. In some trackers, the detection methods and the tracking algorithms are combined to construct the motion model of the object, such as TLD tracker[32]. Tracking algorithms apply the appearance model and motion model to predict the position and state of the object. Tracking algorithms are divided into two kinds: matching based [33] and classification based methods [34] which are also known as generative tracking algorithms and discriminative tracking algorithms. Along with the heating up of deep learning and artificial intelligence, deep learning based tracking algorithms also got a rapid development [35, 36]. There are two ways to update the appearance model. One way is to use the object template calculated in the current frame to partially update the whole object appearance model [37, 38], such as the weighted sum. The other way is to reconstruct the appearance model entirely based on the object template computed in the current frame [39].

## 1.3   Evolution of Visual Object Tracking Technology

The development of the visual object tracking algorithm shows a trend from traditional tracking methods [40–42] to deep learning based tracking methods [43–45], and from generative methods [30, 46–48] to discriminative methods [23, 34, 49]. The evolution of visual object tracking technology can be simply summarized by Fig. 1.14.

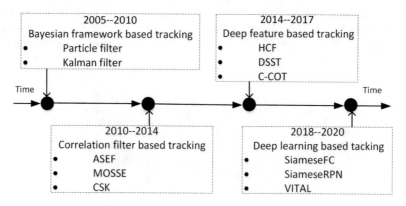

**Fig. 1.14**  The evolution of visual object tracking

From 2005 to 2010, visual object tracking methods are mainly based on the Bayesian framework, Particle filter, and Kalman filter, which are generative methods. During this period, visual object tracking is mainly considered as a template matching problem. Some manual designed features are used to construct the appearance model for comparison. Gaussian distribution is applied as a motion model to provide candidate objects and the final state of the object can be calculated by finding the candidate with the maximum similarity. Abdel-Hadi et al. [46] and Han et al. [47] proposed visual object trackers based on the Kalman filter and particle filter respectively. Yang et al. [48] extracted the superpixel feature to construct the appearance model for comparison.

From 2010 to 2014, the correlation filtering based trackers with kernel methods which belongs to the discriminative methods are widely studied by researchers[50–54]. The purpose of correlation filtering based trackers is to train a correlation filter which could make the object center locate at the peak value in the response map after the correlation filtering operation. Bolme et al. [50] applied the correlation filter to determine the location of eye and proposed the ASEF filter. Then, Bolme et al. [51] further improved the ASEF filter and applied the correlation filter to visual object tracking, and proposed the MOSSE tracker which is also the first correlation filter based tracker. Henriques et al. [52] proposed the CSK tracker which tries to solve the correlation filter with a linear classifier. In 2014, Henriques et al. [53] viewed tracking as a ridge regression problem and applies a circulant matrix to collect the positive and negative samples around the object for training the correlation filter. Aiming at the problems of scale variation in the KCF tracker, Danelljan et al. [54] applied two correlation filters: translation filter and scale filter. Translation filter is used to detect the center location of the object and the scale filter is used to estimate the scale change of the object.

Because of the powerful representation ability of deep feature, deep feature is merged into the correlation filtering based trackers during 2015 and 2017 [55–57]. Well pre-trained networks are used as feature extractors. Ma et al. [55] applied a pretrained deep network to extract the deep feature of the object and combined multi-features from feature maps of different layers in deep network to construct the proposed HCF tracker. In addition, the characteristics of the feature map from different layers in the deep network are also discussed in [55]. Hong et al. [56] proposed a learnable saliency map based on CNN, and combined the saliency map with SVM based classifier to construct the appearance model. Danelljan et al. [57] proposed the continuous convolution operators to integrate multiple resolution feature maps and achieve accurate sub-pixel location.

From 2018 to 2020, along with the development of deep network, deep learning based tracking methods also get rapid developments, especially the Siamese network which obtained a remarkable performance in visual object tracking [36, 58, 59]. Bertinetto et al. [58] combined the Siamese network and correlation filter to propose the SiameseFC tracker. Li et al. [36] introduced the region proposal network into the Siamese network to provide candidates of the object. The region proposal network in [36] can be viewed as a motion model in visual object tracking. Wang et al. [59] combined visual object tracking with instance segmentation problems and proposed a unified solution. Instance segmentation could improve the tracking accuracy, while visual object tracking could improve the speed of instance segmentation.

Recently, aiming at the online update and few shot learning problems in deep learning based trackers, some online update strategies and metal learning are used in the Siamese network based trackers to improve the robustness of tracking performance[60–62]. Zhang et al. [60] treated the update model as a function of ground truth from the first frame, the template of the last frame and the appearance model of the current frame. In addition, the function was expressed as a deep network and proposed the UpdateNet for the model update. Huang et al. [61] and Wang et al. [62] introduced meta learning into the siamese network based tracking method as the initialization of siamese network to improve the robustness of tracking performance.

## 1.4  Chapter Outline

This book presents the state-of-the-art methods in online visual tracking, including the motivations, practical algorithms, and experimental evaluations. The outline of this book is as follows:

In this chapter, we first introduce the wide application and the existing challenges in visual object tracking, including scale variation, background cluster, low resolution, etc. Secondly, we show the basic concepts and main components in visual object tracking to introduce the overall framework of visual object tracking. Then, we comb the evolution of visual object tracking algorithms from correlation filter based trackers to deep learning based trackers. Finally, we show the chapter outline of this book.

In Chap. 2, we mainly introduce some algorithm foundations in visual object tracking from three aspects: correlation filter basics, typical deep learning model for tracking and performance evaluation. In correlation filter basics, we introduce the basic concepts of correlation filter and its application in visual object tracking. In deep learning model for tracking, we introduce four classical deep models in visual object tracking including CNN based model, Siamese based model, GAN based model and reinforcement learning based model. Finally, we describe the performance evaluation of visual object tracking. All these evaluation methods are divided into three aspects: accuracy evaluation, success evaluation and other evaluation.

In Chap. 3, we mainly present the correlation filter based visual object tracking, different from the traditional Bayesian based tracking methods, correlation filter based trackers treat visual object tracking as a foreground and background classification problem, which belongs to the discriminative tracking methods. Correlation filter is used to measure the relevance between the template of the object and search region, and compute the response map. The tracking results can be estimated by finding the peak location in the response map. Correlation filter based trackers have advantages in tracking speed and accuracy, but lack of dealing with scale variation and occlusion challenges. Aiming at the problems above, this chapter mainly introduces three kinds of improved correlation filter based trackers: correlation filter tracker with context aware strategy, correlation filter tracker with scale pyramid, and correlation filter tracker with multi-scale superpixels.

In Chap. 4, we mainly introduce the correlation filter with deep feature for visual object tracking. The correlation filter tracking model can better represent the tracking target by using the deep feature, because the deep feature can better distinguish the target and the background compared with the traditional hand-crafted feature. This chapter mainly introduces three correlation filter methods based on depth features. The first method uses long-short term correlation filter to learn the spatiotemporal feature of the target; the second method uses content-aware and channel attention mechanisms to improve the performance of the tracking method; the third method uses auxiliary relocation with correlation filters to relocate the target and reduces target Tracking failure caused by occlusion.

In Chap. 5, we mainly introduce deep learning based visual object tracking. With the development of deep learning, more and more deep learning methods are applied to visual object tracking. This chapter mainly introduces three deep learning methods, including the Siamese network, generative adversarial network, and reinforcement learning. We enhance the performance of visual object tracking methods by improving those methods, and proposed attention shake Siamese shake based visual object tracking, frequency-aware Siamese network based visual object tracking, improved generative adversarial network based visual object tracking and improved policy-based reinforcement learning based visual object tracking.

In Chap. 6, we summarized our work in this book in three aspects: correlation filter based methods, correlation filter with deep feature and deep learning based visual object tracking methods. Furthermore, we also point out the potential future research directions for visual object tracking in appearance model construction and update.

# References

1. Russell, S., Norvig, P.: Artificial Intelligence: A Modern Approach. Prentice Hall, Upper Saddle River, NJ (2003)
2. Zhang, X., Gao, H., Guo, M., et al.: A study on key technologies of unmanned driving. CAAI Trans. Intell. Technol. 1(1), 4–13 (2016)
3. Collobert, R., Weston, J., Bottou, L., et al.: Natural language processing (almost) from scratch. J. Mach. Learn. Res. 12(76), 2493–2537 (2011)
4. Parkhi, O., Vedaldi, A., Zisserman, A., et al.: Deep face recognition. In: British Machine Vision Conference (2015)
5. Silver, D., Huang, A., Maddison, C., et al.: Mastering the game of go with deep neural networks and tree search. Nature 529(7587), 484 (2016)
6. Tai, J., Tseng, S., Lin, C., et al.: Real-time image tracking for automatic traffic monitoring and enforcement applications. Image Vis. Comput. 22(6), 485–501 (2004)

7. Rautaray, S., Agrawal, A.: Vision based hand gesture recognition for human interaction: a survey. Artif. Intell. Rev. **43**(1), 1–54 (2015)
8. Coifman, B., Beymer, D., McLauchlan, P., et al.: A real-time computer vision system for vehicle tracking and traffic surveillance. Transp. Res. Part C Emerg. Technol. **6**(4), 271–288 (1998)
9. Tang, Z., Naphade, M., Liu, M., et al.: Cityflow: A city-scale benchmark for multi-target multicamera vehicle tracking and re-identification. In: IEEE Conference on Computer Vision and Pattern Recognition, pp. 8797–8806 (2019)
10. Pavlovic, V., Sharma, R., Huang, T.: Visual interpretation of hand gestures for human-computer interaction: a review. IEEE Trans. Pattern Anal. Mach. Intell. **19**(7), 677–695 (1997)
11. Masi, I., Chang, F., Choi, J., et al.: Learning pose-aware models for pose-invariant face recognition in the wild. IEEE Trans. Pattern Anal. Mach. Intell. **41**(2), 379–393 (2018)
12. Smail, H., David, H., Larry, S.: W4: real-time surveillance of people and their activities. IEEE Trans. Pattern Anal. Mach. Intell. **22**(8), 809–830 (2000)
13. Ko, S., Kwon, D.: A surgical knowledge based interaction method for a laparoscopic assistant robot. In: IEEE International Workshop on Robot and Human Interactive Communication, pp. 313–318 (2004)
14. Wu, B., Ji, D., Guo, Z., Shen, H., Xiao, Z.: A method for plane-symmetrical vehicle trajectory tracking in maneuver flight. In: Chinese Control Conference (CCC), pp. 5743–5746 (2016)
15. Lei, Q., Di, Z., Jun-long, L.: Tracking for near space nonballistic target based on several filter algorithms. In: Chinese Control Conference (CCC), pp. 4997–5002 (2015)
16. Collins, R., Lipton, A., Kanade, T., et al.: A system for video surveillance and monitoring: VSAM final report. Robotics Inst. (2000)
17. Tanawongsuwan, R., Bobick, A.: Characteristics of time-distance gait parameters across speeds (2003)
18. Wu, Y., Lim, J., Yang, M.: Online object tracking: a benchmark. In: IEEE Conference on Computer Vision and Pattern Recognition, pp. 2411–2418 (2013)
19. Man, D., Vision, A.: A Computational Investigation into the Human Representation and Processing of Visual Information. WH San Francisco: Freeman and Company, San Francisco (1982)
20. Smeulders, A., Chu, D., Cucchiara, R., et al.: Visual tracking: an experimental survey. IEEE Trans. Pattern Anal. Mach. Intell. **36**(7), 1442–1468 (2014)
21. Briechle, K., Hanebeck, U.: Template matching using fast normalized cross correlation. In: Proceedings of Optical Pattern Recognition XII, vol. 4387. International Society for Optics and Photonics, Bellingham, pp. 95–102 (2001)
22. Comaniciu, D., Ramesh, V., Meer, P.: Real-time tracking of non-rigid objects using mean shift. In: IEEE Conference on Computer Vision and Pattern Recognition, pp.142–149 (2000)
23. Hare, S., Golodetz, S., Saffari, A., et al.: Struck: structured output tracking with kernels. IEEE Trans. Pattern Anal. Mach. Intell. **38**(10), 2096–2109 (2016)
24. Godec, M., Roth, P., Bischof, H.: Hough-based tracking of non-rigid objects. Comput. Vis. Image Underst. **117**(10), 1245–1256 (2013)
25. Kwon, J., Lee, K.: Tracking by sampling trackers. In: IEEE International Conference on Computer Vision, pp. 1195–1202 (2011)
26. Nilski, A.: An evaluation metric for multiple camera tracking systems: the i-lids 5th scenario. In: Optics and Photonics for Counterterrorism and Crime Fighting IV, vol. 7119, pp. 711907–711908 (2008)
27. Babenko, B., Yang, M., Belongie, S.: Visual tracking with online multiple instance learning. In: IEEE Conference on Computer Vision and Pattern Recognition, pp. 983–990 (2009)
28. Chu, D., Smeulders, A.: Color invariant surf in discriminative object tracking. In: European Conference on Computer Vision, pp. 62–75 (2010)
29. Bay, H., Ess, A., Tuytelaars, T., et al.: Speeded-up robust features. Comput. Vis. Image Underst. **110**(3), 346–359 (2008)
30. Ross, D., Lim, J., Lin, R., Yang, M.: Incremental learning for robust visual tracking. Int. J. Comput. **77**(1–3), 125–141 (2008)

31. Mei, X., Ling, H.: Robust visual tracking using l1 minimization. In: IEEE International Conference on Computer Vision, pp. 1436–1443 (2009)
32. Kalal, Z., Matas, J., Mikolajczyk, K.: Pn learning: bootstrapping binary classifiers by structural constraints. In: IEEE Conference on Computer Vision and Pattern Recognition, pp. 49–56 (2010)
33. Baker, S., Matthews, I.: Lucas-Kanade 20 years on: a unifying framework. Int. J. Comput. Vis. **56**(3), 221–255 (2004)
34. Henriques, J., Caseiro, R., Martins, P., et al.: High-speed tracking with kernelized correlation filters. IEEE Trans. Pattern Anal. Mach. Intell. **37**(3), 583–596 (2015)
35. Zhang, Z., Peng, H.: Deeper and wider siamese networks for real-time visual tracking. In: IEEE Conference on Computer Vision and Pattern Recognition, pp. 4591–4600 (2019)
36. Li, B., Yan, J., Wu, W., et al.: High performance visual tracking with siamese region proposal network. In: IEEE Conference on Computer Vision and Pattern Recognition, pp. 8971–8980 (2018)
37. Porikli, F., Tuzel, O., Meer, P.: Covariance tracking using model update based on lie algebra. In: IEEE Conference on Computer Vision and Pattern Recognition, pp. 728–735 (2006)
38. Wu, Y., Cheng, J., Wang, J., et al.: Real-time visual tracking via incremental covariance tensor learning. In: IEEE International Conference on Computer Vision, pp. 1631–1638 (2009)
39. Avidan, S.: Support vector tracking. IEEE Trans. Pattern Anal. Mach. Intell. **26**(8), 1064–1072 (2004)
40. Matthies, L., Kanade, T., Szeliski, R.: Kalman filter-based algorithms for estimating depth from image sequences. Int. J. Comput. Vis. **3**, 209–238 (1989)
41. Kass, M., Witkin, A., Terzopoulos, D.: Snakes: active contour model. Int. J. Comput. Vis. **1**, 321–331 (1988)
42. Mei, X., Ling, H.: Robust visual tracking using $L_1$ minimization. In: IEEE International Conference on Computer Vision, pp. 1436–1443 (2009)
43. Nam, H., Han, B.: Learning multi-domain convolutional neural networks for visual tracking. In: IEEE Conference on Computer Vision and Pattern Recognition, pp. 4293–4302 (2016)
44. Fan, H., Ling, H.: SANet: structure-aware network for visual tracking. In: IEEE Conference on Computer Vision and Pattern Recognition, pp. 42–49 (2017)
45. Guo, Q., Feng, W., Zhou, C., et al.: Learning dynamic siamese network for visual object tracking. In: IEEE International Conference on Computer Vision, pp. 1763–1771 (2017)
46. Abdel-Hadi, A.: Real-time object tracking using color-based Kalman particle filter. In: International Conference on Computational and Experimental Engineering and Sciences, pp. 337–341 (2010)
47. Han, Z., Xu, T., Chen, Z.: An improved color-based tracking by particle filter. In: International Conference on Transportation, Mechanical, and Electrical Engineering, pp. 2512–2515 (2011)
48. Yang, F., Lu, H., Yang, M.: Robust Superpixel Tracking. IEEE Trans. Image Process. **23**(4), 1639–1651 (2014)
49. Wang, Q., Chen, F., Xu, W., Yang, M.: Object tracking via partial least squares analysis. IEEE Trans. Image Process. **21**(10), 4454–4465 (2012)
50. Bolme, D., Draper, B., Beveridge, J.: Average of synthetic exact filters. In: IEEE Conference on Computer Vision and Pattern Recognition, pp. 2105–2112 (2009)
51. Bolme, D., Beveridge, J., Draper, B., et al.: Visual object tracking using adaptive correlation filters. In: IEEE Conference on Computer Vision and Pattern Recognition, pp. 2544–2550 (2010)
52. Henriques, J., Caseiro, R., Martins, P., et al.: Exploiting the circulant structure of tracking-by-detection with kernels. In: European Conference on Computer Vision, pp. 702–715 (2012)
53. Henriques, J., Caseiro, R., Martins, P., et al.: High-speed tracking with kernelized correlation filters. IEEE Trans. Pattern Anal. Mach. Intell. **37**(3), 583–596 (2014)
54. Danelljan, M., Häger, G., Khan, F., et al.: Accurate scale estimation for robust visual tracking. In: British Machine Vision Conference, pp. 1–5 (2014)
55. Ma, C., Huang, J., Yang, X., et al.: Hierarchical convolutional features for visual tracking. In: IEEE International Conference on Computer Vision, pp. 3074–3082 (2015)

56. Hong, S., You, T., Kwak, S., Han, B.: Online tracking by learning discriminative saliency map with convolutional neural network. In: International Conference on Machine Learning, pp. 597–606 (2015)
57. Danelljan, M., Robinson, A., Khan, F., et al.: Beyond correlation filters: learning continuous convolution operators for visual tracking. In: European Conference on Computer Vision, pp. 472–488 (2016)
58. Bertinetto, L., Valmadre, J., Henriques, J., et al.: Fully-convolutional siamese networks for object tracking. In: European Conference on Computer Vision, pp. 850–865 (2016)
59. Wang, Q., Zhang, L., Bertinetto, L., et al.: Fast online object tracking and segmentation: a unifying approach. In: IEEE Conference on Computer Vision and Pattern Recognition, pp. 1328–1338 (2019)
60. Zhang, L., Gonzalez-Garcia, A., Weijer, J., et al.: Learning the model update for siamese trackers. In: IEEE International Conference on Computer Vision, pp. 4010–4019 (2019)
61. Huang, L., Zhao, X., Huang, K.: Bridging the gap between detection and tracking: a unified approach. In: IEEE International Conference on Computer Vision, pp. 3999–4009 (2019)
62. Wang, G., Luo, C., Sun, X., et al.: Tracking by instance detection: a meta-learning approach. In: IEEE Conference on Computer Vision and Pattern Recognition, pp. 6288–6297 (2020)

# Chapter 2
# Algorithms Foundations

From the aspect of tracking principle, visual object tracking can be roughly divided into generative tracking algorithms and discriminative tracking algorithms and there are many basic concepts, models and other background knowledge we should know ahead. This chapter introduces the basic algorithms and models in visual object tracking. Firstly, the concepts of correlation filter and its application in visual object tracking is expressed in this chapter, including three kinds of classical algorithms such as MOSSE, discriminative correlation filter based trackers and kernel correlation filter based trackers. Then, typical deep learning models are expressed including convolutional neural network, siamese network, generative adversarial network and reinforcement learning based network. Finally, the performance evaluation and benchmark datasets are also illustrated in this chapter.

## 2.1 Correlation Filter Basics

This subsection mainly introduces the basic concepts and foundations of correlation filter based trackers. Firstly, the groundbreaking work-MOSSE [1] is introduced in this subsection. Then follows by the expressions of two kinds of correlation filters: the discriminative correlation filter and kernel correlation filter. These two kinds of correlation filters based trackers are similar in formula derivation, but different in designing principle. The discriminative correlation filter based trackers view tracking as a classification problem. While, the kernel correlation filter based trackers view tracking as a ridge regression problem. Specific implementation steps and principles are as follows.

### 2.1.1  MOSSE

MOSSE [1] applies the correlation filtering operation in signal processing to predict the center position of the object. According to the definition of correlation filter, the correlation between two signals can be expressed by Eqs. 2.1 and 2.2.

$$(f_t \otimes h_t)(\tau) = \int_{-\infty}^{\infty} f_t^*(t) h_t(t+\tau) d\tau \qquad (2.1)$$

$$(f_t \otimes h_t)(\tau) = \sum_{-\infty}^{\infty} f_t^*(m) h_t(m+n) \qquad (2.2)$$

These two equations are the correlation filtering operations of continuous signals and discrete signals respectively. Thus, the value of two signals after correlation filtering shows the correlation and similarity of these two signals. The greater the value of two signals after correlation filtering, the more similar the two signals. MOSSE applies this idea to train a filter $h_t$, which could obtain the response map $g_t$ when the object image $f_t$ and the filter $h_t$ are under correlation filtering operation. The highest value in the response map $g_t$ indicates the center of the object, as shown in Eq. 2.3.

$$g_t = f_t \otimes h_t \qquad (2.3)$$

The object image $f_t$ and response map $g_t$ used to train the correlation filter $h_t$ are already known. Object image $f_t$ often comes from the image within the bounding box in the first frame, and the image used for training is usually 1.5 times larger than the object image in order to mix some background information and provide more negative samples. Response map $g_t$ is given by a two-dimensional Gaussian distribution whose expectation locates at the center of the object. It can also be viewed as the training label. According to the frequency domain characteristics of correlation filtering, convolution operation in the time domain corresponds to the multiplication in the frequency domain. Therefore, the solution of correlation filter is carried out in the frequency domain, which could speed up the operation of correlation filtering. The equation of correlation filtering in the frequency domain is as follows:

$$\mathcal{F}(g_t) = \mathcal{F}(f_t \otimes h_t) = \mathcal{F}(f_t) * F(h)^*$$
$$\Rightarrow G_t = F_t * H_t^* \qquad (2.4)$$

$G_t$, $F_t$ and $H_t^*$ represent response map, object image and correlation filter in the frequency domain respectively. $\mathcal{F}()$ is the Fourier transform. $*$ in $H_t^*$ denotes conjugation. The correlation filter $H_t$, can be obtained by minimizing $\sum_{i=1}^{m} |H_t^* F_{ti} -$

$G_{ti}|$. $m$ is the number of training samples. The close solution can be obtained by finding the partial derivative of $H_t^*$. The derivation process is shown as follows:

$$\frac{\partial}{\partial H_t^*} \sum_{i=1}^{m} |H_t^* F_{ti} - G_{ti}|^2 = 0$$

$$\Rightarrow \frac{\partial}{\partial H_t^*} \sum_{i=1}^{m} (H_t^* F_{ti} - G_{ti})(H_t^* F_{ti} - G_{ti})^* = 0$$

$$\Rightarrow \sum_{i=1}^{m} (F_{ti} F_{ti}^* H_t - F_{ti} G_{ti}^*) = 0 \tag{2.5}$$

$$\Rightarrow H_t = \frac{\sum\limits_{i=1}^{m} F_{ti} G_{ti}^*}{\sum\limits_{i=1}^{m} F_{ti} F_{ti}^*}$$

### 2.1.2  Discriminative Correlation Filter

The basic concepts of discriminative correlation filter are based on the MOSSE which is also to learn a position based correlation filter to estimate the location of the object. Just as shown in MOOSE. The best correlation filter should satisfy the following equation.

$$\varepsilon = \sum_{j=1}^{t} \left\| h_t \otimes f_j - g_j \right\|^2 = \frac{1}{MN} \sum_{j=1}^{t} \left\| \overline{H}_t F_j - G_j \right\|^2 \tag{2.6}$$

Where $f_1, f_2, f_3, \ldots f_t$ are the training samples, and the $g_1, g_2, g_3, ..g_t$ are the corresponding outputs which are constructed through Gaussian distribution. The capital letters represent the DFT, and the underlined letters represent complex conjugate. Thus, the correlation filter $H_t$ can be calculated as follows:

$$H_t = \frac{\sum_{j=1}^{t} \bar{G}_j F_j}{\sum_{j=1}^{t} \bar{F}_j F_j} \tag{2.7}$$

Thus the response score and the location of the object can be calculated by Eq. 2.8.

$$y = F^{-1}\left\{ \overline{H}_t Z \right\} \tag{2.8}$$

$Z$ is the frame to be tracked.

Considering the feature of images is multi-dimensional. Thus Eq. 2.6 can be rewritten as follows:

$$\varepsilon = \left\| \sum_{l=1}^{d} h^l \otimes f^l - g \right\|^2 + \lambda \sum_{l=1}^{d} \left\| h^l \right\|^2 \tag{2.9}$$

$f$ represents the feature whose dimension is $d$, $\lambda$ is the regularization term. Comparing Eq. 2.7, the solution of correlation filter $H^l$ for one training sample can be found in Eq. 2.10.

$$H^l = \frac{\bar{G}_j F^l}{\sum_{k=1}^{d} \bar{F}^k F^k + \lambda} \tag{2.10}$$

In order to facilitate the iterative updating, Eq. 2.10 can be divided into two parts: Molecule part $A_t^l$ and denominator part $B_t$. The way to update is as follows:

$$A_t^l = (1 - \eta) A_{t-1}^l + \eta \bar{G}_t F_t^l \tag{2.11}$$

$$B_t = (1 - \eta) B_{t-1} + \eta \sum_{k=1}^{d} \bar{F}_t^k F_t^k \tag{2.12}$$

where $\eta$ is the learning rate. For the new frame $Z$, the response score $y$ can be calculated by Eq. 2.13.

$$y = F^{-1} \left\{ \frac{\sum_{l=1}^{d} A^l Z^l}{B + \lambda} \right\} \tag{2.13}$$

The location with the maximum response score indicates the object center.

### 2.1.3   Kernel Correlation Filter

KCF [2] treats visual object tracking as a ridge regression problem and proves the relationship between ridge regression and classical correlation filtering with cyclic shift samples. Besides, KCF also introduces kernel methods to improve the performance of the algorithm and reduce the operation time. The purpose of KCF algorithm is to find the optimal solution of the function $f(\mathbf{z}) = \mathbf{w}^T \mathbf{z}$ to minimize the minimum mean square error of Eq. 2.14 with regularization term.

$$\min_{\mathbf{w}} \sum_{i} (f(\mathbf{x}_i) - y_i)^2 + \lambda \left\| \mathbf{w} \right\|^2 \tag{2.14}$$

$\lambda$ is the regularization coefficient, $f(\mathbf{x}_i)$ and $y_i$ represent the prediction value after function $y_i$ and ground truth respectively. According to the reference [3], the close solution of $\mathbf{w}$ can be obtained by computing the partial derivation of $\mathbf{w}$ in the minimum mean square error equation and set the partial derivative function to be zero. The specific solution process is shown in Eq. 2.15.

$$
\begin{aligned}
&\frac{\partial}{\partial \mathbf{w}} \sum_i (f(\mathbf{x}_i) - y_i)^2 + \lambda \|\mathbf{w}\|^2 = 0 \\
&\Rightarrow \frac{\partial}{\partial \mathbf{w}} (\mathbf{y} - \mathbf{Xw})^T (\mathbf{y} - \mathbf{Xw}) + \lambda \|\mathbf{w}\|^2 = 0 \\
&\Rightarrow 2\mathbf{X}^T (\mathbf{Xw} - \mathbf{y}) + 2\lambda \mathbf{w} = 0 \\
&\Rightarrow \mathbf{X}^T \mathbf{Xw} - \mathbf{X}^T \mathbf{y} + \lambda \mathbf{w} = 0 \\
&\Rightarrow (\mathbf{X}^T \mathbf{X} + \lambda \mathbf{I})\mathbf{w} = \mathbf{X}^T \mathbf{y} \\
&\Rightarrow \mathbf{w} = (\mathbf{X}^T \mathbf{X} + \lambda \mathbf{I})^{-1} \mathbf{X}^T \mathbf{y}
\end{aligned} \tag{2.15}
$$

$\mathbf{X}$ and $\mathbf{y}$ are the matrix and label of training samples. When the training samples in $\mathbf{X}$ transforms from Fourier domain to complex domain, the transpose symbol $T$ needs to be replaced by the transpose conjugate symbol $H$, $\mathbf{X}^H = (\mathbf{X}^*)^T$. In real domain, transpose and transpose conjugate have the same effect. That is $\mathbf{X}^H = (\mathbf{X})^T$. Thus, Eq. 2.15 in complex domain should be $\mathbf{w} = (\mathbf{X}^H \mathbf{X} + \lambda \mathbf{I})^{-1} \mathbf{X}^H \mathbf{y}$.

Different from MOSSE, KCF applies cyclic matrix as training samples to construct $\mathbf{X}$. Intuitively, the process of constructing multiple training samples by the cyclic shift of the object image in horizontal and vertical directions can be achieved by multiplying the elementary row transformation matrix and elementary column transformation. The sample matrix constructed by cyclic matrix $\mathbf{X}$ can be expressed as Eq. 2.16.

$$
\mathbf{X} = C(\mathbf{x}) = \begin{bmatrix}
x_1 & x_2 & x_3 & \cdots & x_n \\
x_n & x_1 & x_2 & \cdots & x_{n-1} \\
x_{n-1} & x_n & x_1 & \cdots & x_{n-2} \\
\vdots & \vdots & \vdots & \ddots & \vdots \\
x_2 & x_3 & x_4 & \cdots & x_1
\end{bmatrix} \tag{2.16}
$$

An advantage of constructing a training sample matrix using a cyclic matrix is that the training sample can be transformed into a diagonal matrix by Discrete Fourier Transform (DFT), as shown in Eq. 2.17.

$$
\mathbf{X} = \mathbf{F} diag(\hat{\mathbf{x}}) \mathbf{F}^H \tag{2.17}
$$

$\mathbf{F}$ is a sample independent constant matrix which is also known as a discrete Fourier matrix (DFT matrix). According to the properties of discrete Fourier transform,

$\mathbf{F}^H \mathbf{F} = \mathbf{F} \mathbf{F}^H = \mathbf{I}$, $\mathbf{x}$ is the vector that construct $\mathbf{X}$. $\mathbf{x} \in \{x_1, x_2, \dots, x_n\}$. $diag(\hat{\mathbf{x}})$ is the diagonal matrix, which is composed of the elements in $\hat{\mathbf{x}}$. $\hat{\mathbf{x}} = \mathcal{F}(\mathbf{x})$, $\mathcal{F}()$ denotes the Fourier transform function. $\mathbf{X}^H \mathbf{X}$ can be written as Eq. 2.18.

$$
\begin{aligned}
\mathbf{X}^H \mathbf{X} &= \mathbf{F} diag(\hat{\mathbf{x}}^*) \mathbf{F}^H \mathbf{F} diag(\hat{\mathbf{x}}) \mathbf{F}^H \\
&= \mathbf{F} diag(\hat{\mathbf{x}}^*) diag(\hat{\mathbf{x}}) \mathbf{F}^H \\
&= \mathbf{F} diag(\hat{\mathbf{x}}^* \odot \hat{\mathbf{x}}) \mathbf{F}^H
\end{aligned}
\tag{2.18}
$$

Substitute Eqs. 2.17 and 2.18 into Eq. 2.15 in the complex domain, the optimal solution of KCF tracker which is trained by a cyclic matrix can be obtained by Eq. 2.19.

$$
\begin{aligned}
\mathbf{w} &= (\mathbf{X}^H \mathbf{X} + \lambda \mathbf{I})^{-1} \mathbf{X}^H \mathbf{y} \\
\Rightarrow \mathbf{w} &= (\mathbf{F} diag(\hat{\mathbf{x}}^* \odot \hat{\mathbf{x}}) \mathbf{F}^H + \lambda \mathbf{F} \mathbf{I} \mathbf{F}^H)^{-1} \mathbf{F} diag(\hat{\mathbf{x}}^*) \mathbf{F}^H \mathbf{y} \\
\Rightarrow \mathbf{w} &= \mathbf{F} diag(\hat{\mathbf{x}}^* \odot \hat{\mathbf{x}} + \lambda)^{-1} \mathbf{F}^H \mathbf{F} diag(\hat{\mathbf{x}}^*) \mathbf{F}^H \mathbf{y} \\
\Rightarrow \mathbf{w} &= \mathbf{F} diag\left(\frac{\hat{\mathbf{x}}^*}{\hat{\mathbf{x}}^* \odot \hat{\mathbf{x}} + \lambda}\right) \mathbf{F}^H \mathbf{y} \\
\Rightarrow \mathbf{F}^H \mathbf{w} &= diag\left(\frac{\hat{\mathbf{x}}^*}{\hat{\mathbf{x}}^* \odot \hat{\mathbf{x}} + \lambda}\right) \mathbf{F}^H \mathbf{y} \\
\Rightarrow \hat{\mathbf{w}}^* &= diag\left(\frac{\hat{\mathbf{x}}^*}{\hat{\mathbf{x}}^* \odot \hat{\mathbf{x}} + \lambda}\right) \hat{\mathbf{y}}^* \\
\Rightarrow \hat{\mathbf{w}}^* &= \frac{\hat{\mathbf{x}}^* \odot \hat{\mathbf{y}}^*}{\hat{\mathbf{x}}^* \odot \hat{\mathbf{x}} + \lambda} \\
\Rightarrow \hat{\mathbf{w}} &= \frac{\hat{\mathbf{x}} \odot \hat{\mathbf{y}}}{\hat{\mathbf{x}}^* \odot \hat{\mathbf{x}} + \lambda}
\end{aligned}
\tag{2.19}
$$

$\odot$ represents the element-wise multiplication. Since $diag()$ denotes diagonal matrix, multiplication between two matrices can be written as an element-wise multiplication.

KCF not only uses a cyclic matrix to construct the training sample $f(\mathbf{z}) = \mathbf{w}^T \mathbf{z}$, but also introduces the kernel technique and shows the solution method with kernel techniques. The advantage of adding the kernel technique is that it can map a linear indivisible problem with a high dimensional space to simplify the solution and raise the dimension. The optimization function with kernel technique can be expressed as $f(\mathbf{z}) = \mathbf{w}^T \mathbf{z} = \sum_{i=1}^{n} \alpha_i k(\mathbf{z}, \mathbf{x}_i)$. $k(\mathbf{z}, \mathbf{x}_i)$ represent the kernel function of $\mathbf{z}$ and $\mathbf{x}_i$. Therefore, the solving of parameter $\mathbf{w}$ is transformed into the process of solving new parameter $\boldsymbol{\alpha}$. The solution of mean square error with kernel function and regularization term is given in reference [3]. The derivation process is shown in Eq. 2.20.

$$
\frac{\partial}{\partial \mathbf{w}} \sum_i (f(\mathbf{x}_i) - y_i)^2 + \lambda \|\mathbf{w}\|^2 = 0
$$

$$
\Rightarrow \frac{\partial}{\partial \alpha} (\mathbf{y} - \mathbf{K}\alpha)^T (\mathbf{y} - \mathbf{K}\alpha) + \lambda \alpha^T \mathbf{K}\alpha = 0
$$

$$
\Rightarrow (\mathbf{y} - \mathbf{K}\alpha)^T (-\mathbf{K}) + \lambda \mathbf{K}\alpha = 0 \tag{2.20}
$$

$$
\Rightarrow -\mathbf{K}\mathbf{y} + \mathbf{K}^2 \alpha + \lambda \mathbf{K}\alpha = 0
$$

$$
\Rightarrow \alpha = (\mathbf{K} + \lambda \mathbf{I})^{-1} \mathbf{y}
$$

$\mathbf{K}$ is the Kernel matrix which consists of kernel functions. Since KCF tracking algorithm applies a cyclic matrix to construct training sample matrix $\mathbf{X}$, the kernel matrix can be expressed as $\mathbf{K} = C(\hat{\mathbf{k}}^{\mathbf{xx}})$. The close solution of parameter $\alpha$ in $f(\mathbf{z})$ can be solved through Eq. 2.21.

$$
\alpha = (\mathbf{K} + \lambda \mathbf{I})^{-1} \mathbf{y}
$$

$$
\Rightarrow \alpha = (C(\hat{\mathbf{k}}^{\mathbf{xx}}) + \lambda \mathbf{I})^{-1} \mathbf{y}
$$

$$
\Rightarrow \alpha = (\mathbf{F} diag(\hat{\mathbf{k}}^{\mathbf{xx}})\mathbf{F}^H + \lambda \mathbf{F}\mathbf{I}\mathbf{F}^H)^{-1} \mathbf{y}
$$

$$
\Rightarrow \alpha = \mathbf{F} diag(\hat{\mathbf{k}}^{\mathbf{xx}} + \lambda)^{-1} \mathbf{F}^H \mathbf{y}
$$

$$
\Rightarrow \mathbf{F}^H \alpha = diag(\hat{\mathbf{k}}^{\mathbf{xx}} + \lambda)^{-1} \mathbf{F}^H \mathbf{y} \tag{2.21}
$$

$$
\Rightarrow \hat{\alpha}^* = diag(\frac{1}{\hat{\mathbf{k}}^{\mathbf{xx}} + \lambda})\hat{\mathbf{y}}^*
$$

$$
\Rightarrow \hat{\alpha}^* = \frac{\hat{\mathbf{y}}^*}{\hat{\mathbf{k}}^{\mathbf{xx}} + \lambda}
$$

$$
\Rightarrow \hat{\alpha} = \frac{\hat{\mathbf{y}}}{\hat{\mathbf{k}}^{\mathbf{xx}} + \lambda}
$$

The Fourier transform of Eq. 2.21 is shown as follows:

$$
\alpha = \mathcal{F}^{-1}(\frac{\mathcal{F}(\mathbf{y})}{\mathcal{F}(k(\mathbf{x}, \mathbf{x})) + \lambda}) \tag{2.22}
$$

$\mathcal{F}^{-1}()$ and $\mathcal{F}()$ represent inverse Fourier transform and Fourier transform respectively. Equation 2.22 also shows that the KCF maps the sample matrix to the frequency domain for calculation, and then use Fourier inverse transform to convert the results from the frequency domain to the time domain.

The response map of sample $\mathbf{z}$ in the new frame can be obtained by Eq. 2.23, after parameter $\boldsymbol{\alpha}$ is obtained.

$$\hat{f}(\mathbf{z}) = \hat{\mathbf{k}}^{\mathbf{xz}} \odot \hat{\boldsymbol{\alpha}}$$
$$\Rightarrow f(\mathbf{z}) = \mathcal{F}^{-1}(\mathcal{F}(k(\mathbf{z}, \mathbf{x})) \odot \mathcal{F}(\boldsymbol{\alpha})) \tag{2.23}$$

$k(\mathbf{z}, \mathbf{x})$ denotes the values of kernel function of sample $\mathbf{z}$ and training sample $\mathbf{x}$ respectively. The position with maximum response value in response map $f(\mathbf{z})$ is the center of the object predicted by KCF algorithm. Thus, we could achieve the purpose of tracking.

## 2.2  Typical Deep Learning Model for Tracking

In this chapter, we will mainly introduce the tracking methods based on deep learning, including convolutional neural network, Siamese network, generative adversarial network, and reinforcement learning.

### 2.2.1  Convolutional Neural Networks Based Model

CNN-based methods use deep features and deep networks to improve model performance, because deep features include rich spatial and semantic information. Based on those advantages, CNN-based methods achieve better representation and recognition ability than traditional. In order to improve the discriminative ability of the tracker, Hong et al. [4] introduced a deep convolutional network into object tracking. MDNet[5] is a multi-domain method for learning common and unique domain features to represent the target, but due to the size of the network, it suffers from an over-fitting problem. Song et al. [6] incorporated Discriminative Correlation Filter (DCF) method into end-to-end training neural networks, which incorporates CNN correlation filters to boost the efficiency of tracking. In order to increase the robustness of the model, Bhat et al.[7] studied the complementary properties of deep and shallow features. As for the above CNN-based methods, by developing complex network architectures [5], some concentrate on achieving high tracking precision, while others pay attention to realizing real-time trackers by decreasing the complexity of the model [6].

MDNet[5] is a typical CNN-based tracking algorithm. It proposes that for tracking problems, it would make more sense that the CNN should be trained from the data from video tracking to get it. All tracking targets, although different in the category, should actually have some commonality among them, which is something the network needs to learn. It is difficult to train with tracking data because the same object, which is a target in one sequence, may be the background

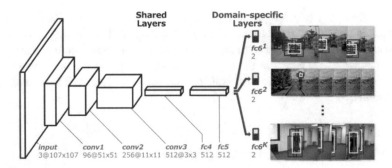

**Fig. 2.1** The overall MDNet architecture

in another, and there is considerable variation in the targets in each sequence, and they experience various challenges, such as occlusion, deformation, etc. Many existing trained networks are large for tasks such as target detection, classification, segmentation, etc., as they have to separate many classes of targets. In contrast, in the tracking problem, a network only needs to be divided into two categories: target and background. And the targets are generally relatively small, then there is actually no need for such a large network, which would increase the computational burden.

To address these issues, the Multi-Domain Network (MDNet) is proposed to learn the commonalities of these targets. The overall framework is shown in Fig. 2.1. The input to the network is set as a $107 \times 107$ bounding box, so that a $3 \times 3$ feature map can be obtained in convolutional layer conv3. The convolutional layers conv1–conv3 are from the VGG-M network, but the size of the input has been changed. The next two fully-connected layers, fc4, fc5, each have 512 output units and are followed with ReLUs and Dropouts. Fc6 is a binary classification layer (Domain-specific layers), with K layers corresponding to K Branches (i.e. K different videos). Only the fc6 corresponding to that video is used in each training session, the previous layers are shared.

A Domain-specific training method is used to learn the commonality of goals in various videos: assume that K videos are used for training, and N cycles are completed. Of mini-batch is made up of 128 frames taken at random from a film, with 32 positive and 96 negative samples drawn at random from these 8 frames. K iterations are rendered in each loop, and the training is repeated N times for each mini-batch of K images. SGD is used for the preparation, and each video corresponds to a different fc6 sheet. The commonality of the goal in each video is learned through this preparation. When the trained network is tested, a new fc6 layer is created and the online fine-tune fc4–fc6 layer is used, while the convolutional layers remain unchanged.

Both long-term and short-term update approaches are used in the network online update approach. The historical tracked targets are saved as positive samples during the tracking process, but the samples are only added as positive samples for training when the score is above a threshold. Short-term corresponds to 20 historical samples, and the network is modified at a fixed interval, the software is set to update every 8 frames, while long-term corresponds to 100 historical samples, and the network is updated when the goal score is below 0.5. All of the negative samples were taken in a short period of time. In addition, hard negative mining was used to generate negative samples in the training, which means that the negative samples become harder and harder to distinguish, thus making the network more and more discriminative.

## 2.2.2   Siamese Networks Based Model

Siamese networks [8–10] have shown considerable potential in monitoring accuracy and speed in recent years, accelerating the measurement process by exchanging network weights. In order to speed up the tracking process, Tao et al. [11] implemented a Siamese network into tracking and compared the similarity between the search area and the template without model update, which could lead to decreased tracking accuracy. In order to adjust to current target changes and improve precision, Guo et al. [12] used an adaptive strategy; however, the network structure in this tracker is shallow and has only fewer layers, which may not be adequate for tracking in quick motion and occlusion conditions. A distractor-aware mechanism was introduced by Zhu et al. [13] to enhance the region proposal network-based tracker and improve its robustness and speed. For model updating, however, the feature in the target variation was not used, which decreased the model's accuracy. Wang et al.[14] combined image segmentation with tracking to achieve a bounding box of non-horizontal rectangular tracking closer to the real target, further improving the model's accuracy. By reducing update times, Siamese networks tend to speed up monitoring. Therefore, to reduce the update overhead is very important by designing an efficient model update strategy.

The siamese network tracking algorithm uses the similarity learning idea to realize the tracking of any target. SiameseFC uses the learned $f(z, x)$ to compare the template image with the search image. If the two images contain the same target, they get a higher score, otherwise, they get a lower score. In order to find the position of the target in the new video frame, SiameseFC traverses all possible positions in the search area and selects the candidate area with the greatest similarity score with the appearance model as the current target area. In the target tracking process, SiameseFC uses the convolutional features of the target area in the initial frame as the appearance model, and does not update the appearance model in subsequent video sequences. The $f(z, x)$ function is essentially a convolutional neural network, which can be obtained by learning from a video sequence dataset with target state labels. The Siamese network first uses the transfer function $\varphi$ to perform feature conversion on the two inputs, and then uses another function $g$ to evaluate the similarity of the two inputs. Therefore, the mapping function $f(z, x)$ is expressed as: $f(z, x) = g(\varphi(z), \varphi(x))$.

As shown in Fig. 2.2, the overall framework of SiameseFC is composed of the upper branch and the lower branch. The convolutional network $\varphi$ of these two

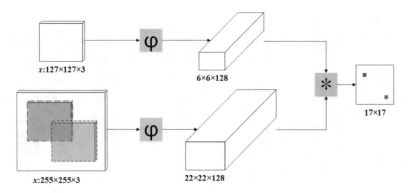

**Fig. 2.2** The overall SiamFC architecture

branches have the same structure and weight parameters. In the tracking stage, a search area $x$ is obtained from the center of the target in the previous frame, and the feature extraction network is used to extract the features of the search area and the real target box in the first frame. Then, SiameseFC uses the $6 \times 6 \times 128$ convolution feature of the template image as the convolution kernel, and performs cross-correlation operation with the $22 \times 22 \times 128$ convolution feature of the search image to obtain a similar map of $17 \times 17$ size. Interpolate the similarity graph to a size of $272 \times 272$, and the position of the maximum value is the position of the target.

In order to construct an effective loss function, the SiameseFC network distinguishes between positive and negative samples for the location points of the search area, that is, points within a certain range close to the target are positive samples, and points outside the range are regarded as negative samples. As shown in Fig. 2.2, the red dots represent positive samples, and the blue dots represent negative samples. They correspond to the red and blue rectangles in the search area X on the left. The form of the loss function for each point in the score map is as follows:

$$\ell(y, v) = log(1 + exp(-yv)) \tag{2.24}$$

Where $v$ is the score value (confidence score) of each point in the score map, the larger the value, the greater the possibility of being a target. $y \in \{+1, -1\}$ is the label corresponding to the point. For the overall loss in the score map, the average value of the loss of all points is used:

$$L(y, v) = \frac{1}{|D|} \sum_{u \in D} \ell(y[u], v[u]) \tag{2.25}$$

where $D$ represents all points in all scoring maps, and $u$ represents a point in $D$.

As shown in Table 2.1, the convolutional network structure $\varphi$ is modified on AlexNet, removing all fully connected layers.

**Table 2.1**  The detail SiameseFC architecture

| Layer | Kernel size | Stride | Exemplar | Search region | Channels |
|-------|-------------|--------|----------|---------------|----------|
|       |             |        | 127×127  | 255×255       | 3        |
| CONV1 | 11×11       | 2      | 59×59    | 123×123       | 96       |
| MP1   | 3×3         | 2      | 29×29    | 61×61         | 96       |
| CONV2 | 5×5         | 1      | 25×25    | 57×57         | 256      |
| MP1   | 3×3         | 2      | 12×12    | 28×28         | 256      |
| CONV3 | 3×3         | 1      | 10×10    | 24×24         | 192      |
| CONV4 | 3×3         | 1      | 8 ×8     | 24×24         | 192      |
| CONV5 | 3×3         | 1      | 6 ×6     | 22×22         | 128      |

## 2.2.3  Generative Adversarial Networks Based Model

To generate realistic-looking images from random noise via CNN, it is introduced
in [15]. Two sub-networks consist of the generative adversarial network (GAN).
One acts as a generator and the other serves as a discriminator. In order to trick the
discriminator, the generator attempts to synthesize images, while the discriminator
seeks to distinguish between real images and images synthesized by the generator.
By competing with each other, the generator and the discriminator are trained
simultaneously. A benefit of adversarial learning is that the generator is conditioned
to generate identical image statistics such that the discriminator does not distinguish
from those of the training samples. Existing empirical objective functions with
supervised learning hardly accomplish this process. The generative adversarial
learning has attracted attentions on deep learning [16–18] and computer vision
applications, such as image generation [19], image stylization [20], object detection
[21], and semantic segmentation [22].

The multi-domain learning model MDNet[5] has achieved good results in various
datasets. However, due to the lack of training samples in the online tracking stage,
its performance is still limited to a certain extent. In order to alleviate this problem,
Song et al. proposed a VITAL[23] model based on a generative confrontation
network, which can enhance the positive samples in the feature space. Its network
structure is shown in Fig. 2.3:

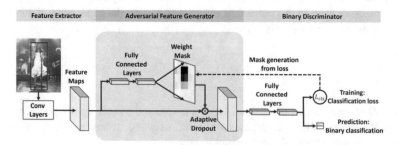

**Fig. 2.3**  The architecture of VITAL

The VITAL model is an improvement based on the MDNet model. The VITAL model uses the idea of generating a confrontation network to enhance the positive samples in the feature space. The process of enhancing the positive samples occurs in the long-term stage of the online update of the model. The connection layer acts on the feature map output by the third convolutional layer of the network to generate a mask matrix. Such a mask matrix is used to simulate the apparent change of the tracked object and further weaken it. The most discriminative feature of the tracked object, thereby preventing the occurrence of drift phenomenon. The mask matrices generated by these two fully connected layers act on the feature map generated by the third convolutional layer to perform an adaptive dropout operation, and then input the result to the subsequent discriminant network and perform online training on it to enhance Discriminate the ability of the network to discriminate the tracked object after the tracked object undergoes various complex apparent changes. In this process, the network composed of two fully connected layers to generate the mask matrix is the generative network in the generative adversarial architecture, and the discriminant network originally in the MDNet network system constitutes the discriminant network in the generative adversarial architecture. The mask matrix generated by the generating network always has the purpose of making it the best to distinguish the network from making mistakes, and the discriminant network has to evolve into a discriminant network with the more anti-interference ability for identifying tracked objects in order to counteract the generation network. Evolution means to update the weight parameters of the discriminating network and the generating network according to the loss function, and the generating network and the discriminating network play a game with each other, and finally reach a dynamic balance. This is the application of the idea of generating adversarial networks in the VITAL model. After online fine-tuning, the discriminant network gradually gains strong anti-interference ability. Unlike traditional generative adversarial networks, when online tracking, the generative network needs to be removed here, leaving the characteristics of time robustness to the tracked object. The discriminative network with the recognition ability. The objective function is defined as follows:

$$\mathcal{L}_{VITAL} = min_G max_D \mathbb{E}_{(C,M) \sim P(C,M)} [log D(M \cdot C)]$$
$$+ \mathbb{E}_{C \sim P(C)} [log(1 - D(G(C) \cdot C))] \tag{2.26}$$
$$+ \lambda \mathbb{E}_{(C,M) \sim P(C,M)} \|G(C) - M\|^2$$

where $C$ represents the feature map output of the third convolutional layer, $G$ and $D$ are the generating network and the discriminant network, respectively, the mask generated according to the feature is $G(C)$, and $M$ is the theoretically optimal mask matrix under the feature $C$. It is the mask matrix that is most likely to make the judgment network error.

## *2.2.4  Reinforcement Learning Based Model*

With the advancement of deep learning in computer vision, deep RL has been introduced in vehicle tracking. The agent communicates with the environment in deep RL and continually obtains the rewards, and then the model is conditioned by optimizing the accumulated potential rewards. Recently, the RL technique for vehicle tracking [24–26] is being exploited by some approaches. A continuous deep Q-learning model was developed by Dong et al. [27] to track the target and a regression approach was used to solve the tracking problem. A policy-based approach was applied by Yun et al. [24] to create the appearance model and target classification model. The relationship between network depth and prediction accuracy was studied by Huang et al. [28] and a method was developed to adaptively change the computation depth to reduce the overhead of computation. The goal of tracking was treated by Supancic et al. [25] as a partly measurable decision-making process and only revised the model when drift tracking occurs. An infinite stream of Internet videos was used as training samples for this method. Chen et al.[29] implemented the Actor-Critic model and used networks for prediction and evaluation, but only the noise of the action space and a basic algorithm of relocation were used, restricting the model's robustness. An iterative shift approach was used by Ren et al.[26] and a new target assessment process was established to further distinguish the target and background. The model's robustness, however, was restricted by the few training samples. A better network architecture is required for a non-real-time RL tracker for high-speed robust tracking performance[24, 26, 29].

Most current deep learning tracking algorithms are deficient in two ways. First, the algorithms are somewhat blind and struggle to efficiently pick candidate samples. The MDNet algorithm, for example, performs dense sampling and then outputs a score to choose the highest scoring sample as the target image, which has the downside of wasting time and doing some unnecessary sample searching. Second, when training the deep network, a large amount of labelled data is needed, and unlabelled video frames cannot be used in semi-supervised mode. It may not be sufficient to use publicly available labelled datasets alone in realistic applications using conventional deep learning tracking methods, particularly in application-specific scenarios where you must create your own labelled dataset, which is more time-consuming and labor-intensive.

To address the first shortcoming above, the ADNet uses the action-driven mechanism to capture the motion information of the target object, which ensures that higher quality candidate samples are searched for first. To address the second shortcoming above, the ADNet use reinforcement learning methods to train the action-driven model mentioned above on a partially labelled dataset. The core idea of the paper is action-decision, i.e. successive sampling by different actions and ultimately locating the location of the target. Its network structure is shown in Fig. 2.4, the core part of the network is a VGG-m convolutional neural network, and the structure of the network ADNet has an $m \times k$-dimensional vector (corresponding

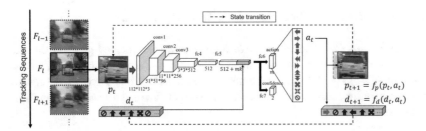

**Fig. 2.4** The overall ADNet architecture

to $m \times k$ kinds of actions and $k \times k$ histories) in the output result after fc5 fully connected layer.

## 2.3 Performance Evaluation

This section introduces several evaluation methods in visual object tracking including: center error, average center error, area overlap and other evaluation criteria. These evaluation criteria evaluate and rank different tracking methods from the four perspectives of accuracy, success rate, speed and robustness. Such as: center error, root mean square error and accuracy rate can be used to evaluate the accuracy of the tracking method; area overlap and success rate can be used to evaluate the success rate of the tracking method; frame rate and equivalent filtering operations can be used to evaluate the tracking method speed; finally, One-Pass Evaluation (OPE), Temporal Robustness Evaluation (TRE), Spatial Robustness Evaluation (SRE) and AR curve are regarded as the robustness of the tracking method evaluation.

### 2.3.1 Performance Evaluation Criteria

Different datasets often correspond to different evaluation criteria. For example, the evaluation criteria used in the OTB dataset are the accuracy rate curve and the success rate curve of a one-time evaluation; the VOT dataset uses the same filtering operation, and the average overlap and A-R curve are expected as the evaluation criteria. The evaluation criteria in the OTB dataset are also applicable to other datasets, such as TC128, UAV123, etc. The specific expressions of each evaluation standard are as follows.

#### 2.3.1.1   Evaluate the Accuracy of the Tracking Algorithm

**Center Error, CE**   The center error indicates the distance by pixel of the center point position between the ground truth of the target state and the target state (Bounding Box) predicted by the tracker. The state of the target is often composed of the center point coordinates and scale of the target. The specific calculation formula is as follows:

$$\delta_t = \|x_t^G - x_t^O\|  \tag{2.27}$$

where $x_t^G$ represents the center position of the true value of the target state in the $t$-th frame, and $x_t^O$ is the center position of the target state in the t-th frame predicted by the tracker, which is the center error of the $t$-th frame of a certain video sequence. The center error can well reflect the accuracy of the tracking algorithm in the positioning of the target center in a certain frame. If all the central error values in a video sequence are connected into a curve, the central error curve of the video sequence will be obtained.

**Average Center Error, ACE**   The center error only reflects the tracking accuracy of the tracking method in a single frame, and does not consider the tracking effect of the tracking method in other frames. Therefore, the average center error is proposed to measure the tracking performance of the tracking method for the tracking sequence. The average center error not only evaluates the tracking performance of the tracking method on a single frame, but also evaluates the tracking performance of the tracking method in the tracking sequence. The average center error represents the average of the center errors of all frames in the tracking sequence, and the unit is a pixel. The calculation formula is as follows:

$$ACE = \frac{1}{N} \sum_{t=1}^{N} \delta_t  \tag{2.28}$$

where $\delta_t$ represents the central error in the $t$-th frame, and $N$ is the total number of frames in a certain video sequence. The lower the average center error, the better the performance of the tracking algorithm.

**Root Mean Square Error, RMSE**   Root means square error not only considers the tracking performance of the tracking method on a single frame, but also considers the root-mean-square error of the tracking method for the tracking accuracy of the tracking sequence. This evaluation index first averages the square of the center error of all frames in the tracking sequence, and then extracts the square root of this average value. The unit of the root mean square error is also the pixel, and the specific calculation formula is as follows:

$$RMSE = \sqrt{\frac{1}{N} \sum_{t=1}^{N} \|x_t^G - x_t^O\|^2}  \tag{2.29}$$

The root mean square error together with the average center error and the center error indicate the accuracy of the tracking method's estimation of the target center position, that is, the tracking method's ability and accuracy to locate the target center, so they can evaluate the accuracy of the object tracking method.

### 2.3.1.2  Evaluate the Success Rate of the Tracking Algorithm

**Region Overlap, RO**  The evaluation standard of the accuracy of the tracking algorithm reflects the accuracy of the tracker's prediction of the center position of the target. It is simple and easy to implement and has a high computational efficiency. However, it does not consider the size of the target, nor can it directly indicate whether the tracking algorithm fails to track. For example, if the center positions coincide, but the target frame scales are different, the tracking accuracy evaluation method will fail. Area overlap uses the intersection ratio of the target frame enclosed by the true value of the target state in a certain frame and the target frame enclosed by the tracking algorithm prediction state as the evaluation criterion. The evaluation standard considers the size of the target and directly indicates whether the tracking algorithm is successful in tracking the target. The regional overlap evaluation will get a real number between 0 and 1, $t \in [0, 1]$. If $\phi_t = 0$, it means that there is no intersection between the target frame enclosed by the true value of the target state in the frame and the target frame enclosed by the tracking algorithm predicting the target state, that is, there is no overlap area between the two. Conversely, $\phi_t = 1$, it means that the two target frames completely overlap. The calculation formula for domain overlap is as follows:

$$\phi_t = \frac{R_t^G \cap R_t^O}{R_t^G \cup R_t^O} = \frac{TP}{TP + FN + FP} \tag{2.30}$$

Among them, $R_t^G$ and $R_t^O$ respectively represent the target area enclosed by the true value of the target state in the $t$-th frame and the target area enclosed by the state value predicted by the tracking algorithm. TP stands for True Positive, which belongs to both the area predicted as the target by the tracking algorithm and the area surrounded by the true value of the target. FN stands for False Negative, which belongs to the area enclosed by the true value of the target, but does not belong to the area predicted as the target by the tracking algorithm. FP stands for False Positive, which belongs to the area predicted as the target by the tracking algorithm, but does not belong to the area enclosed by the true value of the target. If all areas in a video sequence are overlapped and connected into a curve, the area overlap curve of the video sequence will be obtained, which the abscissa is the frame number and the ordinate is the area overlap.

**Average Overlap, AO**  Similar to the central error, the region overlap only considers the evaluation of a certain frame, but does not consider the overall evaluation of the video sequence. Similar to the average central error, the average overlap is based on the overlap of each frame area, and the overall evaluation of the tracking algorithm in the entire video sequence is realized by calculating the average value of the overlap of the entire video sequence. The specific algorithm can be expressed as follows,

$$\bar{\phi} = \frac{1}{N} \sum_{t=1}^{N} \phi_t \tag{2.31}$$

where $\phi_t$ indicates that the area of the $t$-th frame overlaps, and $N$ is the number of all frames included in the video sequence. The higher the average overlap, the better the performance of the tracking algorithm.

### 2.3.1.3  Other Evaluation Criteria for Tracking Algorithms

**Tracking Length, TL**  The tracking length is defined on the basis of the central error, which mainly represents the number of frames from the start of the target tracking algorithm to the first tracking failure, and its unit is the frame. In order to define the tracking failure from the perspective of the center error, a threshold $T_c$ is usually preset. When the central error is higher than the threshold Tc, that is, $\phi_t > T_c$, that means the algorithm tracking fails. Conversely, if $\phi_t \leq T_c$, the algorithm is considered to be successful in tracking. Therefore, the tracking length is the number of frames experienced by the tracking algorithm from the start of tracking to the first time when the center error is greater than the threshold $T_c$. The longer the tracking length, the better the performance of the tracking algorithm.

**Failure Rate, FR**  The failure rate is an evaluation method of the video target tracking algorithm in the VOT dataset. It will judge whether the algorithm has successfully tracked in a frame based on the area overlap. If it is judged that the frame is a tracking failure, it will record the index number of the frame, and use the true value of the target state in the frame to re-run the tracking algorithm initialization. In this way, a set of indexes of frames that have failed to track will be obtained, that is, $\mathfrak{F}_\tau = \mathfrak{f}_i$ . The number of elements in the set, $F_r = |\mathfrak{F}_\tau|$, represents the number of failures of the tracking algorithm. Similar to the tracking success and failure defined based on the central error, the tracking success and failure defined based on the area overlap is also realized by the threshold $T_0$. If the area of a frame overlaps $\phi_t > T_0$, the tracking is successful, otherwise, the tracking fails. The failure rate can be calculated as follows,

$$F_r(\mathfrak{F}_\tau) = \frac{1}{\log(F_\tau)} \sum_{\mathfrak{f}_i \in \mathfrak{F}_\tau} -\frac{\delta \mathfrak{f}_i}{N} \log(\frac{\delta \mathfrak{f}_i}{N}) \tag{2.32}$$

$$\delta \mathfrak{f}_i = \begin{cases} \mathfrak{f}_{i+1} - \mathfrak{f}_i & \mathfrak{f}_i < \max(\mathfrak{F}_\tau) \\ \mathfrak{f} + N - \mathfrak{f}_i & \mathfrak{f}_i = \max(\mathfrak{F}_\tau) \end{cases} \tag{2.33}$$

where $\mathfrak{f}_i$ represents the index of the frame corresponding to the $i$-th tracking failure. The equation shows that the fewer frames elapsed between two tracking failures, the greater the failure rate. The greater the failure rate, the worse the performance of the video tracking algorithm.

**Precision Rat, PR and Success Rate, SR** The accuracy and success rate evaluations in video target tracking are based on the tracking success defined by the central error and by the area overlap respectively. As described in the tracking length and failure rate, the threshold $T_c$ based on the central error and the threshold $T_0$ to based on the area overlap are used to evaluate the success of the algorithm tracking. In the definition of tracking success based on the central error, if the central error is $\phi_t \leqslant T_0$, the tracking is considered successful. In the definition of tracking success based on area overlap, if the area overlap $\phi_t > T_0$, the tracking is considered successful. Therefore, the accuracy rate and the success rate are the percentages of the number of frames successfully tracked to the total number of frames. The difference between the two is mainly the angle at which the tracking success is described. The accuracy rate refers to the number of frames whose central error is less than $T_c$ in the total number of frames. The percentage of the total number of frames, and the power refers to the percentage of the total number of frames whose area overlap is greater than $T_0$. The accuracy and success rate can be calculated as follows:

$$PR = \frac{\mathfrak{R}(\delta_t \leq T_c)}{N}, t \in \{1, 2, \ldots, N\} \tag{2.34}$$

$$SR = \frac{\mathfrak{R}(\phi_t \geq T_o)}{N}, t \in \{1, 2, \ldots, N\} \tag{2.35}$$

where $\mathfrak{R}(*)$ represents the number of frames meeting the condition $*$, and $N$ is the total number of frames. Therefore, the higher the accuracy and success rate of the tracking algorithm, the better the performance of the algorithm.

**Precision Rate Plot, PRP and Success Rate Plot, SRP** If you change the size of the central error and the area overlap threshold, the accuracy and success rate will also change with the changes in these two thresholds. Therefore, the threshold value and its corresponding accuracy rate and success rate are plotted as curves, and the precision rate curve (PRP) can be obtained and the success rate curve (SRP). As far as the accuracy rate curve is concerned, gradually increasing the value of the threshold $T_c$, the number of frames that meet the condition $\phi_t > T_c$ will gradually increase, so the accuracy rate curve is a monotonically increasing curve. As far as the success rate curve is concerned, gradually increasing the value of the threshold To will gradually reduce the number of frames that meet the condition $\phi_t > T_0$. Therefore, the success rate is inversely proportional to the threshold To, and the success rate curve is a monotonically decreasing curve.

**Frame Pre Seconds, FPS** Frame rate is an important evaluation criterion to measure the tracking speed of an algorithm. It represents the number of frames that the tracker can track the target in 1 s, and the unit is frame per second. The frame rate is a measure of whether the tracking algorithm can achieve real-time tracking. In general, if the frame rate of the tracking algorithm can exceed 25FPS or 30FPS, it is considered that it can achieve real-time tracking of the target. The frame rate can be calculated by the timer during programming, or the average frame rate can be calculated by dividing the total time spent tracking the video sequence by the total number of frames. The frame rate will be affected by the tracking algorithm and hardware equipment, so when using the frame rate, it is necessary to introduce the hardware equipment and configuration of the algorithm running.

**Equivalent Filter Operations, EFO** The same filtering operation is also an evaluation index to measure the speed of the tracking algorithm, which is proposed along with the VOT dataset. It mainly solves the problem that the same tracking algorithm has different frame rates on different hardware devices. Compared with the frame rate, the same filtering operation can show the running speed of the algorithm more directly and fairly. It first needs to use a $30 \times 30$ window on the hardware device running the algorithm to filter a $600 \times 600$ image and record the time required for the operation. This time indicates the performance of the hardware device you are using inferior. Then, by dividing the time required for the algorithm to process one frame and the filtering time, the evaluation index of the equivalent filtering operation can be obtained.

**OPE, TRE, and SRE** OPE, TRE and SRE are evaluation indicators of the robustness of video target tracking algorithms. Among them, OPE refers to one-pass evaluation (OPE), which means the evaluation after running all video sequences in the entire dataset once. TRE refers to Temporal Robustness Evaluation, which divides each video sequence in the entire dataset into 20 segments, and uses the start frame of these 20 sub video sequences as the start frame of the algorithm to initialize and track the tracking algorithm. For a video sequence, the tracking algorithm runs 20 times, but the starting frame is different during these 20 runs, so as to analyze and evaluate the time robustness of the tracking algorithm. SRE refers to (Spatial Robustness Evaluation), which affinely changes the state of the initial frame of each video sequence in the data to obtain 12 target states for initialization, and uses these 12 affine-changed state pairs respectively to initialize and perform tracking. Each video sequence in the dataset has been run 12 times from beginning to end, but the initialization state of each run is different, in order to evaluate the spatial robustness of the tracking algorithm. The robustness evaluations of the three video target tracking algorithms, OPE, TRE and SRE, all correspond to their respective accuracy rate curves and success rate curves, of which OPE accuracy rate curves and success rate curves are the most widely used.

**A-R Plot** The A-R chart is an evaluation standard that comprehensively considers the accuracy and robustness of the video target tracking algorithm. It is used to measure the comprehensive performance of the tracking algorithm and can achieve the purpose of sorting multiple tracking algorithms. Here, A refers to the Expected Average Overlap (EAO), which can be obtained by the expected value of the average overlap of all video sequences in the dataset. R refers to the robustness value $R_S$, which can be calculated as follows:

$$R_S = e^{-SM}, M = \frac{|\mathfrak{J}_\tau|}{N} \tag{2.36}$$

where $M$ represents the average number of failures, which can be obtained by calculating the ratio of the total number of failures $|\mathfrak{J}_\tau|$ to the total length $N$ of the sequence. $S$ is a manually set parameter, indicating that the video target tracking algorithm is expected to continuously track $S$ frames. The graph made with the expected average overlap rate A as the ordinate and the robustness value $R$ as the abscissa is the A-R graph. The tracker located in the upper right corner of the A-R diagram is better than the tracker located in the lower left corner. According to this principle, A-R chart can realize the comparison and sorting of tracking algorithms.

### 2.3.2 Benchmark Datasets

This section introduces some datasets used in visual object tracking, 8 video tracking datasets including the OTB dataset, VOT dataset, TC128, UAV123, LaSOT and GOT-10K datasets. These datasets provide a large number of manually annotated video sequences. Moreover, evaluation standards and evaluation toolboxes are provided to facilitate the comparison between various tracking methods, such as: OTB dataset and VOT dataset. Among them, the OTB dataset first standardizes the standards of video tracking methods, and provides a comparison environment for tracking methods. It contains many types of tracking challenges and is widely used by tracking method.

**OTB** The OTB dataset (Object Tracking Benchmark, OTB) mainly includes three datasets, namely: OTB-2013 [30], OTB100 (OTB-2015) [31] and OTB50. The OTB dataset was first proposed by Y. Wu et al. [30] in CVPR in 2013 and named OTB-2013. OTB-2013 contains 51 video sequences and has more than 2900 frames with artificially labelled target boxes. The Skating video sequence can be regarded as two different video sequences because of the different labeling objects. The OTB-2013 dataset. also divides visual object tracking into 11 types of challenges, such as: scale change, illumination change, occlusion, etc., and annotates the tracking challenges corresponding to each video sequence in the dataset to facilitate the analysis of tracking methods to deal with different challenges. Part of the video sequence in the OTB dataset is shown in Fig. 2.5.

It is worth noting that a video sequence may correspond to multiple tracking challenges. The OTB-2015 dataset is Y. Wu et al. [31] based on OTB-2013 to expand the video sequence, the number of video sequences expands to 100, so the OTB-2015 dataset is also called OTB100. With the wide application of OTB-2013 and OTB-2015 datasets, many tracking methods have achieved good tracking results on these two datasets. In order to increase the difficulty of the OTB tracking dataset,

**Fig. 2.5** Samples of some sequences in the OTB benchmark

another 50 complex video sequences were extracted from the OTB-2015 dataset to form a new dataset called OTB50. The OTB dataset also proposes an evaluation tool, which has good compatibility and is also suitable for some other datasets, such as: TC128, UAV123, etc. Therefore, the OTB dataset is currently the most widely used dataset in visual object tracking.

**VOT** The VOT (Visual Object Tracking, VOT) dataset is mainly derived from the Visual Object Tracking Challenge (VOT Challenge). It provides a precisely defined and repeatable comparison method for visual object tracking methods, and it also provides a common platform to analyze the performance of visual object tracking methods. Since 2013, the VOT challenge has released a new dataset every year for comparison and evaluation of various tracking methods. So far, the VOT dataset mainly includes VOT2013 [32], VOT2014 [33], VOT2015 [34], VOT2016 [35], VOT2017 [36], VOT2018 [37] and VOT2019 [38]. Different from the OTB dataset, the VOT dataset updates very quickly. It retains some of the video sequences in the previous dataset based on some weaknesses of the existing tracking methods, and adds some new video sequences to increase the tracking difficulty of the target in the video sequence. For example, the VOT2019 dataset is based on the current deep feature-based tracking method that is relatively weak for small target object tracking. On the basis of the previous dataset, video sequences such as ant tracking are added. In addition, the VOT Challenge 2019 also aims on the RGB image based tracking problems and the tracking dataset for the RGBD tracking algorithm is added. The VOT dataset has its own unique evaluation criteria and evaluation tools [37], such as: EAO, EFO and A-R diagrams. Different from the general target state labeling method, the VOT dataset no longer uses a regular rectangular frame to label the target area, but uses an irregular rectangular frame with rotation. This labeling can obtain more accurately the target area in the frame, and make the target image contains less background information. Part of the video sequence in the VOT dataset is shown in Fig. 2.6.

**Fig. 2.6**  Samples of some sequences in the VOT benchmark

**Fig. 2.7**  Samples of some sequences in the TC128 benchmark

**TC128**  The TC128 dataset (Temple Color 128, TC128) was proposed by Liang et al. [39] of Temple University in the United States in 2015 in the IEEE Transactions on Image Processing journal. It contains 128 video sequences with manual annotations. The source of these 128 video sequences is mainly divided into two parts, one is the 50 video sequences commonly used in other video datasets, and the other is the 78 manually labelled video sequences. The video tracking dataset is mainly to explore the influence of color information on the video target tracking algorithm, so the video sequences in the video dataset are all color pictures. Part of the video sequence in the TC128 dataset is shown in Fig. 2.7.

**UAV123**  The UAV123 dataset (Unmanned Aerial Vehicles, UAV) was proposed by Mueller et al. [40] of King Abdullah University of Science and Technology at the 2016 ECCV conference. The video sequences in this dataset are all taken from overhead and most of these videos were shot and produced by unmanned aerial

**Fig. 2.8** Samples of some sequences in the UAV123 benchmark

vehicles. There are also some video sequences that are synthesized by computer. The UAV123 dataset has more specific tasks and application scenarios, which includes 123 video sequences with manual annotations. In addition, the dataset also provides 20 ultra-long video sequences to test the tracking ability of the visual object tracking methods in long period videos and is named UAV20L. Part of the video sequence of the UAV123 dataset is shown in Fig. 2.8.

**NFS** The NFS dataset (Need For Speed, NFS) was proposed by Kiani et al. [41] at the 2017 ICCV meeting. Unlike the previous dataset with a video frame rate of 30 FPS, the NFS dataset first proposed visual object tracking dataset based on high frame rates. This dataset is more focused on studying the impact of high frame rate video sequences on visual object tracking methods. The NFS dataset contains 100 video sequences with a frame rate of 240 FPS. These 100 video sequences are artificially labelled with target frames and 9 different tracking challenges. The video sequence of the NFS dataset is based on real scenes and is collected by mobile phones, tablets and other commonly used devices. The video sequence of part of the NFS dataset is shown in Fig. 2.9.

**LaSOT** The LaSOT dataset (Large-scale Single Object Tracking, LaSOT) was proposed by Heng et al. [42] of Temple University at the 2019 CVPR conference. It contains a total of 1400 video sequences and more than 3.52 million target frames with artificially labelled annotations, and the total size of the dataset has reached 227G. This is currently one of the largest visual object tracking datasets with artificially labelled. The LaSOT dataset divides the 1400 video sequences into 70 categories according to different tracking targets, and each category includes 20 video sequences. Meanwhile, the LaSOT dataset. also pays attention to the tracking of long-term video targets. The average number of frames contained in each video sequence is 1512 frames, which has 83 s of video duration. The shortest video sequence has 1000 frames, and the longest video sequence exceeds 10,000 frames. Another feature of the LaSOT dataset is that it not only provides a target frame

**Fig. 2.9** Samples of some sequences in the NFS benchmark

**Fig. 2.10** Samples of some sequences in the LaSOT benchmark

reflecting the state and category label of the target, but also gives the corresponding semantics in combination with the movement of the target in the video description. So the dataset makes can be used to evaluate single-target video tracking as well as suitable for other tasks such as video description. The video sequence of part of the LaSOT dataset is shown in Fig. 2.10.

**TrackingNet** The TrackingNet dataset is a large dataset proposed by Muller et al. [43] at the 2018 ECCV conference. This dataset filters and obtains video sequences from YouTube, which can be regarded as a subset of the video target detection dataset YT-BB. The TrackingNet dataset is aimed at outdoor video sequences, and it has more than 30,000 video sequences and more than 14 million video frames with target frames. The TrackingNet dataset helps to improve some tracking methods that

**Fig. 2.11** Samples of some sequences in the TrackingNet benchmark

require lots data as support. The size of the TrackingNet dataset is 1.1T, which is currently the largest video target tracking dataset. The video sequence of part of the TrackingNet dataset is shown in Fig. 2.11.

**GOT-10k** The GOT-10K dataset (Generic Object Tracking, GOT) is a dataset published online on arXiv by Huang et al. [44] in 2019. The size of the dataset is 66G, including more than 10,000 video sequences and more than 1.5 million frames with manually labelled target frames. The GOT-10K dataset is smaller than the LaSOT and TrackingNet datasets, but it contains the most types of targets. The dataset is based on WordNet, and the targets used for tracking cover more than 560 objects in reality. This dataset divides all video sequences into training set and test set, which helps to unify the training samples based on the deep learning tracking methods, and provides a relative commonality for the deep learning based tracking methods. The video sequence of part of the TrackingNet dataset is shown in Fig. 2.12. In order to achieve a fair evaluation of the Generic Object Tracking Algorithm (GOTA), the GOT-10K dataset also formulated the one-shot rule, which means in addition to people, other target categories that have appeared in the training set will not reproduce in the test data. This can remove the prior knowledge introduced by the target detection to improve the tracking performance, and only discuss the performance of the tracking algorithm that does not distinguish between target categories. The testing set contains 180 video sequences covering 84 types of targets and 32 types of motion modes, so it can effectively evaluate visual object tracking methods. In addition, the GOT-10K dataset. also provides some additional tags, such as target visibility and motion category as auxiliary tags for analyzing visual object tracking methods, which makes it not only suitable for target tracking, but also for other tasks, such as: video description, motion classification, etc.

**Fig. 2.12**  Samples of some sequences in the GOT-10k benchmark

## 2.4  Summary

In this section, the algorithmic foundations are introduced in three aspects: correlation filter basics, typical deep learning model for tracking and performance evaluation, which explain the correlation filter based methods, deep learning based methods, performance evaluation methods, and benchmark datasets of visual object tracking.

For the correlation filter basics, we first explain the concept of correlation filter and its application in visual object tracking. Then, MOSSE which is the first correlation filter based tracking method is introduced in this chapter. Furthermore, we also introduce the DSST tracker which is the Milestone of discriminative correlation filter based tracking methods. DSST introduces the correlation filter based trackers into multi-dimension and proposes the scale filter to cope with the scale variation challenge. Finally, the kernel correlation filter based tracker treat tracking as a ridge regression problem and introduce kernel method in correlation filter based trackers.

For the typical deep learning model based tracking methods, we mainly divided the deep learning model into four aspects: CNN based model, Siamese network based model, GAN based model and reinforcement learning based model. For each model, we first introduce the basic concepts and then a milestone typical tracker is described in detail. For CNN based model, MDNet applies the CNN network and fine tuning methods in visual object tracking is introduced in this chapter. SiameseFC could be trained pairwised, combining the advantage of correlation filter and deep learning method. VITAL and ADNet represent the GAN based and reinforcement learning based tracking methods, respectively.

For the tracking performance evaluation methods, 13 evaluation methods including center error and area overlap rate are described from tracking algorithm accuracy, success rate, speed and robustness. These evaluation methods can test the tracking ability of the tracker. And for the tracking dataset, 8 datasets such as OTB are introduced. The most commonly used OTB dataset is also the video tracking dataset used most in this article.

## References

1. Bolme, D., Beveridge, J., Draper, B., et al.: Visual object tracking using adaptive correlation filters. In: IEEE Conference on Computer Vision and Pattern Recognition, pp. 2544–2550 (2010)
2. Henriques, J., Caseiro, R., Martins, P., et al.: High-speed tracking with kernelized correlation filters. IEEE Trans. Pattern Anal. Mach. Intell. **37**(3), 583–596 (2015)
3. Rifkin, R., Yeo, G., Poggio, T., et al.: Regularized least-squares classification. In: Nato Science Series Sub Series III Computer and Systems Sciences, vol. 190, pp. 131–154 (2003)
4. Hong, S., You, T., Kwak, S., Han, B.: Online tracking by learning discriminative saliency map with convolutional neural network. In: International Conference on Machine Learning, pp. 597–606 (2015)
5. Nam, H., Han, B.: Learning multi-domain convolutional neural networks for visual tracking. In: IEEE Conference on Computer Vision and Pattern Recognition, pp. 4293–4302 (2016)
6. Song, Y., Ma, C., Gong, L., Zhang, J., Lau, R.W., Yang, M.H.: Crest: convolutional residual learning for visual tracking. In: IEEE International Conference on Computer Vision, pp. 2555–2564 (2017)
7. Bhat, G., Johnander, J., Danelljan, M., Khan, F.S., Felsberg, M.: Unveiling the power of deep tracking. In: European Conference on Computer Vision, pp. 483–498 (2018)
8. Li, B., Wu, W., Wang, Q., Zhang, F., Xing, J., Yan, J.: Siamrpn++: evolution of siamese visual tracking with very deep networks. In: IEEE Conference on Computer Vision and Pattern Recognition, pp. 4282–4291 (2019)
9. Zhang, Z., Peng, H.: Deeper and wider siamese networks for real-time visual tracking. In: IEEE Conference on Computer Vision and Pattern Recognition, pp. 4591–4600 (2019)
10. Fan, H., Ling, H.: Siamese cascaded region proposal networks for real-time visual tracking. In: IEEE Conference on Computer Vision and Pattern Recognition, pp. 7952–7961 (2019)
11. Tao, R., Gavves, E., Smeulders, A.: Siamese instance search for tracking. In: IEEE Conference on Computer Vision and Pattern Recognition, pp. 1420–1429 (2016)
12. Guo, Q., Feng, W., Zhou, C., Huang, R., Wan, L., Wang, S.: Learning dynamic siamese network for visual object tracking. In: IEEE International Conference on Computer Vision, pp. 1763–1771 (2017)
13. Zhu, Z., Huang, G., Zou, W., Du, D., Huang, C.: UCT: learning unified convolutional networks for real-time visual tracking. In: IEEE International Conference on Computer Vision Workshops, pp. 1973–1982 (2017)
14. Wang, Q., Teng, Z., Xing, J., Gao, J., Hu, W., Maybank, S.: Learning attentions: residual attentional siamese network for high performance online visual tracking. In: IEEE Conference on Computer Vision and Pattern Recognition, pp. 4854–4863 (2018)
15. Goodfellow, I.J., Pouget-Abadie, J., Mirza, M., Xu, B., Warde-Farley, D., Ozair, S., Bengio, Y.: Generative adversarial networks. In: Proceedings of Neural Information Processing Systems, pp. 2672–2680 (2014)
16. Arjovsky, M., Chintala, S., Bottou, L.: Wasserstein generative adversarial networks. In: International Conference on Machine Learning, pp. 214–223 (2017)
17. Gurumurthy, S., Kiran Sarvadevabhatla, R., Venkatesh Babu, R.: Deligan: generative adversarial networks for diverse and limited data. In: IEEE Conference on Computer Vision and Pattern Recognition, pp. 166–174 (2017)

18. Nowozin, S., Cseke, B., Tomioka, R.: f-GAN: training generative neural samplers using variational divergence minimization. In: Neural Information Processing Systems, pp. 271–279 (2016)
19. Zhang, H., Xu, T., Li, H., Zhang, S., Wang, X., Huang, X., Metaxas, D.N.: Stackgan: text to photo-realistic image synthesis with stacked generative adversarial networks. In: IEEE International Conference on Computer Vision, pp. 5907–5915 (2017)
20. Isola, P., Zhu, J.Y., Zhou, T., Efros, A.A.: Image-to-image translation with conditional adversarial networks. In: IEEE Conference on Computer Vision and Pattern Recognition, pp. 1125–1134 (2017)
21. Wang, X., Shrivastava, A., Gupta, A.: A-fast-RCNN: hard positive generation via adversary for object detection. In: IEEE Conference on Computer Vision and Pattern Recognition, pp. 2606–2615 (2017)
22. Souly, N., Spampinato, C., Shah, M.: Semi supervised semantic segmentation using generative adversarial network. In: IEEE International Conference on Computer Vision, pp. 5688–5696 (2017)
23. Song, Y.B., Ma, C., Wu, X.H., Gong, L.J., Bao, L.C., Zuo, W.M., Shen, C.H., Rynson, W.H.L., Ming-Hsuan,Y.: VITAL: visual tracking via adversarial learning. In: IEEE Conference on Computer Vision and Pattern Recognition, pp. 8990–8999 (2018)
24. Yun, S., Choi, J., Yoo, Y., Yun, K., Young Choi, J.: Action-decision networks for visual tracking with deep reinforcement learning. In: IEEE Conference on Computer Vision and Pattern Recognition, pp. 2711–2720 (2017)
25. Supancic, J. III, Ramanan, D.: Tracking as online decision-making: learning a policy from streaming videos with reinforcement learning. In: IEEE International Conference on Computer Vision, pp. 322–331 (2017)
26. Ren, L., Yuan, X., Lu, J., Yang, M., Zhou, J.: Deep reinforcement learning with iterative shift for visual tracking. In: European Conference on Computer Vision, pp. 684–700 (2018)
27. Dong, X., Shen, J., Wang, W., Liu, Y., Shao, L., Porikli, F.: Hyperparameter optimization for tracking with continuous deep q-learning. In: IEEE Conference on Computer Vision and Pattern Recognition, pp. 518–527 (2018)
28. Huang, C., Lucey, S., Ramanan, D.: Learning policies for adaptive tracking with deep feature cascades. In: IEEE International Conference on Computer Vision, pp. 105–114 (2017)
29. Chen, B., Wang, D., Li, P., Wang, S., Lu, H.: Real-time 'Actor-Critic' tracking. In: European Conference on Computer Vision, pp. 318–334 (2018)
30. Wu, Y., Lim, J., Yang, M.H.: Online object tracking: a benchmark. In: IEEE Conference on Computer Vision and Pattern Recognition, pp. 2411–2418 (2013)
31. Wu, Y., Lim, J., Yang, M.H.: Object tracking benchmark. IEEE Trans. Pattern Anal. Mach. Intell. **37**(9), 1834–1848 (2015)
32. Kristan, M., Pflugfelder, R., Leonardis, A., et al.: The visual object tracking vot2013 challenge results. In: IEEE International Conference on Computer Vision Workshops, pp. 98–111 (2013)
33. Kristan, M., Pflugfelder, R., Leonardis, A., et al.: The visual object tracking vot2014 challenge results. In: European Conference on Computer Vision, Visual Object Tracking Challenge Workshop, pp. 191–217 (2014)
34. Kristan, M., Matas, J., Leonardis, A., et al.: The visual object tracking vot2015 challenge results. In: IEEE International Conference on Computer Vision Workshops, pp. 564–586 (2015)
35. Kristan, M., Matas, J., Leonardis, A., et al.: The visual object tracking vot2016 challenge results. In: European Conference on Computer Vision Workshops, pp. 777–823 (2016)
36. Kristan, M., Matas, J., Leonardis, A., et al.: The visual object tracking vot2017 challenge results. In: IEEE International Conference on Computer Vision Workshops, pp. 1949–1972 (2017)
37. Kristan, M., Matas, J., Leonardis, A., et al.: The visual object tracking vot2018 challenge results. In: European Conference on Computer Vision Workshops, pp. 3–53 (2018)

38. Kristan, M., Matas, J., Leonardis, A., et al.: The visual object tracking vot2019 challenge results. In: IEEE International Conference on Computer Vision Workshops, pp. 2206–2241 (2019)

39. Liang, P., Blasch, E., Ling, H.: Encoding color information for visual tracking: algorithms and benchmark. IEEE Trans. Image Process. **24**(12), 5630–5644 (2015)

40. Mueller, M., Smith, N., Ghanem, B.: A benchmark and simulator for UAV tracking. In: European Conference on Computer Vision, pp. 445–461 (2015)

41. Kiani Galoogahi, H., Fagg, A., Huang, C., Ramanan, D., Lucey, S.: Need for speed: a benchmark for higher frame rate object tracking. In: IEEE International Conference on Computer Vision, pp. 1125–1134 (2017)

42. Fan, H., Lin, L., Yang, F., Chu, P., Deng, G., Yu, S., Ling, H.: Lasot: a high-quality benchmark for large-scale single object tracking. In: IEEE Conference on Computer Vision and Pattern Recognition, pp. 5374–5383 (2019)

43. Muller, M., Bibi, A., Giancola, S., Alsubaihi, S., Ghanem, B.: Trackingnet: a large-scale dataset and benchmark for object tracking in the wild. In: European Conference on Computer Vision, pp. 300–317 (2018)

44. Huang, L., Zhao, X., Huang, K.: Got-10k: A large high-diversity benchmark for generic object tracking in the wild. Preprint, arXiv:1810.11981 (2018)

# Chapter 3
# Correlation Filter Based Visual Object Tracking

Different from the traditional Bayesian-based tracking methods, correlation filter based trackers treat visual object tracking as a foreground and background classification problem, which belongs to the discriminative tracking methods. The Correlation filter is used to measure the relevance between the template of the object and search region, and compute the response map. The tracking results can be estimated by finding the peak location in response map. Correlation filter based trackers have advantages in tracking speed and accuracy, but lack of dealing with scale variation and occlusion challenges. Aiming at the problems above, this chapter mainly introduces three kinds of improved correlation filter based trackers: correlation filter tracker with context-aware strategy; correlation filter tracker with scale pyramid and correlation filter tracker with multi-scale superpixels.

## 3.1 Introduction

There are various tracking algorithms have been proposed to track object online [1–3] or offline [4, 5]. Many surveys try to show the classification and definition of single object tracking [6–10]. Smeulders et al. [8] showed a brief definition of visual object tracking. While Wu et al. [9, 10] provided the OTB benchmark and summarized visual object tracking into 11 challenges. From the principle of tracking algorithm, visual object tracking can be divided into generative methods [1, 11–13] and discriminative methods [14–16]. For generative methods, the tracking results are estimated by matching the template and candidate objects. The candidate object with the highest matching score is the tracking result [11]. While the discriminated methods treat tracking as either a classifier [17] or regressor [15].

Correlation filter based tracking methods [15, 18], which belongs to the discriminated methods, estimated tracking results by training a discriminated correlation filter. The location of the maximum value in the response map after correlation

W. Xing et al., *Visual Object Tracking from Correlation Filter to Deep Learning*,
https://doi.org/10.1007/978-981-16-6242-3_3

filtering indicates the position of the object center. Bolme et al. [18] first applied the correlation filter into the visual object tracking field and proposed the MOSSE tracker. Henriques et al. [19] introduced the circulant matrix to increase the speed of training the correlation filter under dense samples. Henriques et al. [20] treated tracking as a ridge regression problem and introduced the kernel method into the correlation filter based tracking methods. Tang et al. [21] extended the kernel correlation filter based method into the multi-kernel correlation filter based method. In order to cope with the scale variation challenge. Danelljan et al. [22] proposed two correlation filters, one for translation filter which is used for estimating the center position of the object and the scale filter which is used for estimating the scale of the object. In order to further improve the representation ability of the object, deep features are also combined into the correlation filter based tracking methods[23].

The traditional correlation filter based tracking methods have advantages in tracking speed and accuracy, but lack of dealing with scale variation and occlusion challenges. Aiming at the problems above, this chapter mainly introduces three kinds of improved correlation filter based trackers. The first method proposed the context aware based global background information on the basis of DCF to improve the discriminative ability and the adaptive update model is proposed to improve the tracking robustness. The second method combined the position estimation and scale estimation with the scale pyramid filter to make the tracker cope with multi-scale problem. A manually designed rich image feature is proposed to improve the tracking performance. The third method treats tacking as the problem of finding the optimal combination of the object patches. The object is segmented into several sub-patches based on the multi-scale superpixels segmentation, then multi-KCF trackers are used to track the sub-patches respectively, Finally, the optimal combination of sub-patches can be calculated by the proposed min-max criterion which considering the structure information of the object.

## 3.2   Correlation Filter Tracker with Context Aware Strategy

Correlation filter based trackers have achieved great success in tracking speed when comparing with other trackers. However, there still exists some space for improvement in correlation filter based tracker, such as the full use of background information. Due to the cosine window and the fixed ROI area in the training procedure of correlation filter based tracker, the use of background information is very limited which also reduces the discriminating ability of the classifier. In order to solve this problem, a novel DCF_BM tracker is proposed. Firstly, more global background information on the basis of DCF is introduced to improve the discriminating ability of classifier. Then a novel red-detection component is proposed to handle the situation when the tracking failure occurs under some complex tracking challenges. Finally, different from the linear interpolation update method which is widely used in correlation filter based tracker, an adaptive model update strategy is proposed to improve the tracking robustness. The experimental results show the comparable tracking performance when comparing with state-of-the-art trackers.

### 3.2.1  Context Aware Strategy

In this section, we combine the DCF framework with the framework in the CACF to add global context information. While training the correlation filter, we sample around the object. The specific background modeling process is shown in Fig. 3.1 we use object and background image blocks to train the peak regression classifier. In this section, we return the expected value of the global background image block to zero. It may not be optimal to drastically normalize the expected output value of the background image block to zero, but this may lead to a closed solution, which contributes to the real-time performance of the tracker. For improved objective functions, see Eq. 3.1.

$$\min_{W} \|A_0 W - y\|_2^2 + \lambda_1 \|W\|_2^2 + \lambda_2 \sum_{i=1}^{k} \|A_i W\|_2^2 \tag{3.1}$$

Where $A_0$ represents the circulant matrix formed by the object image block, $A_i$ represents the circulant matrix formed by the global background image block, and $\lambda_1$ and $\lambda_2$ are regularization parameters. For the objective function, the expected

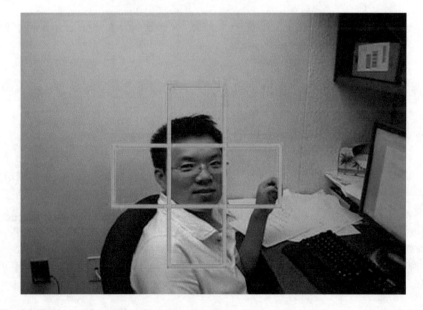

**Fig. 3.1** Background modeling diagram

output value of the target image block is $y$. Rejoin the object image block and the background image block to form a new matrix. The expression can be rewritten as:

$$f_p(W, B) = \|BW - \bar{y}\|_2^2 + \lambda_1 \|W\|_2^2 \tag{3.2}$$

Here, $B$ denotes a new matrix formed by combining the global background image block and the object, and $y$ denotes a label vector obtained by expanding the label $y$ with 0. $B$ and $y$ satisfy the equations below:

$$B = \begin{bmatrix} A_0 \\ \sqrt{\lambda_2 A_1} \\ \cdots \\ \sqrt{\lambda_2 A_k} \end{bmatrix} \tag{3.3}$$

$$\bar{y} = \begin{bmatrix} y \\ 0 \\ 0 \\ \cdots \\ 0 \end{bmatrix} \tag{3.4}$$

since $fp(W, B)$ is a convex function, by deriving the objective function and setting the derivative to 0, a closed solution for $W$ can be obtained:

$$W = (B^T B + \lambda_1 I)^{-1} B^T \bar{y} \tag{3.5}$$

using the properties of the circulant matrix, the above equation can finally be transformed as follows:

$$W = [F diag(\hat{\alpha}_0^* \odot \hat{\alpha}_0 + \lambda_1 + \lambda_2 \sum_{i=1}^{k} \hat{\alpha}_i^* \odot \hat{\alpha}_i) F^H]^{-1} diag(\hat{\alpha}_0^* \odot \hat{y}) \tag{3.6}$$

by performing a Fourier transform on $W$, then, we can obtain $\hat{W}$.

$$\hat{W} = \frac{\hat{\alpha}_0^* \odot \hat{y}}{\hat{\alpha}_0^* \odot \hat{\alpha}_0 + \lambda_1 + \lambda_2 \sum_{i=1}^{k} \hat{\alpha}_i^* \odot \hat{\alpha}_i} \tag{3.7}$$

After training the correlation filters, the next step is the object detection process. The object detection method used in this article is the same as the DCF tracker object detection method, except that it has a wide search range. The response map can be obtained by convolving the trained filter with the image block $z$ (search window) in the next frame. Similar to the DCF tracker, the detection formula used to solve the response map can be expressed as:

$$\hat{r}_d = \hat{z} \odot \hat{\alpha}_0^* \odot \hat{\alpha}_0 + \sqrt{\lambda_2} \sum_{i=1}^{k} \hat{z} \odot \hat{\alpha}_i^* \odot \hat{\alpha}_i \tag{3.8}$$

### 3.2.2   Adaptive Update Model

During the tracking process, objects often undergo various changes. Therefore, the tracking algorithm needs to update the model in time to adapt to this change in order to improve the robustness of the tracking algorithm. This is very difficult. In traditional correlation filter based tracking algorithms, both the KCF tracker and the DSST tracker use the following linear interpolation to update the method, as shown in Eqs. 3.9 and 3.10.

$$\hat{x}^n = (1 - \gamma)\hat{x}^{n-1} + \gamma\hat{x} \tag{3.9}$$

$$\hat{\alpha}^n = (1 - \gamma)\hat{\alpha}^{n-1} + \gamma\hat{\alpha} \tag{3.10}$$

Where $n$ is the sequence number of the current frame, $\hat{x}$ is the target representation model represented by the predicted position image block, $\hat{\alpha}$ is the classification parameter, and $\gamma$ is the model update rate. Currently, the model update rate is determined by experience and is constant. The higher the value, the faster the model will be updated. Conversely, the smaller the value of $\gamma$ the slower the model update speed. If the object changes significantly, such as a change in attitude or in-plane rotation, it should be selected as a large value. If the tracking environment changes significantly and the tracking object does not change much, you should choose the smaller value. However, if it is too large, the update rate will be too fast and the model will be prone to drift. In other words, setting the model update rate to a fixed value is not appropriate because it does not accurately reflect object changes. In addition, this update method can easily overfit the model to a few frames of the image. For example, the updated model is particularly sensitive to biting and deformation. This article proposes an adaptive model update strategy. Here, we will introduce the penalty factor $\xi$ for controlling the update rate of the model. $\xi$ is determined by the following equation.

$$\xi = \frac{max(\phi(t))}{max(\{\phi(1), \phi(2), \ldots \phi(t-1)\})} \tag{3.11}$$

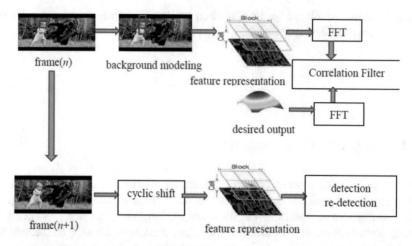

**Fig. 3.2** Pipeline of the proposed tracking algorithm

## 3.2.3   Framework and Procedure

Figure 3.2 shows the details of the flowchart of the tracking algorithm proposed In this section. Our algorithm primarily includes relevant filter training and target detection. Image feature representations continue to use the most commonly used FHOG features in correlation filter based object tracking. Compared to traditional correlation filter based tracking algorithms, the proposed tracker improves the correlation filter training process. The training negative samples consider not only the image blocks after the object's periodic shift, but also the image blocks around the object. This helps improve the identification performance of the correlation filter. In addition, this paper proposes an adaptation model update strategy to better adapt to object changes. In addition, the rediscovery component is also used on the proposed tracker to reduce the frequency of tracking errors.

In traditional correlation filter based tracking algorithms, the principle of tracking is to apply a "correlation filter" template to the detected image block and treat the peak position of the response map as the location of the object. However, this detection method has the disadvantage that the position with the highest response value does not always track the actual position of the object, especially in complex situations. Therefore, using this method for position estimation of the object can directly lead to contamination of the model, which affects the accuracy of the tracking algorithm. This chapter introduced a rediscovery and search operation to remedy this problem. Using the APCE indicator to determine the tracking performance of the current frame. This indicator has been improved based on the PSR indicator, which measures the vibration of the response map. The calculation method is shown in Eq. 3.12.

$$APCE = \frac{|max(\phi(t)) - min(\phi(t))|^2}{mean(\sum_{m,n}(g_{m,n} - min(\phi(t)))^2)} \tag{3.12}$$

$\phi(t)$ represents the response image of the t-th frame. If the $APCE$ does not reach the historical average, the tracking result for the current frame may be inaccurate. At this time, the rediscovery component is used to search for objects in positions corresponding to other peaks in the response graph. The response maps obtained from the associated filter templates are then calculated for each candidate image block. Finally, determine the image block with the highest response value as the object. The rediscovery method used here does not require training additional correlation filters to detect tracking reliability, nor does it require training additional classifiers to rediscover objects.

### 3.2.4 Experimental Results and Discussions

This section mainly introduces the experimental results of this article. Firstly, the dataset used in the experiment is introduced. We compared the trackers proposed in this article with other trackers in the OTB-2013 and OTB-2015 datasets. Then, this paper introduced the parameter settings of the proposed algorithm. Finally, the performance of the proposed algorithm is tested and analyzed in this chapter.

In experimental settings, the kernel function type is set to a linear kernel, image block padding is set to be 2. $\lambda_1$ and $\lambda_2$ are 1e−4 and 26 respectively. In this chapter, we also set the linear interpolation factor used for adaptation to 0.012. Set the cell size is set to 4 and the orientation is set to 9, when calculating the HOG function.

When comparing the proposed algorithm with some correlation filter based trackers, KCF and its improved variants show significantly better performance than some traditional trackers such as Struck [16], TLD[24], MEEM[25]. Thus, some recent trackers with relatively better performance such as CSK[19], KCF[15], SAMF[26], DSST[22] and Staple [27], are compared in this chapter.

The experimental results of the proposed tracker named as DCF_BM are shown in Fig. 3.3a, b. We can see that the proposed DCF_BM tracker in this chapter shows the best tracking performance on OTB-2013 when comparing with other traditional trackers. The accuracy and success rate are reached 83.0% and 61.3% respectively. Comparing with the baseline trackers, the proposed tracker shows a significant improvement, about 9%. Figure 3.4 shows the experimental results of DCF_BM on OTB-2015 dataset. Comparing with the baseline trackers, the proposed algorithm could still achieve the best performance with the accuracy and success rate of 80.7% and 59.3%. Comparing with the origin KCF tracker, the accuracy and success rate improved by 11.0% and 16.0% respectively. From the experimental results on the datasets above, we can say that the proposed tracking algorithm is effective and can improve the tracking performance.

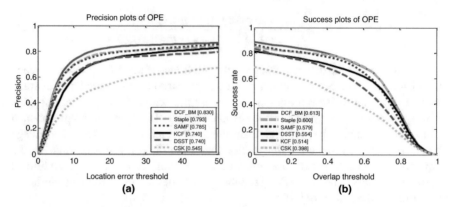

**Fig. 3.3** Experimental results achieved by different trackers on OTB-2013

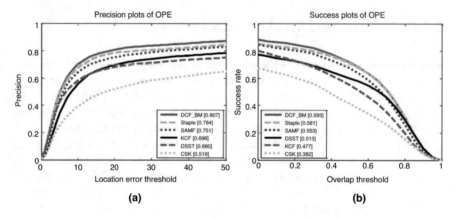

**Fig. 3.4** Experimental results achieved by different trackers on OTB-2015

The Staple tracker ranks the second in Figs. 3.3 and 3.4. This is mainly due to the HOG feature and color histogram feature are combined in the Staple tracker. The final response map is obtained by linearly weighting the response map. The boundary effect is inherently a defect in the Correlation Filter based tracking framework and the pixel-level color probability feature is unaffected by this factor. Therefore, DAT[28] reduces the boundary effect. Staple[27] tracker roughly uses the linear weight method in the specific implementation. However, setting the response of the correlation filter and the response of color probability to a certain fixed proportion, such as 0.7 and 0.3 has an obvious disadvantage. It cannot determine the weights of correlation filter and color probability adaptively.

To further show the performance of the proposed DCF_BM tracker under different challenges, the quantitative experiments and analysis on OTB-2015 dataset are given in Tables 3.1 and 3.2. It can be seen that the DCF_BM tracker shown in the tables above achieves the best performance in LR scenes. In addition, the performance of the DCF_BM tracker is improved under various attributes compared

**Table 3.1** Average precision score of different trackers on OTB-2015

| Attribute | DCF_BM | Stape | DSST | KCF | SAMF |
|-----------|--------|-------|------|-----|------|
| IV(38) | 0.817 | 0.791 | 0.721 | 0.719 | 0.715 |
| OPR(63) | 0.762 | 0.738 | 0.644 | 0.677 | 0.739 |
| SV(64) | 0.757 | 0.727 | 0.638 | 0.633 | 0.705 |
| OCC(49) | 0.738 | 0.726 | 0.597 | 0.630 | 0.726 |
| DEF(44) | 0.779 | 0.748 | 0.542 | 0.617 | 0.686 |
| MB(29) | 0.738 | 0.707 | 0.567 | 0.601 | 0.655 |
| FM(39) | 0.747 | 0.697 | 0.552 | 0.621 | 0.654 |
| IPR(51) | 0.799 | 0.770 | 0.691 | 0.701 | 0.721 |
| OV(14) | 0.708 | 0.661 | 0.481 | 0.501 | 0.628 |
| BC(31) | 0.785 | 0.766 | 0.704 | 0.713 | 0.689 |
| LR(9) | 0.638 | 0.631 | 0.567 | 0.560 | 0.685 |

**Table 3.2** Average success rate score of different trackers on OTB-2015

| Attribute | DCF_BM | Stape | DSST | KCF | SAMF |
|-----------|--------|-------|------|-----|------|
| IV(38) | 0.615 | 0.598 | 0.558 | 0.479 | 0.534 |
| OPR(63) | 0.549 | 0.534 | 0.470 | 0.453 | 0.536 |
| SV(64) | 0.537 | 0.525 | 0.468 | 0.394 | 0.495 |
| OCC(49) | 0.560 | 0.548 | 0.453 | 0.443 | 0.540 |
| DEF(44) | 0.566 | 0.554 | 0.420 | 0.436 | 0.509 |
| MB(29) | 0.567 | 0.546 | 0.469 | 0.459 | 0.525 |
| FM(39) | 0.571 | 0.537 | 0.447 | 0.459 | 0.507 |
| IPR(51) | 0.564 | 0.552 | 0.502 | 0.469 | 0.519 |
| OV(14) | 0.515 | 0.481 | 0.386 | 0.393 | 0.480 |
| BC(31) | 0.585 | 0.574 | 0.523 | 0.498 | 0.525 |
| LR(9) | 0.417 | 0.418 | 0.383 | 0.307 | 0.430 |

to the standard KCF tracker. This is mainly because of the application of background modeling which increases negative numbers and improves the discriminative power, especially in occlusion and fast motion challenges, in these challenges, the average precision scores of KCF is 0.651 and 0.621 respectively, while the scores of the proposed tracker, DCF_BM, are 0.738 and 0.747.

The improvement of the proposed tracker is mainly due to the application of re-detection and re-search components. Since the trackers could not guarantee the accuracy of the detection results because of the outliers in the response map in fast motion and occlusion scenarios, re-detection and re-search component is applied to expand the search area and re-detect the object.

## 3.3   Correlation Filter Tracker with Scale Pyramid

Although Correlation filter based tackers have advantages in tracking speed and robustness, these kinds of trackers also show weak performance in handling multi-scale problems especially under scale variation challenges. Besides, how to design a more powerful feature for the construction of the appearance model to improve the tracking accuracy is also one of the problems to be solved in correlation filter based trackers. In this chapter, we proposed a tracker named as CFRF_RC to solve the problems mentioned above. Firstly, position estimation and scale estimation are combined in the proposed tracking method to cope with the multi-scale problem quickly and effectively. Due to the limited effectiveness of traditional manually designed features, the construction of appearance model is relatively simple. Thus, a novel and powerful feature which could significantly improve the tracking performance is designed in this chapter. Finally, in order to better deal with occlusion and the tracking drift in some other complex sequences, a relocation component is proposed to re-detect the object at the locations at the second peak in the response map. Then proposed tracker is tested on the widely used datasets such as OTB-2013, OTB-2015, etc.

### 3.3.1   Scale Pyramid Filter

KCF based tracker does not take the scale change of the objects into consideration. during the whole tracking process, the KCF tracker assumes the bounding box of the object is always the same. To solve the multi-scale challenge in KCF tracker, The scale correlation filter in DSST [22] is incorporated into the KCF tracking framework. We calculate the position of the object with the kernelized correlation filter firstly, and then a series of samples of various scales are extracted around the position of the object to train one-dimensional scale filter. The objective function is as follows:

$$\varepsilon = \left\| \sum_{l=1}^{d} h^l * f^l - g \right\|^2 + \lambda \sum_{l=1}^{d} \left\| h^l \right\|^2 \tag{3.13}$$

where $l = 1, 2, \ldots d$ indicates the dimension of feature. $h$ represents the scale filter to be trained. $f$ is the patch of input image and $g$ is the expected output of Gaussian distribution. $\lambda$ is the regularization coefficient to eliminate the zero frequency of spectrum. By simplifying, $H^l$ can be calculated as Eq. 3.14.

$$H^l = \frac{\bar{G} F^l}{\sum_{k=1}^{d} \bar{F}^k F^k + \lambda} = \frac{A_t^l}{B_t} \tag{3.14}$$

In general, lowercase letters indicate variables in the time domain. While the uppercase letters represent the variables in frequency domain. In particular, $\hat{G}$ and $\hat{F}^k$ are the conjugate complex numbers of $G$ and $F^k$. Thus, the response map can be obtained by Eq. 3.15.

$$y = F^{-1} \left\{ \frac{\sum_{l=1}^{d} \bar{A}^l Z^l}{B + \lambda} \right\} \qquad (3.15)$$

Where $Z$ represents the Fourier transform of feature map at the predicted position.

A double threshold judgment for the object to be tracked is applied before the feature is extracted. When the size of the object is larger than $threshold_{max}$, the resolution of the object is reduced to loss some details but increase the tracking speed. When the size is under $threshold_{min}$, we upsample the object image to get more information and details of the object and improve the accuracy of tracking results.

Traditional KCF tracker sets the expansion coefficients of width and height to be 2.5. However, through the analysis of the video sequences, we find that the high objects may move in a certain direction. Therefore, the search area should be increased if the height and width ratio of the object exceeds $threshold_{sz(1)/sz(2)}$. This phenomenon exists in the pedestrians scenes, pedestrians walk in a fixed direction. Through experiments, we find that the expansion coefficient of height should be set to 2.1 and the expansion coefficient of width is better set to 2.5, when the height and width ratio exceeds $threshold_{sz(1)/sz(2)}$.

In order to train the scale filter independently, the number of training samples cannot be set too small or too large. Setting the number of training numbers too large will reduce the tracking speed. While setting the number too small will lead to underfitting. The number of scales is reduced from 33 to 17 in the proposed method by tuning the parameters on OTB-2013 dataset. The response map is set to be $1 \times 17$. Then, the triangle interpolation algorithm is used to increase the number of scales from 17 to 33 to increase the accuracy of scale estimating.

### 3.3.2  Rich Image Feature Representation

Recently, researchers pay more attention to the feature extraction without considering the construction methods of the appearance model. This also shows that the feature extraction plays the most important role in appearance model construction. A good feature could improve the tracking results directly. Fast Histogram of Oriented Gradients (FHOG) feature is one of the popular non-deep learning feature that used in visual object tracking. FHOG is a classic dense descriptor and achieves good performance in visual object tracking. But a single FHOG feature is not enough for the tracker to cope with the complex scenes in tracking. In this chapter, a more powerful feature extraction and representation method is proposed by modifying the kernel in KCF, as shown in Eq. 3.16. One of the benefits is that no more complicated calculations need to be added in Eq. 3.16, when it deals with multi-channel problems.

$$k_{xx'} = exp(-\frac{1}{\sigma^2}(\|x\|^2 + \|x'\|^2 - 2F^{-1}(\sum_c \hat{x}_c^* \odot \hat{x}_c))) \qquad (3.16)$$

Where $x'$ could be ether $x$ or $z$. Thus, Eq. 3.16 can be applied to solve both $k_{xx}$ and $k_{xz}$. $c$ indicates the number of connected channels, such as $x = [x_1, x_2, \ldots x_c]$.

During the designing of feature representation, FHOG feature and Color Name feature are fused in the proposed method to construct the rich image feature representation. Color Name feature [29] contents 11 colors which are obtained from human language when people describe the color of the objects in real life. Probability Latent Semantic Analysis (PLSA) is used to extract the Color Name feature. In the proposed method, mapping matrices are applied to convert the RGB value of images into Color Name features.

In this chapter, the intensity gradient of the object image does not change dramatically during the whole tracking process. Therefore, we also assume the gradient value of the object as well as the combination of the object image gradients will not vary drastically. Thus, the Sobel operator is used to calculate the gradients of the object image in horizontal, vertical, 45° and 135° planes. Take the process in horizontal direction as an example. The gradient value matrix $D_x$ in horizontal direction is $m \times n$. If one of the elements in $D_x$ is smaller than $-thrGrad$, then the element is set to be 1, while, if the value of element is over $thrGrad$, then it is set to be 2. The other elements whose value is between $-thrGrad$ and $thrGrad$, are all set to be 0. Then, the gradient value matrix is divided into $cellSize \times cellSize$ cells. For each cell, the number of pixels with specific values is recorded for feature extraction. Thus, the feature of the integral image is presented as $feat$ which could be normalized by Eq. 3.17.

$$feat_{normalized} = feat./(cellSize \times cellSize) \qquad (3.17)$$

At last, we can obtain a feature matrix whose size is $(m/cellSize) \times (n/cellSize) \times$ 3. Since the operation in the other three directions are the same. Thus, the dimensional of the proposed feature should be 12.

### 3.3.3   Framework and Procedure

The Framework and procedure of the proposed method is shown in Fig. 3.5. The entire proposed algorithm is divided into three main components: position estimation, re-location, and scale estimation. The translation filter and scale filter are both trained in the initial frame. The translation filter is used to determine the center location of the objects in the following sequences, while the scale filter is used to estimate the size of the objects. Then, the response map is applied to detect the tracking confidence. If the tracking confidence is over a certain threshold, it goes to the scale estimation step. Otherwise, the relocation component starts to intervene

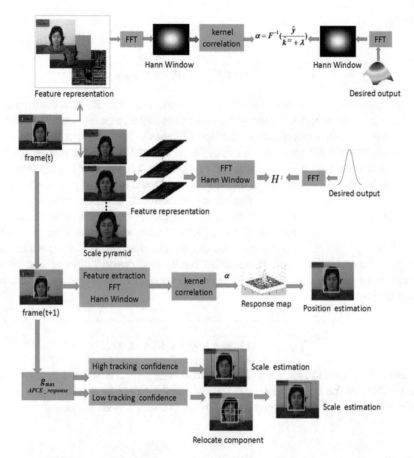

**Fig. 3.5** The pipeline of the proposed tacking method

to relocate the object. Finally, the scale correlation filter is used to estimate the size of the object to increase the success rate.

For the traditional KCF based trackers, the center location of the object is at the point where the response map gets the maximum value. However, in some complex scenes, such as occlusion and fast moving, the distribution of response map does not always follow the Gaussian distribution and the center location of the object may not at the peak point of the response map either. This situation may also lead to the tracking drift or lose the object, according to the Large Margin with Circulant Feature Maps (LMCF) [30]. To solve this problem, the relocation component is proposed to re-estimate the position of the object. Different from the Long-term Correlation Tracker (LCT) tracker [31], the proposed relocation component does not need to train an additional filter and detector to reflect the tracking confidence. In the relocation component, the maximum value of the response map and $APCE\_response$ are both used as tracking confidence indicator.

$APCE\_response$ can be calculated by Eq. 3.18.

$$APCE\_response = \frac{|g_{max} - g_{min}|^2}{mean(\sum_{m,n}(g_{m,n} - g_{min})^2)} \tag{3.18}$$

Where $g_{max}$ and $g_{min}$ represent the maximum and minimum values of the response map respectively. $m$ and $n$ are the width and height of the response map. We believe the tracking results is less accurate when the values of these two tracking confidence indicators of current frame are less than the mean values of these two indicators within a certain few frames. Thus, the proposed relocation component starts to relocate the object. Global search method is not adopted in the proposed relocation component by considering the calculation cost. Instead, we believe the searching scope should be related to the movement of the object. For example, when the object moves fast, the object locations of two adjacent frames are relatively far away. On the opposite, when the object moves slowly, the locations are closer. Based on the analysis above, we set large search areas for the fast moving objects, and small search areas for the slow moving objects. the length of the search range can be computed by Eq. 3.19.

$$l = \sqrt{\frac{c_1}{g_{max} * (target\_sz(1) + target\_sz(2))}} \tag{3.19}$$

Where $c_1$ is a constant, and step size in the rectangle search area is set to determine the position of the object. The final location of the object in current frame could estimate by point of the response map with the maximum value of $g_{max}$.

### 3.3.4 Experimental Results and Discussions

In this section, the experimental setup for the proposed method is introduced. All the proposed method is implemented by MATLAB language. The hyperparameters used in the tracker are shown in Table 3.3. One thing should be mentioned about

**Table 3.3** Main parameters used in proposed method

| Parameter | Value |
|---|---|
| $threshold_{max}$ | $150 \times 150$ |
| $threshold_{min}$ | $80 \times 80$ |
| thrGrad | 8 |
| $c_1$ | 20.5 |
| cellSize | 4 |
| $threshold_{sz(1)/sz(2)}$ | 2.50 |
| Orientation | 9 |
| Appearance model update rate | 0.012 |

the proposed tracker is that it is parameter sensitive. When the hyperparameter changes slightly, the tracking performance may change a lot. OTB-2013 and OTB-2015 datasets are adopted to test the performance of the proposed tracking algorithm. OTB-2013 and OTB-2015 are widely used in the tracking field, which contains 50 and 100 tracking sequences respectively. These datasets contain 11 tracking challenges which almost included all the complex scenarios in visual object tracking.

In order to verify the effectiveness and availability of the proposed algorithm. Some classical KCF and DCF based trackers such as Context-Aware Discriminative Correlation Filter (DCF_CA) [32], Target response Adaptation Correlation Filter (DCF_AT) [33], etc. are used for comparison. Some other tracking algorithms for scale Variation challenge are also applied for comparison, such as DSST [22], SAMF [26] and their variants FDSST [34], SAMF_CA. In addition, some deep learning based trackers like DLSSVM [35], SiamFC [36] are also taken into account. The comparison results on OTB-2013 and OTB-2015 are shown in Fig. 3.6. The legend parts of Fig. 3.6 show the performance of the top 10 trackers. From Fig. 3.6, we can conclude that the proposed tacker shows the best tracking performance on both precision plots and success plots. On OTB-2013, the precision rate and success rate reach 86.1% and 64.9% respectively, which show 12.1% and

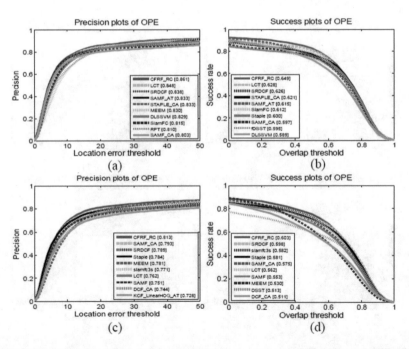

**Fig. 3.6** Experimental results of the state-of-the-art trackers on OTB-2013 and OTB-2015 datasets. (**a**) Precision plots of OPE on OTB-2013 dataset. (**b**) Success plots of OPE on OTB-2013 dataset. (**c**) Precision plots of OPE on OTB-2015 dataset. (**d**) Success plots of OPE on OTB-2015

13.5% increase comparing with KCF. While on OTB-2015 dataset, the precision rate of the proposed tracker is 81.3% and success rate is 60.3%. Comparing with KCF tracker, these two rates increased by 11.7% and 12.6%. In addition, LCT, SRDCF and SAMF_CA also show relatively good performance.

The performance of LCT tracker, which is a long-term object tracker, ranks the second on OTB-2013 in both precision rate and success rate. Similar to the proposed tracker, the re-detection and relocation component are applied to mitigate the occlusion and tracking drift. However, the LCT tracker uses three correlation filters in the tracking framework. On OTB-2015 dataset, SRDCF and SAMF_CA show the best performance on precision and success rate except for the proposed tacker. The similarity between the two algorithms is that they use two different methods to solve the problem of boundary effects caused by cyclic shift. Therefore, these methods for reducing the boundary effects are effective and worth referencing.

Figure 3.7 shows the performance of the proposed tracker under four kinds of tracking challenges on OTB-2015 dataset. Figure 3.7a–d are success plots of occlusion, scale variation, in-plane rotation and deformation respectively. Since the goal of the proposed tracker mainly to improve the success rate of tracking algorithms when dealing with scale variation and occlusion challenges, Fig. 3.7 only shows the success rate results under these four challenges. From Fig. 3.7,

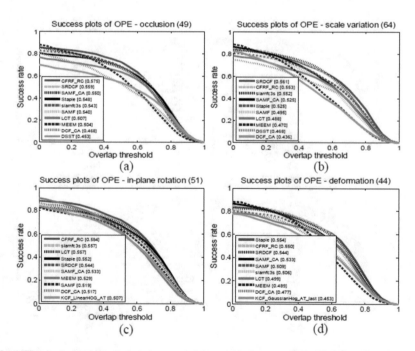

**Fig. 3.7** Experimental results of the state-of-the-art trackers on OTB-2015. (**a**) Success plots of OPE under occlusion challenge. (**b**) Success plots of OPE under scale variation challenge. (**c**) Success plots of OPE under in-plane rotation challenge. (**d**) Success plots of OPE under deformation challenge

we can see that the proposed tracker shows the best performance under occlusion, scale variation and in-plane rotation challenges. But, the proposed tracker ranks the second when copes with deformation.

On the OTB-2015 dataset, the success rate of proposed tracker is 55.3% under scale variation challenge. It shows a good performance comparing with KCF. We believe this improvement is mainly due to the position estimation and scale estimation applied in the proposed tracker. In the tracking process, the results of position estimation are not adopted directly. After position estimation, the proposed tracker also constructed an image pyramid at the position where obtained by position estimation to estimate the scale of the object. In addition, the scale correlation filter which is used for scale estimation is updated linearly. This also helps to improve the accuracy of scale estimation.

The proposed compressed scale correlation filter is also applied in the KCF tracker and construct a new tracker named as KCF_Scale. The details of implementation can be found in the experiment section. Table 3.4 shows the precision rate, success rate (AUC) and tracking speed of KCF_Scale on OTB-2013 and OTB-2015 datasets, when comparing with SAMF and DSST trackers. SAMF and DSST also aim to improve the tracking performance when handling scale variation challenge. From Table 3.4, we can see that the KCF_Scale tracker could achieve the best tracking performance on precision and success rate with high tracking speed, nearly at 86.5 and 85.4 fps on OTB-2013 and OTB-2015 respectively. We believe there are two reasons. One is the reduction of scale samples increase the tracking speed, and the other reason is Hermitian symmetry of the Fourier coefficient of a real function is used to reduce the computation complexity and memory consumption. It can improve the tracking speed without reducing tacking accuracy.

Figure 3.8 shows the results of qualitative experiments when comparing with the DCF_CA, DSST and KCF. All the five sequences in Fig. 3.8 contain several tracking challenges such as scale variation, motion blur, fast motion, etc. The black boxes represent the proposed tracker which is similar to the object in size. This also proves the effectiveness of the proposed algorithm in dealing with scale variation challenge.

## 3.4  Correlation Filter Tracker with Multi-Scale Superpixels

Discriminative correlation filter based tracker, such as KCF, has achieved great success in handling some tracking challenges, but, there still remain some challenges which are difficult for KCF, such as scale variation, fast motion, occlusion etc. We believe the reason is mainly caused by the ROI with a fixed size and the lack of structure information. Thus, a Multi-Scale Superpixels and Color Feature Guided Kernelized Correlation Filters (MSSCF-KCF) tracker is proposed in this chapter to cope with the problems mentioned above. MSSCF-KCF view tracking as a problem of optimizing the combination of the object components. Firstly, the object is segmented into several patches based on the global confidence map which is calculated by the proposed multi-scale superpixel segmentation method. Then, for

**Table 3.4** Experimental results on the OTB-2013 and OTB-2015 dataset

| Tracker | Precision (2013) | AUC (2013) | Speed (fps) | Precision (2015) | AUC (2015) | Speed(fps) |
|---|---|---|---|---|---|---|
| KCF_Scale | 0.793 | 0.581 | 86.5 | 0.762 | 0.561 | 85.4 |
| SAMF | 0.785 | 0.579 | 18.5 | 0.751 | 0.553 | 17.9 |
| DSST | 0.740 | 0.554 | 28.9 | 0.680 | 0.513 | 21.5 |

**Fig. 3.8** Comparison of tracking bounding boxes generated by different tackers for challenging sequences. The black, red, green and blue tracking boxes represents the proposed tracker, DCF_CA, DSST and KCF respectively

each patch, the color feature extracted from object along with the confidence map obtained from KCF to construct the observation model. Finally, the proposed center distance matrix and min-max criterion are applied to search the best combination of the object patches to use the structure information of the object. Besides, the monitoring update strategy is used to monitor the tracking procedure and update the appearance model in MSSCF-KCF. The comparison experiments with some state-of-the-art KCF based tackers prove the effectiveness of the proposed MSSCF-KCF tacker.

## 3.4.1   Multi-Scale Superpixels Segmentation

KCF, which is a discriminative method, shows the advantages in tracking speed and competitive performance. However, there are still some shortcomings of KCF tracker. For example, the KCF is weak in handling the scale variation, fast motion and occlusion scenes. In order to enhance the capacity of KCF to handle the challenge of scale variation, the object are segmented into several patches. For each patch, KCF is used to track the image patch. The optimal combination of tracking results of patches are adopted as the final tracking results. We believe this may compensate the deficiency of traditional KCF to a certain extent. Since the tracking speed of KCF far exceeds the requirements of real-time tracking, we can still ensure the real-time tracking by applying multiple KCF trackers. In this chapter, the goal is to provide stable and efficient patches. Object patches can be calculated by Fig. 3.9.

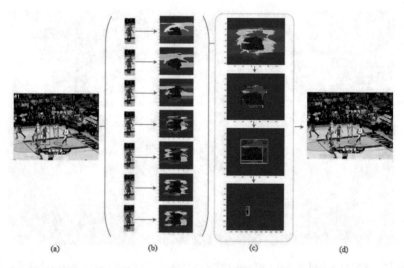

**Fig. 3.9** The procedure of obtaining multi-scale superpixel based object patches. (**a**) Object image and region of interest, which are represented by the images within yellow box and red box respectively. (**b**) Segment results of multi-scale superpixels and relative separate confidence masks. The segment results are obtained by SLIC with multiple scales. (**c**) Obtaining of global confidence mask and object patches. Object patches are inferred by the different values in the global confidence mask. The sizes and numbers of the object patches are constrained by threshold $Thre$ and step size $\alpha_{step}$. (**d**) Result of the object patches, which is used to train the traditional KCFs and extract the color features in order to get preparation for the next step

The training center and size of the bounding box have a significant impact on the tracking results of KCF. The proposed multi-scale superpixels segmentation method could determine the center and size of each object patches automatically. As shown in Fig. 3.9. Firstly, we select the Region Of Interest (ROI) based on object bounding box, which is $\lambda$ times larger than object image, as shown in Fig. 3.9a. $\mathbf{X}_{ROI}$ and $\mathbf{X}_O$ are states of ROI and the object respectively, labelled as yellow and red boxes in Fig. 3.9a. $I(\mathbf{X}_{ROI})$ and $I(\mathbf{X}_O)$ represent the corresponding images. Secondly, The ROI is segmented by SLIC with $N_{ss}$ different scales. Figure 3.9b shows the separate confidence mask of each scale, which represents the score of each superpixels with different scales, and can be computed by Eq. 3.20.

$$Score(SP_s^k) = \frac{\sum_{p(i,j) \in SP_s^k} \mathbb{I}(p(i, j) \in I(\mathbf{X}_O))}{N(SP_s^k)} \qquad (3.20)$$

$SP_s^k$ is the $k$th superpixel under scale $s$, $\mathbb{I}(*)$ is the indicator function, $N(SP_s^k)$ is the number of pixels in $SP_s^k$, and the denominator of Eq. 3.20 shows the number of pixels which belong to both $SP_s^k$ and $I(\mathbf{X}_O)$. The separate confidence map can be represented as $SP_s^k(i, j) = score(SP_s^k)$, $SP_s^k(i, j)$ is the value of pixel located at $(i, j)$ and belonged to the $k$th superpixel under scale $s$. while $SM_s = SP_s^k(i, j), k = 1, 2 \ldots N_s; i, j \in SP_s^k$ is the separate confidence mask under scale $s$. For each element in $SM_S$ can be computed by Eq. 3.21.

$$SM_s(i, j) = \sum_{k=1}^{N_s} \mathbb{I}(i, j \in SP_s^k) score(SP_s^k) \tag{3.21}$$

Finally, the separate confidence masks of different scales are integrated into a global confidence mask, which can be viewed as the weighted average of separate confidence masks, as shown in Fig. 3.9c. The global confidence mask can be obtained by Eq. 3.22.

$$G_{SM} = \sum_{s=1}^{N_{ss}} \beta_s \cdot SM_s;$$

$$st. \sum_{s=1}^{N_{ss}} \beta_s = 1 \tag{3.22}$$

$\beta_s$ indicates weight coefficient. In this chapter, $\beta = \frac{1}{N_{ss}}$, thus, we obtained Eq. 3.23.

$$G_{SM} = \frac{\sum_{s=1}^{N_{ss}} SM_s}{N_{ss}} \tag{3.23}$$

the number of the object patches is related to the threshold $Thre$ and step size $\alpha_{step}$, $0 < \alpha_{step} < 1$. $N_{pa}$ indicates the number of the object patches which could computed by Eq. 3.24.

$$N_{pa} = \frac{1 - Thre}{\alpha_{step}} \tag{3.24}$$

If $\alpha_{step} = 0.1$ and $Thre = 0.7$, the number of the object patches are 3, $N_{pa} = 3$. Thus, Object patches can be obtained by gathering the elements with certain values in global confidence mask. Set $PM_{Thre}^\gamma$ to be the patch mask, which means the $\gamma$th patch mask under the threshold $Thre$ and step size $\alpha_{step}$, $\gamma \in (0, 1 \ldots . N_{pa} - 1)$. Then, $OP_\gamma$, which is the set of pixels whose value is 1, and $PM_{Thre}^\gamma$ can be computed by Eqs. 3.25 and 3.26.

$$PM_{Thre}^\gamma(i, j) = \mathbb{I}(Thre \leqslant G_{SM}(i, j) \leqslant (Thre + \gamma * \alpha_{step})) \tag{3.25}$$

$$OP_\gamma = \mathbf{I}(\mathbf{X}_{ROI}) \cdot PM_{Thre}^\gamma \tag{3.26}$$

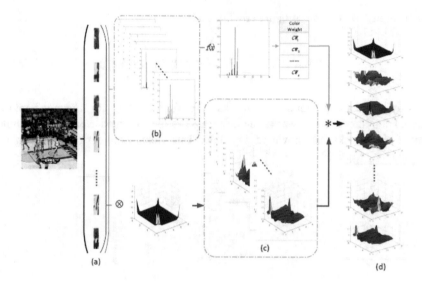

**Fig. 3.10** The procedure of obtaining color feature guided confidence maps. (a) The possible states of sub-candidates which estimated by Gaussian distribution based motion model. (b) The HSI histograms of sub-candidates which is used to compute color weights by measuring with HSI histogram of corresponding object patch templet. (c) The confidence scores of sub-candidates. (d) The color feature guided confidence maps of sub-candidates, which are obtained by further filtering of confidence scores via color weights

The segmentation results and bounding boxes of the object patches of the whole frame are shown in Fig. 3.9. The image within the bounding boxes of the object patches are used for training the KCF trackers, Thus, we can get $\gamma$ KCF trackers. Choosing the optimal combination of these KCF trackers helps to improve the performance of KCF tracker, when dealing with scale variation challenge.

In order to improve the accuracy of the confidence map obtained by the KCF tracker, the color feature is used to further filter the confidence scores. The final confidence map which is calculated by both KCF and HSI feature is named as color feature guided confidence map. The procedure of computing color feature guided confidence map for a single patch is shown in Fig. 3.10.

For better understanding of Fig. 3.10. The $\gamma$th object patch, $\mathbf{X}_{OP_\gamma}$ is chosen as example. $HSI(I(\mathbf{X}_{OP_\gamma}))$ and $KCF(I(\mathbf{X}_{OP_\gamma}))$ indicate the HSI feature extracted from the $\gamma$th object patch and the confidence map of $\mathbf{X}_{OP_\gamma}$ obtained by KCF. Assume $\mathbf{X}_{OP_\gamma}$ follows Gaussian distribution in Eq. 3.27.

$$p(\mathbf{X}^t_{OP_\gamma}|\mathbf{X}^{t-1}_{OP_\gamma}) = N(\mathbf{X}^t_{OP_\gamma}; \mathbf{X}^{t-1}_{OP_\gamma}, \Psi) \qquad (3.27)$$

$\Psi$ indicates the diagonal covariance matrix. Thus, we can get $N_{sc}$ sub-candidates of the object patch $OP_\gamma$ in the next frame for matching. As shown in Fig. 3.10a, $SC_{\gamma,\xi}$, $\xi \in \{1, 2, \cdots, N_{sc}\}$ represent the sub-candidates. The blue lines in Fig. 3.10a shows the procedure of obtaining color weight, which is calculated by measuring the 2-Norm distance between the HSI histograms of templet patch and sub-candidates. In order to normalize the color weight, the normalized exponential distance is applied as the color weights after normalization, computed by Eq. 3.28.

$$CW_{\gamma,\xi} = e^{-\dfrac{\left\| HSI(I(\mathbf{X}_{SC_{\gamma,\xi}})) - HSI(I(\mathbf{X}_{OP_{\gamma}})) \right\|_2}{\max\limits_{i=1,2\cdots,Ncs}(\left\| HSI(I(\mathbf{X}_{SC_{\gamma,i}})) - HSI(I(\mathbf{X}_{OP_{\gamma}})) \right\|_2)}} \tag{3.28}$$

$CW_{\gamma,\xi}$ is the color weight of sub-candidate $SC_{\gamma,\xi}$. $\mathbf{X}_{SC_{\gamma,\xi}}$ and $HSI(I(\mathbf{X}_{SC_{\gamma,\xi}}))$ indicate the state and HSI histogram of $\xi$-th sub-candidate for $SC_{\gamma,\xi}$. The denominator of Eq. 3.28 show the maximum value of all sub-candidates, $SC_{\gamma,\xi}$, $\xi = 1, 2, \ldots, N_{sc}$. Equation 3.28 could limit the color weights $CW_{\gamma,\xi} \in (0, 1]$, and set the color weight with a large value when the 2-Norm distance is small. $\hat{f}(I(\mathbf{X}_{SC_{\gamma,\xi}}))$ represents the confidence scores of sub-candidates, which can be calculated by following the red lines in Fig. 3.10. Thus, the color feature guided confidence map of $SC_{\gamma,\xi}$ could be computed by Eq. 3.29.

$$H_{CF}(I(\mathbf{X}_{SC_{\gamma,\xi}})) = CW_{\gamma,\xi} \cdot \hat{f}(I(\mathbf{X}_{SC_{\gamma,\xi}})) \tag{3.29}$$

Where $H_{CF}(I(\mathbf{X}_{SC_{\gamma,\xi}}))$ is the final color feature guided confidence map, which can obtain better predicted results. $H_{CF}(I(\mathbf{X}_{OP_{\gamma}})) = \{H_{CF}(I(\mathbf{X}_{SC_{\gamma,\xi}}))\}, \xi \in \{1, 2, \cdots, N_{sc}\}$ means the color feature guided confidence map of $OP_{\gamma}$, which is the collection of color feature guided confidence map of sub-candidates. Thus, $H_{CF}(I(\mathbf{X}_{OP_{\gamma}})), \gamma \in \{1, 2, \cdots, N_{pa}\}$ is the color feature guided confidence map of the whole frame. Color feature guided confidence map introduces color feature into KCF to further filter out intrusions caused by the sub-candidates.

### 3.4.2   Structure Based Optimization Strategy

The final tracking results are viewed as the optimal combination of the sub-candidates. Structure characteristics of the object are used in this chapter to find the optimal combination of sub-candidates and improve the performance when handling the scale variation challenge. As shown in Fig. 3.11, a novel center distance matrix is proposed by computing the center distances of two sub-candidates from different object patches to utilize the structure feature of the object. Then, the min-max criterion is proposed to find the optimal combination of sub-candidates and compute the tracking results.

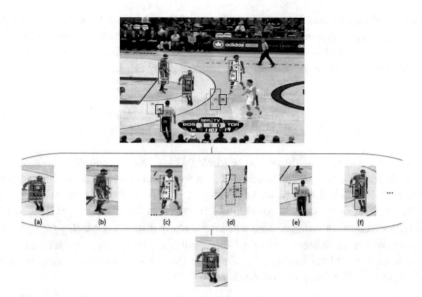

**Fig. 3.11** The procedure of selecting best combination from sub-candidates. (**a**)–(**f**) Show six groups of sub-candidates. Each group consists of sub-candidates selected from all object patches, and the sub-candidates are selected by choosing only one sub-candidate from different object patches and combined according to the shortest center distances. At last, we get the best combination of sub-candidates and derive the final state of the object according to the proposed min-max criterion

Equation 3.30 shows the center distance matrix which is obtained by measure the distances between any two sub-candidates in object patches to use the structure information of the object. The object can be treated as composition of the object patches.

$$
C_{DM} = \begin{bmatrix}
C_{DM}(1,1) & C_{DM}(1,2) & \cdots & C_{DM}(1,N_{pa}) \\
C_{DM}(2,1) & C_{DM}(2,2) & \cdots & C_{DM}(1,N_{pa}) \\
\vdots & \vdots & \vdots & \vdots \\
C_{DM}(N_{pa},1) & C_{DM}(N_{pa},2) & \cdots & C_{DM}(N_{pa},N_{pa})
\end{bmatrix}
\tag{3.30}
$$

$C_{DM}(i,j)$ is a matrix which includes the distances of all sub-candidates of the object patch $i$ and $j$. Thus, $C_{DM} \in \mathbb{R}^{(N_{pa} \cdot N_{sc}) * (N_{pa} \cdot N_{sc})}$ while $C_{DM}(i,j) \in \mathbb{R}^{N_{sc} * N_{sc}}$. $C_{DM}(i,j)$ can be computed by Eq. 3.31.

$$
C_{DM}(i,j) = \begin{bmatrix}
dist_{1,1} & dist_{1,2} & \cdots & dist_{1,N_{sc}} \\
dist_{2,1} & dist_{2,2} & \cdots & dist_{2,N_{sc}} \\
\vdots & \vdots & \vdots & \vdots \\
dist_{N_{sc},1} & dist_{N_{sc},2} & \cdots & dist_{N_{sc},N_{sc}}
\end{bmatrix}
\tag{3.31}
$$

$dist_{p,q}$ is the center distance between the $p$th sub-candidate of the object patch $i$ and the $q$th sub-candidate of the object patch $j$. From Eqs. 3.30 and 3.31, we can see that $dist_{p,q} = dist_{q,p}$ and $C_{DM}(i, j) = C_{DM}(j, i)^T$. If $p = q, dist_{p,q} = \infty$. The center distance matrix which contains structure information is applied as dictionary for calculating the optimal combination of sub-candidates.

The optimal combination in this method is defined as the combination with highest color feature guided confidence score and lowest center distance, which can be represented as Eq. 3.32.

$$\min_k C_{DM}(G_k) \max_k \sum_{i=1}^{N_{pa}} H_{CF}(G_k(i)) \tag{3.32}$$

Equation 3.32 is the min-max criterion proposed in this chapter. $G_k$ is the $k$th possible combination. $G_k = \{G_k(1), G_k(2), \cdots, G_k(N_{pa})\}$. $G_k(i)$ is the sub-candidate of $i$th object patch in $G_k$, $\sum_{i=1}^{N_{pa}} H_{CF}(G_k(i))$ and $C_{DM}(G_k)$ is the sum of color feature guided confidence score and the sum of center distances between elements respectively. These two optimization can also be integrated by Eq. 3.33.

$$\max_k \frac{\sum_{i=1}^{N_{pa}} H_{CF}(G_k(i))}{N_{pa}} \cdot \frac{dist_{max} \mathbf{C}_{N_{pa}}^2}{C_{DM}(G_k)}$$

$$= \max_k \frac{dist_{max} \mathbf{C}_{N_{pa}}^2 \sum_{i=1}^{N_{pa}} H_{CF}(G_k(i))}{N_{pa} C_{DM}(G_k)} \tag{3.33}$$

$$= \max_k \kappa' \frac{\sum_{i=1}^{N_{pa}} H_{CF}(G_k(i))}{C_{DM}(G_k)}$$

The first item is the mean value of color feature guided the confidence score of sub-candidates in $G_k$, and the second item shows the reciprocal of mean value of center distance between sub-candidates in $G_k$. $dist_{max}$ which means the maximum distance in $C_{DM}$ is used for normalization. $\kappa'$ is the constant, as shown in Eq. 3.34.

$$\kappa' = \frac{dist_{max} \mathbf{C}_{N_{pa}}^2}{N_{pa}}$$

$$= \frac{dist_{max} N_{pa}(N_{pa} - 1)}{2N_{pa}} \tag{3.34}$$

$$= \frac{dist_{max}(N_{pa} - 1)}{2}$$

The number of summation terms in $C_{DM}(G_k)$ is $\mathbf{C}_{N_{pa}}^2$, GEP algorithm[37] is used to solve the NP hard problem in finding the optimal combination of sub-candidates. $G_k = \{G_k(1), G_k(2), \cdots, G_k(N_{pa})\}$ is used as the gene in GEP, and the elements in $G_k$ is treated as chromosomes accordingly. Thus, the state of the object could be estimated by selecting the smallest bounding box which could wrap all selected sub-candidates. The final state of the object can be calculated by Eq. 3.35.

$$\mathbf{X}_O = \left\{ X_{G_k}^{i_{min}}, X_{G_k}^{j_{min}}, (X_{G_k}^{p_{max}} - X_{G_k}^{i_{min}}), (X_{G_k}^{q_{max}} - X_{G_k}^{j_{min}}) \right\} \tag{3.35}$$

$X_{G_k}^{i_{min}}$ and $X_{G_k}^{j_{min}}$ are the minimum values of the upper left corner coordinates of all $\mathbf{X}(G_k(i))$, $X_{G_k}^{p_{max}}$ and $X_{G_k}^{q_{max}}$ are the maximum values of the lower right corner coordinates of all $\mathbf{X}(G_k(i))$. When the color feature guided confidence scores of the selected object patches are lower than a particular threshold $T_d$, which means these selected object patches many be the interference and should be dropped out. The equation of $T_d$ is shown as follows:

$$T_d = \lambda' \frac{\sum_{i=1}^{N_{pa}} H_{CF}(G_k(i))}{N_{pa}} \tag{3.36}$$

Empirically, $T_d$ is $2/3$ of the mean of color feature guided confidence score. Thus, $\lambda' = 2/3$.

### 3.4.3   Framework and Procedure

Since the proposed MSSCF-KCF tracker treats the object as the combination of some interrelated and overlapping patches, the main purpose of MSSCF-KCF is to select the optimal combination of the tracking results of each patch. The pipeline of MSSCF-KCF tracker is shown in Fig. 3.12. As shown in Fig. 3.12a, the ROI which is $\lambda$ times larger than the bounding box is segmented into several superpixels of different scales. We calculate the confidence masks of these superpixels and integrate these separate confidence masks into one confidence mask named as the global confidence mask. Then we segment the object image into several object patches based on the values of elements in global confidence mask. After getting the object patches, we calculate the confidence map and extract the HSI feature of each patch to obtain the color feature guided confidence map, as shown in Fig. 3.12b. By assuming the motion of the object following Gaussian distribution, we can obtain several sub-candidates patches for each object patch. Through the proposed center distance matrix and min-max criterion, the tracking problem turned into an optimal problem which can be viewed as a NP hard problem. In order to solve this NP hard problem, GEP algorithm is applied in the proposed method to find the optimal combination and get the final tracking results.

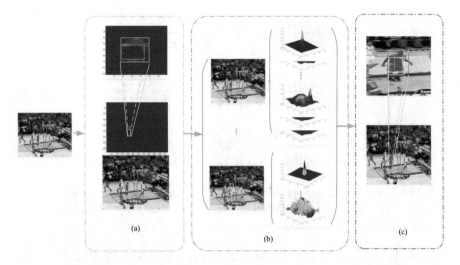

**Fig. 3.12** The pipeline of MSSCF-KCF tracker. The procedure of proposed MSSCF-KCF is mainly divided into three parts. (**a**) Multi-scale superpixels based multiple kernelized correlation filters, which can be viewed as process of obtaining multi-scale superpixel patches of the object and training KCFs for the patches. (**b**) Color-feature guided confidence map, also known as hybrid confidence map In this section, which is generated by considering the confidence score and filtered by color-feature guided method. (**c**) Structure based selection and combination of sub-candidates, which is based on the proposed min-max criterion and center distance matrix, and optimized by GEP

In order to update the color feature guided confidence map and monitoring the tracking process, the update and monitoring strategy is proposed, which can be divided into update strategy and monitoring strategy. For the update strategy, it can also be divided into two parts: the update of confidence map computed by the KCF and the color weights obtained by HSI feature. The update of confidence map simply follows the update of KCF tracker, while the update of color weights can be computed by Eq. 3.37.

$$HSI(temp_i) = \nu HSI(OP_\gamma^i) + (1 - \nu)HSI(temp_{i-1}) \tag{3.37}$$

$HSI(temp_i)$ indicates the HSI feature of $temp_i$, and $HSI(OP_\gamma^i)$ shows the corresponding HSI feature of $OP_\gamma^i$. $\nu$ means the forgetting factor. For monitoring strategy, $\{X_O^i\}$ recorded by MSSCF-KCF tracker. The tracking results of KCF, which is represented as $\{X_K^i\}$ are also recorded by MSSCF-KCF. In order to sense the tracking operation and adjust parameters in MSSCF-KCF dynamically, three testing indexes, which can be calculated by Eqs. 3.38–3.40, are designed to measure the movement and scale change of the objects.

$$R_P(i) = \frac{\|(\mathbf{\Psi}_2 - \frac{1}{2}\mathbf{\Psi}_3)(\mathbf{X}_O^i - \mathbf{X}_O^{i-1})\|_2}{max(1, mean(\sum_{j=2}^{i} \|(\mathbf{\Psi}_2 - \frac{1}{2}\mathbf{\Psi}_3)(\mathbf{X}_O^j - \mathbf{X}_O^{j-1})\|_2))} \tag{3.38}$$

$$R_S(i) = \frac{\|\mathbf{\Psi}_3(\mathbf{X}_O^i - \mathbf{X}_O^{i-1})\|_2}{max(1, mean(\sum_{j=2}^{i} \|\mathbf{\Psi}_3(\mathbf{X}_O^j - \mathbf{X}_O^{j-1})\|_2))} \tag{3.39}$$

$$RM_P(i) = \frac{\|(\mathbf{\Psi}_2 - \frac{1}{2}\mathbf{\Psi}_3)(\mathbf{X}_O^i - \mathbf{X}_K^i)\|_2}{max(1, mean(\sum_{j=1}^{i} \|(\mathbf{\Psi}_2 - \frac{1}{2}\mathbf{\Psi}_3)(\mathbf{X}_O^j - \mathbf{X}_K^j)\|_2))} \tag{3.40}$$

Equation 3.38 is the changing rate of the object center, Eq. 3.39 is the changing rate of scale. Equation 3.40 is the changing rate of center between MSSCF-KCF and monitor. In these Equations, $\mathbf{\Psi}_2 = [\mathbf{E}_{2\times2}, \mathbf{0}_{2\times2}] \in \mathbb{R}^{2\times4}$, and $\mathbf{\Psi}_3 = [\mathbf{0}_{2\times2}, \mathbf{E}_{2\times2}] \in \mathbb{R}^{2\times4}$. $\mathbf{E}_{2\times2}$ and $\mathbf{0}_{2\times2}$ are $2 \times 2$ identity matrix and zero matrix respectively. $\|(\mathbf{\Psi}_2 - \frac{1}{2}\mathbf{\Psi}_3)(\mathbf{X}_O^i - \mathbf{X}_O^{i-1})\|_2$ is the center error between $i$th frame and $i - 1$th frame. $\|(\mathbf{\Psi}_2 - \frac{1}{2}\mathbf{\Psi}_3)(\mathbf{X}_O^i - \mathbf{X}_K^i)\|_2$ means the center error between proposed tracker and monitor in $i$th frame. Whether the proposed tracker is running properly can be determined by comparing these three testing indexes with 1. If any of these testing indexes is over 1, we believe the proposed tracker is under an abnormal situation. The forgetting factor and variance of Gaussian distribution should be reduced and number of sub-candidates should be increased. Generally, the proposed monitor strategy is a tradeoff between speed and accuracy. The pseudo code of MSSCF-KCF is shown in Algorithm 1.

Algorithm 1 can be mainly divided into two parts. The first part, which is from step 1 to step 4, is segmenting the object and initialising the object templet for training the KCF trackers. The other steps are the second part, which is used to estimate the final tracking results and update the color feature guided confidence map iteratively.

### 3.4.4   Experimental Results and Discussions

The implement details and parameter settings of the proposed MSSCF-KCF trackers are discussed in this section. The experiments run on a computer with 3.3 GHz CPU and 8G memory, $\alpha_{step} = 0.1$, $Thre = 0.7$ and $N_{ss} = 7$. The superpixel numbers are $\{10, 20, 40, 60, 80, 100, 120\}$. SLIC [38] and GEP [37] are used in the proposed tracker for superpixel segmentation and optimal solution respectively. Widely used dataset such as OTB-2013[9], OTB-2015[10], ALOV++[39], etc. In addition, a small self-made dataset which is taken by a mobile phone is also used to test the proposed tracker. The average tracking speed could reach 15.3372 fps, which is slower than the KCF tracker, which is 118.8189 fps. We believe the multiply KCF trackers and process of optimal solution may slow down the tracking speed. However, the proposed tracker can still meet the demand of real-time tracking. The

---

**Algorithm 1:** Framework of the proposed method, MSSCF-KCF

---

**Input:**

  The initial object state $\mathbf{X}_O^1$;

  Enlargement factor $\lambda$;

  Step size $\alpha_{step}$;

  Threshold $Thre$;

  the scales of superpixels $\{S_s\}$, $s \in \{1, 2, \cdots, N_{ss}\}$;

  Frame number $\mathbf{N}_f$;

**Output:**

  The states of the objects $\{\mathbf{X}_O^i\}$, $i \in \{2, 3, \cdots, \mathbf{N}_f\}$;

  1: Getting the ROI by using $\lambda$, $\mathbf{X}_{ROI}$;

  2: Segmenting $I(\mathbf{X}_{ROI})$ based on multi-scale superpixel method, and computing the global confidence mask $G_{SM}$.

  3: Computing the number of the object patches $N_{pa}$, and estimating the state of each object patch $\mathbf{X}_{OP_\gamma}$, $\gamma \in \{1, 2, \cdots, N_{pa}\}$;

  4: Extracting HSI features and training KCFs for each object patch, and using as the initial object patch templet;

  5: **for** $i = 2; i < \mathbf{N}_f; i + +$ **do**

  6:     Getting sub-candidates of all object patches according to the Gaussian distribution based motion model;

  7:     Computing the confidence scores of sub-candidates $\hat{f}(I(\mathbf{X}_{SC_{\gamma,\xi}}))$ and color weights $CW_{\gamma,\xi}$, and obtaining the color feature guided confidence map;

  8:     Computing center distance matrix $C_{DM}$ and obtaining the optimal combination $G_k$ by applying GEP algorithm;

  9:     **if** color feature confidence score of $G_k(i)$ lower than $T_d$ **then**

  10:        Dropping out the $G_k(i)$;

  11:    **end if**

  12:    Estimating the state of the object $\mathbf{X}_O^i$ by Eq. 3.35;

  13:    Monitoring the tracking results by monitoring strategy by Eqs. 3.38–3.40;

  14:    Updating KCFs and HSI of the object patch templet by Eq. 3.37;

  15: **end for**

  16: **return** $\mathbf{X}_O^i$;

---

experiments can be divided into three sub-sections: basic experiments, experiments on benchmarks, experiments on self-made dataset.

**Basic Experiments** In order to test the effectiveness of each component in the proposed tracking algorithm, the experiments and comparisons of multi-scale superpixel based method, color feature guided method and sub-candidates selection and combination are illustrated in this section.

Figure 3.13 shows the comparisons between the proposed MSSCF-KCF tracker and BB-KCF tracker on the widely used dataset. The BB-KCF tacker is the grid block based KCF which means the ROI of the object is segmented into equal blocks by grid. The precision and success rate of OPE, TRE and SRE, which are proposed in the OTB benchmark [10] are used for comparison. From Fig. 3.13, we can see that all the plots of MSSCF-KCF are better than BB-KCF. This is mainly due to the superpixel based segmentation method used in MSSCF-KCF. Since the tracking performance is determined by the size and center of the object patch, the proposed

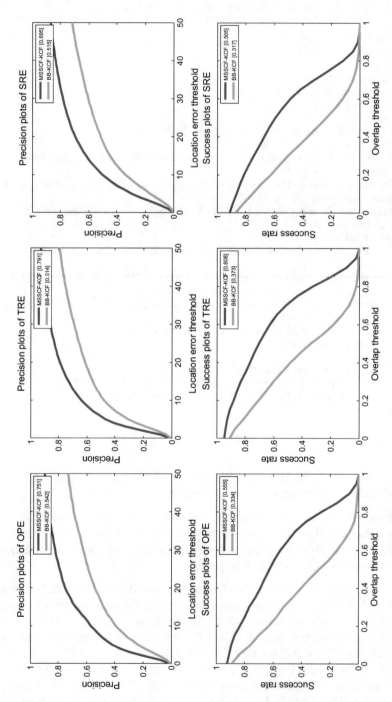

**Fig. 3.13** The precision and success plots of OPE, TRE and SRE, when comparing between MSSCF-KCF and BB-KCF

**Table 3.5**   Results of score of KCF, color weights and color feature guided confidence score

|                | $SC_1$ | $SC_2$ | $SC_3$ | $SC_4$ | $SC_5$ | $SC_6$ |
|----------------|--------|--------|--------|--------|--------|--------|
| CS of KCF      | 0.9932 | 0.3548 | 0.6597 | 0.3195 | 0.3839 | 0.7110 |
| CW of MSSCF-KCF | 1     | 0.3937 | 0.6941 | 0.3679 | 0.4029 | 0.6100 |
| CS of MSSCF-KCF | 0.9932 | 0.1397 | 0.4579 | 0.1175 | 0.1546 | 0.4337 |

superpixel based segmentation could segment the object into several patches and considering the object center at the same time, which is different from the grid block based KCF, BB-KCF.

Table 3.5 is used to illustrate the feasibility of the color feature guided confidence map. CS of KCF, CW of MSSCF-KCF and CS of MSSCF-KCF indicate the confidence score of KCF tracker, the color weight of MSSCF-KCF and the Confidence score of MSSCF-KCF respectively. While $SC_1$ to $SC_6$ are the six sub-candidates to be compared. From Table 3.5, we find that the sub-candidate may have the better score in color feature guided confidence map when it have high scores in both CS of KCF and color weight, such as the $SC_1$ in Table 3.5. This also means the color weight could further filter out the outliers, especially the sub-candidates with high scores in confidence map, but low color weights.

Similar to Fig, 3.13, Fig. 3.14 shows the comparison results of precision and success plots of OPE, TRE and SRE in the OTB benchmark. The MSSCF-KCF(r) tracker in Fig. 3.14 is designed for comparison. Unlike MSSCF-KCF tracker, MSSCF-KCF(r) selects and combines the sub-candidates randomly without the min-max criterion. The plots in Fig. 3.14 show that the proposed MSSCF-KCF tracker has better performance in both precision and success rate. This also means that the proposed center distance matrix and min-max criterion which considers the structure information of the object have great effect on improving the tracking performance of MSSCF-KCF.

**Experiments on Benchmarks**   In order to show the performance of the proposed tracker, the benchmarks, such as OTB-2013 and OTB-2015 are applied to test the proposed tracker. The experiments on benchmarks can also be divided into the precision and success plots of OPE, TRE and SRE when comparing with the baseline trackers and the performance of the proposed tracker under 11 tracking challenges. Figure 3.15 and Table 3.6 show the precision and success plots of OPE, TRE and SRE, when comparing with the baseline trackers. The red plots in Fig. 3.15 represent the proposed tracker which are all higher than the plots of the baseline trackers. That is, the proposed tracker has a better tracking performance in precision and success rate. From the precision and success plots of SRE and TRE in Fig. 3.15, we can conclude that the proposed tracker also has better temporal and spatial robustness.

For clearer and more intuitive representation of the tracking results, the average precision and success rates of OPE, TRE and SRE are shown in Table 3.6. The 'p' and 's' in Table 3.6 indicate the average precision and success rate respectively.

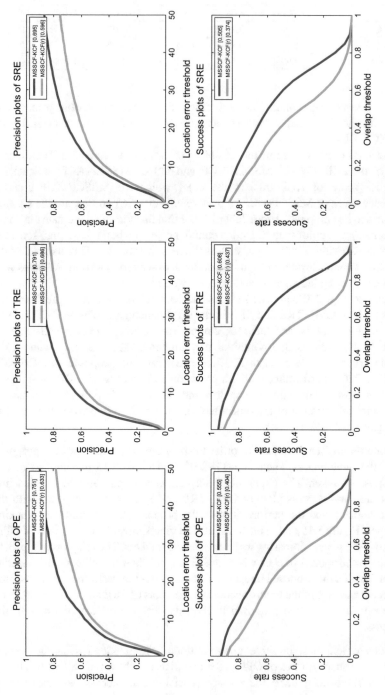

**Fig. 3.14** The precision and success plots of OPE, TRE and SRE, when comparing between MSSCF-KCF and MSSCF-KCF(r)

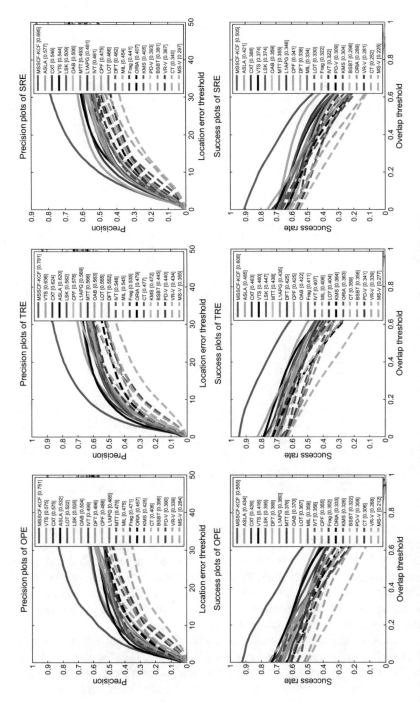

**Fig. 3.15** The precision and success plots of OPE, TRE, SRE, when comparing with baseline trackers in OTB

**Table 3.6** The precision and success scores of OPE, TRE and SRE, when comparing with 28 trackers in OTB

|          | OPE_p | OPE_s | TRE_p | TRE_s | SRE_p | SRE_s |
|----------|-------|-------|-------|-------|-------|-------|
| MSSCF-KCF | 0.751 | 0.555 | 0.791 | 0.608 | 0.695 | 0.505 |
| CXT      | 0.575 | 0.426 | 0.624 | 0.463 | 0.546 | 0.388 |
| Struck   | 0.656 | 0.474 | 0.707 | 0.514 | 0.635 | 0.439 |
| KCF      | 0.74  | 0.51  | 0.774 | 0.556 | 0.683 | 0.463 |
| SCM      | 0.649 | 0.499 | 0.653 | 0.514 | 0.575 | 0.420 |
| VTD      | 0.576 | 0.416 | 0.643 | 0.462 | 0.553 | 0.381 |
| TLD      | 0.608 | 0.437 | 0.624 | 0.448 | 0.573 | 0.402 |
| IVT      | 0.499 | 0.358 | 0.548 | 0.407 | 0.481 | 0.322 |
| L1APG    | 0.485 | 0.380 | 0.569 | 0.435 | 0.481 | 0.348 |
| CSK      | 0.545 | 0.398 | 0.618 | 0.454 | 0.525 | 0.367 |
| VR-V     | 0.339 | 0.368 | 0.434 | 0.339 | 0.367 | 0.281 |
| VTS      | 0.575 | 0.416 | 0.638 | 0.460 | 0.544 | 0.374 |
| Frag     | 0.471 | 0.352 | 0.535 | 0.411 | 0.441 | 0.322 |
| MS-V     | 0.284 | 0.212 | 0.355 | 0.277 | 0.297 | 0.225 |
| CPF      | 0.488 | 0.355 | 0.578 | 0.425 | 0.475 | 0.341 |
| KMS      | 0.425 | 0.326 | 0.472 | 0.364 | 0.405 | 0.304 |
| LOT      | 0.522 | 0.367 | 0.555 | 0.404 | 0.466 | 0.330 |
| PD-V     | 0.396 | 0.308 | 0.440 | 0.314 | 0.393 | 0.309 |
| ASLA     | 0.532 | 0.434 | 0.620 | 0.485 | 0.577 | 0.421 |
| DFT      | 0.496 | 0.389 | 0.552 | 0.425 | 0.462 | 0.338 |
| LSK      | 0.505 | 0.395 | 0.582 | 0.447 | 0.509 | 0.374 |
| OAB      | 0.504 | 0.370 | 0.563 | 0.422 | 0.506 | 0.359 |
| MTT      | 0.475 | 0.376 | 0.568 | 0.438 | 0.493 | 0.355 |
| MIL      | 0.475 | 0.359 | 0.545 | 0.406 | 0.454 | 0.334 |
| CT       | 0.406 | 0.306 | 0.477 | 0.359 | 0.340 | 0.252 |
| BSBT     | 0.396 | 0.322 | 0.445 | 0.358 | 0.381 | 0.298 |
| ORIA     | 0.457 | 0.333 | 0.479 | 0.363 | 0.407 | 0.289 |
| TM-V     | 0.445 | 0.352 | 0.510 | 0.396 | 0.428 | 0.313 |

For example, 'OPE_p' is the average precision rate of OPE, while 'OPE_s' is the average success rate of OPE. The numbers in red and blue represent the highest and lowest score in Table 3.6. The numbers of the proposed tracker are all in red which means that the proposed tracker has the best performance when comparing with the baseline trackers. Because of the multi-scale superpixel method and structure based optimization strategy the performance of the proposed tracker shows a significant improvement when comparing with the traditional KCF.

The precision rate of the proposed tracker and other 28 state-of-art trackers under 11 tracking challenges are provided in Table 3.7. FM, BC, MB, De, Il, IpR, LR, Oc, OpR, OV and SV in Table 3.7 represent fast motion, background clutter, motion blur, deformation, illumination, in-plane rotation, low resolution, occlusion, out-of-plane rotation, out of view and scale variation respectively. From Table 3.7, we can

**Table 3.7** The precision rate of 28 trackers when location error threshold in precision plot is 20

|          | FM    | BC     | MB    | De    | Il    | IpR   | LR    | Oc    | OpR   | OV    | SV    |
|----------|-------|--------|-------|-------|-------|-------|-------|-------|-------|-------|-------|
| MSSCF-KCF | 0.697 | 0.712 | 0.707 | 0.687 | 0.668 | 0.732 | 0.542 | 0.748 | 0.712 | 0.605 | 0.721 |
| CXT      | 0.515 | 0.443  | 0.509 | 0.422 | 0.501 | 0.61  | 0.371 | 0.491 | 0.574 | 0.51  | 0.55  |
| Struck   | 0.604 | 0.585  | 0.551 | 0.521 | 0.558 | 0.617 | 0.545 | 0.564 | 0.597 | 0.539 | 0.639 |
| KCF      | 0.602 | 0.753  | 0.65  | 0.74  | 0.728 | 0.725 | 0.381 | 0.749 | 0.729 | 0.65  | 0.679 |
| SCM      | 0.333 | 0.578  | 0.339 | 0.586 | 0.594 | 0.597 | 0.305 | 0.64  | 0.618 | 0.429 | 0.672 |
| VTD      | 0.352 | 0.571  | 0.375 | 0.501 | 0.557 | 0.599 | 0.168 | 0.545 | 0.62  | 0.462 | 0.597 |
| TLD      | 0.551 | 0.428  | 0.518 | 0.512 | 0.537 | 0.584 | 0.349 | 0.563 | 0.596 | 0.576 | 0.606 |
| IVT      | 0.22  | 0.421  | 0.222 | 0.409 | 0.418 | 0.457 | 0.278 | 0.455 | 0.464 | 0.307 | 0.494 |
| L1APG    | 0.365 | 0.425  | 0.375 | 0.383 | 0.341 | 0.518 | 0.46  | 0.461 | 0.478 | 0.329 | 0.472 |
| CSK      | 0.381 | 0.585  | 0.342 | 0.476 | 0.481 | 0.547 | 0.411 | 0.500 | 0.54  | 0.379 | 0.503 |
| VR-V     | 0.254 | 0.318  | 0.26  | 0.348 | 0.222 | 0.294 | 0.136 | 0.332 | 0.332 | 0.236 | 0.324 |
| VTS      | 0.353 | 0.578  | 0.375 | 0.487 | 0.573 | 0.579 | 0.187 | 0.534 | 0.604 | 0.455 | 0.582 |
| Frag     | 0.346 | 0.421  | 0.288 | 0.468 | 0.326 | 0.401 | 0.163 | 0.475 | 0.444 | 0.355 | 0.407 |
| MS-V     | 0.258 | 0.275  | 0.254 | 0.200 | 0.254 | 0.281 | 0.139 | 0.241 | 0.297 | 0.301 | 0.315 |
| CPF      | 0.377 | 0.418  | 0.261 | 0.494 | 0.366 | 0.463 | 0.130 | 0.517 | 0.529 | 0.483 | 0.475 |
| KMS      | 0.368 | 0.419  | 0.365 | 0.430 | 0.374 | 0.376 | 0.259 | 0.412 | 0.414 | 0.390 | 0.431 |
| LOT      | 0.420 | 0.529  | 0.395 | 0.487 | 0.367 | 0.508 | 0.201 | 0.532 | 0.520 | 0.567 | 0.465 |
| PD-V     | 0.300 | 0.320  | 0.342 | 0.427 | 0.326 | 0.324 | 0.205 | 0.373 | 0.361 | 0.222 | 0.364 |
| ASLA     | 0.253 | 0.496  | 0.278 | 0.455 | 0.517 | 0.511 | 0.156 | 0.460 | 0.518 | 0.333 | 0.552 |
| DFT      | 0.373 | 0.597  | 0.383 | 0.537 | 0.475 | 0.469 | 0.211 | 0.481 | 0.497 | 0.391 | 0.441 |
| LSK      | 0.375 | 0.504  | 0.324 | 0.481 | 0.449 | 0.534 | 0.304 | 0.534 | 0.525 | 0.515 | 0.480 |
| OAB      | 0.416 | 0.446  | 0.360 | 0.470 | 0.388 | 0.471 | 0.376 | 0.483 | 0.503 | 0.454 | 0.541 |
| MTT      | 0.401 | 0.424  | 0.308 | 0.332 | 0.351 | 0.522 | 0.510 | 0.426 | 0.473 | 0.374 | 0.461 |
| MIL      | 0.396 | 0.456  | 0.357 | 0.455 | 0.349 | 0.453 | 0.171 | 0.427 | 0.466 | 0.393 | 0.471 |
| CT       | 0.323 | 0.339  | 0.306 | 0.435 | 0.359 | 0.356 | 0.152 | 0.412 | 0.394 | 0.336 | 0.448 |
| BSBT     | 0.321 | 0.3112 | 0.307 | 0.371 | 0.302 | 0.380 | 0.243 | 0.390 | 0.391 | 0.442 | 0.330 |
| ORIA     | 0.274 | 0.389  | 0.234 | 0.355 | 0.421 | 0.500 | 0.195 | 0.435 | 0.493 | 0.315 | 0.445 |
| TM-V     | 0.420 | 0.378  | 0.447 | 0.383 | 0.321 | 0.440 | 0.280 | 0.395 | 0.411 | 0.502 | 0.417 |

see that the proposed tracker could rank in the top 5 when comparing with the 28 state-of-the-art trackers. The proposed tracker could also show the best performance under some specific challenges such as fast motion, motion blur, in-plane rotation and scale variation, etc. This also proves that the proposed multi-scale superpixel segmentation method and the application of the structure information help improve the tracking performance under some tracking challenges, especially scale variation.

In order to further test the practicability of the proposed tracker in real life, MSSCF-KCF is also tested on the self-made dataset. Some state-of-the-art trackers such as PF[40], MS[41], SPT[42], KCF[15], DSST[22], DFT[43], CT[44] and CCOT[34] are also tested on this self-made dataset for comparison.

**Fig. 3.16** The tracking results of MSSCF-KCF, PF, MS, SPT, BB-KCF, ProT_SPT, KCF, DSST, DFT, CT, CSK and CCOT under 6 self-made sequences in real life scenes

Figure 3.16 shows a qualitative experiment of the self-made dataset. The sequences from top to bottom are named as girl dinner, girl friend, girl gliding, girl skating, girl skiing and girl skiing 1 respectively. girl dinner and girl skating sequences contain the fast motion and camera moving challenges. Since the object moving fast and the camera shakes in these two sequences, these may cause the tacking failure. The proposed tracker shows a better performance in these two sequences when comparing with other trackers, which means the proposed tracker could handle the camera shaking and fast motion challenge. In the girl gliding sequence, the proposed tracker provides the most appropriate bounding box, whose size is consistent with the scale of the object. This means the MSSCK-KCF tracker has better ability in handling scale variation challenge. We believe this results may be mainly due to the multi-scale superpixel segmentation and structure based optimization strategy.

Generally speaking, the tracking performance may get improved by the proposed MSSCF-KCF tracker, when handling some specific tracking challenges, such as fast motion, motion blur, scale variation. The experiments of TRE and SRE on OTB benchmarks also prove that the proposed tracker has a better robustness comparing with some state-of-the-art trackers.

## 3.5 Summary

In this chapter, we mainly proposed three improved correlation filter based trackers. All those three trackers are designed to take advantage of the fast tracking speed of the KCF tracker to further improve the tracking performance when handling the challenges such as occlusion and scale variation, etc.

In the first method, context aware based global background information is used to improve the discriminate ability of classifier and enhance the use of background information. Then the adaptive update model is used to improve the tracking robustness, when tracking failure occurs. The experiments show that context aware information and adaptive update model could help correlation based trackers to cope with the occlusion challenge.

In the second method, two correlation filters are combined together to estimate the position and the scale of the object to handle the scale variation challenge, and a manually designed feature is used to construct the appearance model and improve the tracking robustness. The experiments show that the scale pyramid filter with multi-scale information of the object could help the proposed tracker estimate the scale change and the carefully designed feature could improve the robustness of appearance model in correlation filter based trackers.

In the third method, in order to use the structure information of the object, the state of the object is viewed as the best combination of sub-object patches which is segmented by superpixel methods. The optimal problem can be solved through min-max criterion and GEP algorithm. Segmenting the object into several patches and using the multiple KCF trackers to use structure information of the object could improve the performance when handling scale variation challenge, but loss some tracking speed. It is a trade-off between tracking accuracy and speed.

Generally, context aware information and carefully designed feature could improve the robustness of appearance model in correlation filter based trackers. Re-detection methods can also help correlation based trackers to cope with the occlusion challenge. Segmenting the object into several patches and using the multiple KCF trackers to use structure information of the object could improve the performance when handling scale variation challenge, but loss some tracking speed. It is a trade-off between tracking accuracy and speed.

## References

1. Ross, D., Lim, J., Lin, R., Yang, M.: Incremental Learning for robust visual tracking. Int. J. Comput. **77**(1–3), 125–141 (2008)
2. Li, H., Shen, C., Shi, Q.: Real-time visual tracking using compressive sensing. In: IEEE Conference on Computer Vision and Pattern Recognition, pp. 1305–1312 (2011)
3. Du, B., Sun, Y., Wu, C., et al.: Real-time tracking based on weighted compressive tracking and a cognitive memory model. Signal Process. **139**, 173–181 (2017)

4. Zamir, A., Dehghan, A., Shah, M.: GMCP-tracker: global multi-object tracking using generalized minimum clique graphs. In: European Conference on Computer Vision, pp. 343–356 (2012)

5. Berclaz, J., Fleuret, F., Turetken, E., et al.: Multiple object tracking using k-shortest paths optimization. IEEE Trans. Pattern Anal. Mach. Intell. **33**(9), 1806–1819 (2011)

6. Yilmaz, A., Javed, O., Shah, M.: Object tracking: a survey. ACM Comput. Surv. **38**(4), 13-es (2006)

7. Kristan, M., Matas, J., Leonardis, A., et al.: A novel performance evaluation methodology for single-target trackers. IEEE Trans. Pattern Anal. Mach. Intell. **38**(11), 2137–2155 (2016)

8. Smeulders, A., Chu, D., Cucchiara, R., et al.: Visual tracking: an experimental survey. IEEE Trans. Pattern Anal. Mach. Intell. **36**(7), 1442–1468 (2013)

9. Wu, Y., Lim, J., Yang, M.: Online object tracking: a benchmark. In: IEEE Conference on Computer Vision and Pattern Recognition, pp. 2411–2418 (2013)

10. Wu, Y., Lim, J., Yang, M.: Object tracking benchmark. IEEE Trans. Pattern Anal. Mach. Intell. **37**(9), 1834–1848 (2015)

11. Abdel-Hadi, A.: Real-time object tracking using color-based Kalman particle filter. In: International Conference on Computational and Experimental Engineering and Sciences, pp. 337–341 (2010)

12. Han, Z., Xu, T., Chen, Z.: An improved color-based tracking by particle filter. In: International Conference on Transportation, Mechanical, and Electrical Engineering, pp. 2512–2515 (2011)

13. Yang, F., Lu, H., Yang, M.: Robust superpixel tracking. IEEE Trans. Image Process. **23**(4), 1639–1651 (2014)

14. Wang, Q., Chen, F., Xu, W., Yang, M.: Object tracking via partial least squares analysis. IEEE Trans. Image Process. 21(10), 4454–4465 (2012)

15. Henriques, J., Caseiro, R., Martins, P., et al.: High-speed tracking with kernelized correlation filters. IEEE Trans. Pattern Anal. Mach. Intell. **37**(3), 583–596 (2015)

16. Hare, S., Golodetz, S., Saari, A., et al.: Struck: structured output tracking with kernels. IEEE Trans. Pattern Anal. Mach. Intell. **38**(10), 2096–2109 (2016)

17. Zhong, B., Yao, H., Chen, S., et al.: Visual tracking via weakly supervised learning from multiple imperfect oracles. Pattern Recogn. **47**(3), 1395–1410 (2014)

18. Bolme, D., Beveridge, J., Draper, B., et al.: Visual object tracking using adaptive correlation filters. In: IEEE Computer Society Conference on Computer Vision and Pattern Recognition, pp. 2544–2550 (2010)

19. Henriques, J., Caseiro, R., Martins, P., et al.: Exploiting the circulant structure of tracking-by-detection with kernels. In: European Conference on Computer Vision, pp. 702–715 (2012)

20. Henriques, J., Caseiro, R., Martins, P., et al.: High-speed tracking with kernelized correlation filters. IEEE Trans. Pattern Anal. Mach. Intell. **37**(3), 583–596 (2014)

21. Tang, M., Feng, J.: Multi-kernel correlation filter for visual tracking. In: IEEE International Conference on Computer Vision, pp. 3038–3046 (2015)

22. Danelljan, M., Hager, G., Khan, F., et al.: Accurate scale estimation for robust visual tracking. In: British Machine Vision Conference, pp. 1–5 (2014)

23. Wang, Q., Gao, J., Xing, J., et al.: DCFnet: discriminant correlation filters network for visual tracking. Preprint, arXiv: 1704.04057 (2017)

24. Kalal, Z., Matas, J., Mikolajczyk, K.: Pn learning: bootstrapping binary classifiers by structural constraints. In: IEEE Computer Society Conference on Computer Vision and Pattern Recognition, pp. 49–56 (2010)

25. Zhang, J., Ma, S., Sclaroff, S.: Meem: robust tracking via multiple experts using entropy minimization. In: European Conference on Computer Vision, pp. 188–203 (2014)

26. Li, Y., Zhu, J.: A scale adaptive kernel correlation filter tracker with feature integration. In: European Conference on Computer Vision Workshops, pp. 254–265 (2014)

27. Bertinetto, L., Valmadre, J., Golodetz, S., Miksik, O., Torr, P.: Staple: complementary learners for realtime tracking. In: IEEE Conference on Computer Vision and Pattern Recognition, pp. 1401–1409 (2016)

28. Pu, S., Song, Y., Ma, C., et al.: Deep attentive tracking via reciprocative learning. In: Neural Information Processing Systems, pp. 1931–1941 (2018)
29. Weijer, J., Schmid, C., Verbeek, J.: Learning color names from real-world images. In: IEEE Conference on Computer Vision and Pattern Recognition, pp. 17–22 (2007)
30. Wang, M., Liu, Y., Huang, Z.: Large margin object tracking with circulant feature maps. In: IEEE Conference on Computer Vision and Pattern Recognition, pp. 4800–4808 (2017)
31. Ma, C., Yang, X., Zhang, C., et al.: Long-term correlation tracking. In: IEEE Conference on Computer Vision and Pattern Recognition, pp. 5388–5396 (2015)
32. Mueller, M., Smith, N., Ghanem, B., et al.: Context-aware correlation filter tracking. In: IEEE Conference on Computer Vision and Pattern Recognition, pp. 1387–1395 (2017)
33. Bibi, A., Mueller, M., Ghanem, B., et al.: Target response adaptation for correlation filter tracking. In: European Conference on Computer Vision, Amsterdam, pp. 419–433 (2016)
34. Danelljan, M., Robinson, A., Khan, F., et al.: Beyond correlation filters: learning continuous convolution operators for visual tracking. In: European Conference on Computer Vision, pp. 472–488 (2016)
35. Ning, J., Yang, J., Jiang, S., Zhang, L., Yang, M.: Object tracking via dual linear structured SVM and explicit feature map. In: IEEE Conference on Computer Vision and Pattern Recognition (CVPR), pp. 4266–4274 (2016)
36. Bertinetto, L., Valmadre, J., Henriques, J., et al.: Fully-convolutional siamese networks for object tracking. In: European Conference on Computer Vision, pp. 850–865 (2016)
37. Ferreira, C.: Gene expression programming in problem solving. In: Soft Computing and Industry, pp. 635–653. Springer, London (2003)
38. Achanta, R., Shaji, A., Smith, K., et al.: SLIC superpixels compared to state-of-the-art superpixel methods. IEEE Trans. Pattern Anal. Mach. Intell. **34**(11), 2274–2282 (2012)
39. Smeulders, A., Chu, D., Cucchiara, R., et al.: Visual tracking: an experimental survey. IEEE Trans. Pattern Anal. Mach. Intell. **36**(7), 1442–1468 (2014)
40. Nummiaro, K., Koller-Meier, E., VanGool, L.: An adaptive color-based particle filter. Image Vis. Comput. **21**(1), 99–110 (2003)
41. Collins, R.: Mean-shift blob tracking through scale space. In: IEEE Conference on Computer Vision and Pattern Recognition, pp. II–234 (2003)
42. Wang, S., Lu, H., Yang, F., et al.: Superpixel tracking. In: IEEE Conference on Computer Vision and Pattern Recognition, pp. 1323–1330 (2011)
43. Sevilla-Lara, L., Learned-Miller, E.: Distribution fields for tracking. In: IEEE Conference on Computer Vision and Pattern Recognition, pp. 1910–1917 (2012)
44. Zhang, K., Zhang, L., Yang, M.: Real-time compressive tracking. In: European Conference on Computer Vision, Florence, pp. 864–877 (2012)

# Chapter 4
# Correlation Filter with Deep Feature for Visual Object Tracking

The correlation filter tracking model can better represent the tracking target by using the deep feature, because the deep feature can better distinguish the target and the background compared with the traditional hand-crafted feature. This chapter mainly introduces three correlation filter methods based on depth features. The first method uses long-short term correlation filter to learn the spatiotemporal feature of the target; the second method uses content-aware and channel attention mechanisms to improve the performance of the tracking method; the third method uses auxiliary relocation with correlation filters to relocate the target and reduces target tracking failure caused by occlusion.

## 4.1 Introduction

To design accurate and stable tracking models, CF has been selected. To explain the association between two signals, CF was originally applied to signal processing. Since CF is effective and robust, a minimum output sum of squared error (MOSSE) filter [1] first uses CF in the visual object tracking. The minimum output sum of squared error (MOSSE) filter is used to calculate the degree of similarity between the target and the candidate samples based on the target tracking matching problem. The main idea is to construct a target correlation filter template and use it to convolve with the candidate samples in the video sequence frame by frame to obtain the corresponding response values and select the candidate sample with the highest response value as the target prediction position for the current frame. To generate adequate samples, KCF adopts circulant matrices and computes the solution in the Fourier space, which is fast and can be applied to real-time tracking. The positive and negative samples are generated using the circular matrix of the target proximity region, and the diagonalisable nature of the circular matrix in Fourier space is used to transform the matrix operations into vector element points Hadamard products, which greatly reduces the amount of operations and improves the speed. Unlike other methods, KCF designs a multichannel feature fusion of grey-scale maps, which can better discriminate between tracking targets and backgrounds, providing a solution to the multichannel feature fusion problem of target tracking. To learn the position and scale, DSST[2] chooses two separate filters. MUSTer [3], inspired by a psychological memory model, designs short-term and long-term memory stores for robust modeling of appearance.

To mitigate this problem, SRDCF [4] is proposed. SRDCF ignores the boundary component of all moved samples since these effects occur near the boundary. To implement an efficient filter, BACF[5] selects background information outside the bounding box. In order to update the tracking model, LMCF[6] adopts a highly optimistic update strategy. Staple[7] blends the HOG function with the color feature effectively and proposes an efficient method of features fusion. In order to improve tracking efficiency, CSR-DCF[8] combines Staple with CFLB using the CN function. These techniques, however, only use hand-craft features, which restrict the model's discrimination ability. DeepSRDCF[4] enhances SRDCF with deep features and more efficiently explains the features of the object. Deep features are also used by C-COT[9]; it brings the cubic interpolation function map into the continuous space domain and adopts the Hessian matrix to obtain the position of the object. ECO[10] uses a factorized convolution operator, a generative sample space model and a short-term update model based on C-COT to increase the speed and efficiency of the algorithm. These methods illustrate that in visual object tracking, CF methods still play a critical role. It is still necessary to improve these models' representation capability and choose a suitable update strategy for CF-based methods.

## 4.2  Long-Short Term Correlation Filter Based Visual Object Tracking

To improve the tracking efficiency, we combine the long-short term with fusion features in this section. To be precise, both long-term and short-term correlation filter models are built based on spatio-temporal information representation, and deep features and hand-crafted features are combined to reflect the tracking target. Figure 4.1 depicts the process of tracking this work.

### 4.2.1  Fusion of Deep Features and Hand-Crafted Features

Deep features have also been selected in recent years to reflect the tracking target, and the efficacy of deep trackers exceeds that when only hand-crafted features are used. Features integrating multi-layer deep features with HOG + CN features are

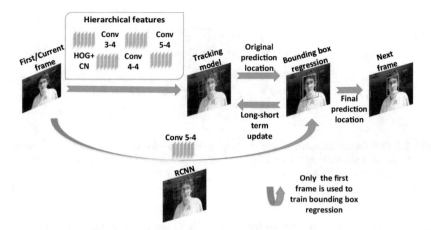

**Fig. 4.1** The first frame initializes the regression model and the tracker for the Bounding-box. Then the multi-model tracker will track the target through deep and hand-crafted features. The pre-trained bounding-box regression model would then fine-tune the predicted location as the final predicted position. At last, with the final predicted location, the long-short-term correlation filters will be updated

used to train the correlation filters to enhance the tracker's representation ability. Lower convolution layer features provide more temporal location details, according to CF2[11], and higher convolution layer features provide more spatial information that can explain the tracking target position. More image semantic information is stored in the features of higher convolutional layers to identify the tracking target appearances that can distinguish the tracking target from the background. It is useful to incorporate deep multi-layer features that provide both semantic information and location information to increase tracking efficiency. For example, by combining hand-crafted HOG [12] with CN [13], some other tracking methods boost the representation ability. The HOG features of 31 channels are robust for lighting transition, occlusion, non-rigid deformation, motion blur, in-plane rotation, and out-of-plane rotation. While the CN function converts the three RGB image channels into 11 color channels to obtain 11-channel features, it achieves good performance in scale change, rapid motion, and rigid deformation. So, to represent the tracking target, HOG and CN features are usually combined.

Conv3-4, conv4-4, and conv5-4 features from VGG19 and HOG features combined with CN features are used in this work to enhance the tracker's representation ability. The structures of the functions are shown in Fig. 4.2 and for four functions, respectively, there are four function structures. The extracted HOG and CN features are combined as one feature, and three deep three-layer features are used as three features. These features are independent. The size of the cosine window defines the height and width of the feature. Assuming the size of the cosine window is $28 \times 26$, sizes of the three features are $28 \times 26$, and receptively, the number of channels is 512, 512, and 256. The sizes of the features of HOG and CN are $56 \times 56$ and

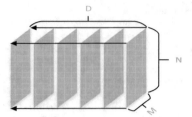

**Fig. 4.2** One feature structure of our method. In order to achieve fusion features, four feature structures like HOG+CN and deep features of three layers from VGG19 are adopted. M and N denote the width and height of the feature map, and the channel number D of each feature is different

twice the size of the window of the cosine. HOG has 31 channels, and CN has 10 channels, and 41 channels have the HOG + CN feature after connection. Then, to downsample the HOG + CN function from 56 × 56 to 28 × 28 according to the size of the cosine window, we use the bilinear interpolation function. Finally, with the size of 28 × 28 × 41, we obtain the HOG + CN feature. All four features are obtained through the extraction process and are selected to train four correlation filters to predict the target's location.

### 4.2.2   Correlation Filters with Long-Short Term Update

A single correlation filter based on a single feature does not reliably predict the tracking target. Four correlation filters are used to approximate object position by looking for the highest response value of the correlation map, as inspired by the use of the object tracking multi-correlation filters to improve performance based on KCF [14]. To combine deep and hand-crafted features, three convolutional layer outputs are used as three deep features, while HOG + CN is chosen as one hand-crafted feature. Suppose $X$ is a feature vector of $M \times N \times D$, and M, N, and D denote the distance, height, and the number of channels, respectively. We can obtain the column vector of the non-linear mapping function $f(xi) = \omega^{\mathrm{T}} xi$ and $\omega$ implies the coefficient of weight. The minimum squared error is: The Ridge regression function is used to find a solution that makes the shifted samples linearly separable in the new space.

$$\min_{\omega} \sum_{i} (f(x_i) - y_i)^2 + \lambda \|\omega\|^2 \qquad (4.1)$$

Each moving sample has a Gaussian distribution value. To solve the minimization problem, a correlation filter of the same size as X is trained, and the correlation filter minimization problem can be transformed independently using fast Fourier transformation (FFT). The correlation filter is built using a Gaussian kernel matrix, and the form of the kernel matrix is as follows:

$$K^{xx'} = exp(-\frac{1}{\sigma^2}(\|x\|^2 + \|x'\| - 2(\mathcal{F}^{-1})(\hat{x}^* \odot \hat{x}')))  \qquad (4.2)$$

Where $x$ and $x'$ are the templates and the candidate generating vector, $\hat{x}$ denotes the Discrete Fourier Transform (DFT) of $x$, $\hat{x}^*$ is the complex-conjugate vector after the transpose of Hermitian, $\odot$ is the corresponding multiplication operation for the product, and $\mathcal{F}^{-1}$ is the inverse DFT.

After conversion, a dual $\alpha$ to $\omega$ solution is found (refer to KCF for a comprehensive conversion process). $\alpha$ is updated for each filter by:

$$\alpha_{t+1} = (1 - \gamma) * \alpha_t + \gamma * \alpha_{new}  \qquad (4.3)$$

Where $\gamma$ is the learning rate and $\alpha_{new}$ in the current frame is measured as $\alpha$. In this work, it is vital to update four correlation filters according to the change in tracking target. Then, in the next frame, the image patch correlation filter response map is obtained and is calculated by searching for the location with the highest value in the $M \times N$ size correlation response map.

Given that the tracking target will be deformed and occluded during the tracking phase, it is critical to establish an upgrade strategy for the tracker in order to achieve reliable tracking performance. However, multiple variables affect the monitoring result, and it is impossible to apply a single update technique to all scenarios. Some situations can be resolved with a single upgrade approach, while others can deteriorate. It's also difficult to respond to a monitoring goal change with a fixed-term update strategy. In occlusion, the short-term update strategy is more vulnerable to rapid deformation but less susceptible to object drift, while the long-term update strategy is insensitive to rapid deformation and more resistant to occlusion but not ideal for rapid changes in the object's appearance.

To solve this problem, a long-term update strategy is created, as shown in Fig. 4.3. Long- and short-term memory correlation filters will be qualified, and the final correlation filter will be weighted. The update strategy will improve the tracker's performance by combining the benefits of both the short-term update model for rapid deformation handling and the long-term occlusion handling model. For each 1, 3, and 5 frames, the parameters of the three correlation filters in this work will be modified separately. When the three correlation filter parameters are combined by weighting, the final correlation filter parameters are obtained. It changes the parameters as follows:

$$\alpha = \sum_{i=1,3,5} \sum_{j=1}^{4} w_i \alpha_j  \qquad (4.4)$$

For each model, where $w$ is the weight and $\alpha_i (i = 1, 3, 5)$ corresponds to $model_i (i = 1, 3, 5)$. $\alpha_j$ denotes four solutions for functions. One-frame correlation

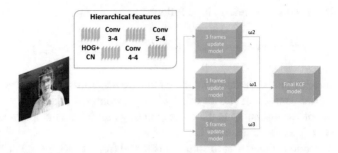

**Fig. 4.3** Correlation filters for long-short term updates. The position of the tracking target can be predicted using three separate correlation filters and fusion features. The one-frame correlation filter is updated every frame, while the three-frame correlation filter is updated every three frames and the five-frame correlation filter is updated every five frames. The final correlation filter is synthesized by weighing the three correlation filters

is good for monitoring rapid deformation and fast movement, and it updates faster to provide information about deformation. Long-term occlusion and minor deformation are efficiently tracked using three-frame and five-frame correlation filters, which are more robust for long-term monitoring. Finally, as compared to using a single in occlusion and fast deformation case alone or in pairs, the long-short-term upgrade strategy combines all three update correlation efficiency better.

Due to the drift issue, the bounding box will inevitably drift and lose track after the tracker obtains the tracking results. For expected outcomes, a fine-tuning method may be used to reduce the probability of missing an object due to object drift and to boost the tracker's accuracy. Furthermore, since the bounding box is larger, more useless data would be added, negatively impacting the tracking model. A bounding-box regression is used in this study to fine-tune the location and scale of the tracker's prediction performance.

With a Gaussian distribution, 10,000 sample bounding boxes are created randomly around the initial position of the object in the first frame of each video sequence. The bounding-box may be called a positive sample if it has more than 0.6 overlaps with the ground truth. For bounding-box regression training, the top 1000 positive samples are selected. The 37-Th layer performance is selected as the deep feature for bounding-box regression, using ImageNet-trained VGG19 to extract deep features from 1000 positive candidate samples. Ridge regression is determined using RCNN [15] bounding-box regression with the position and deep features of candidate samples.

The bounding box regression method is as follows. Let $P = (P_x, P_y, P_w, P_h)$ denotes the final output of the correlation filter, $G = (G_x, G_y, G_w, G_h)$ denote the truth of the ground, and $\hat{G} = (\hat{G}_x, \hat{G}_y, \hat{G}_w, \hat{G}_h)$ is the bounding box regression result of $P$. Via the following four equations, we change $P$.

$$
\begin{aligned}
\hat{G}_x &= P_x + \Delta x \\
\hat{G}_y &= P_y + \Delta y \\
\hat{G}_w &= P_x * \Delta x \\
\hat{G}_h &= P_y * \Delta y
\end{aligned}
\tag{4.5}
$$

Then it obtains a general form of the four equations. Translations are denoted by $d_x(P)$ and $d_y(P)$, $d_w(P)$ and $d_h(P)$ scale changes.

$$
\begin{aligned}
\hat{G}_x &= P_w d_x(P) + P_x \\
\hat{G}_y &= P_h d_y(P) + P_y \\
\hat{G}_w &= P_w exp(d_w(P)) \\
\hat{G}_h &= P_h exp(d_h(P))
\end{aligned}
\tag{4.6}
$$

There is an optimal adjustment for each frame, $t* = (t_x, t_y, t_w, t_h)$,

$$
\begin{aligned}
G_x &= P_x + P_w t_x(P) \\
G_y &= P_y + P_h t_y(P) \\
G_w &= P_w * e^{(t_w(P))} \\
G_h &= P_h * e^{(t_h(P))}
\end{aligned}
\tag{4.7}
$$

Then, the $t*$ solution form is obtained,

$$
\begin{aligned}
t_x &= (G_x - P_x)/P_w \\
t_y &= (G_y - P_y)/P_y \\
t_w &= log(G_w/P_w) \\
t_h &= log(G_h/P_h)
\end{aligned}
\tag{4.8}
$$

The function can be expressed as $d * (P) = w^T * \Phi(P)$, $\Phi(P)$ denotes the map of the input feature, $w*$ denotes the RCNN parameters to represent four equations of adjustment, $d * (P)$ means the predicted value is obtained. To minimize the difference between the predicted and the ground truth value, the loss function is designed as follows.

$$Loss = \sum_{i}^{N}(t_*^i - \hat{w}_*^T \Phi(P^i))^2 \tag{4.9}$$

Then, by the gradient descent method, we obtain the function optimization target and optimum $w*$.

$$W_* = argmin_{w_*} \sum_{i}^{N}(t_*^i - \hat{w}_*^T \Phi(P^i))^2 + \lambda \left\| \hat{w}_* \right\|^2 \tag{4.10}$$

Finally, a well-trained bounding-box regression model is obtained by pre-training. In the following frames, the expected position and its deep features are fed into the previously trained bounding-box regression model. When the tracker produces the predicted result in the current frame, Eq. 4.6 will be used to fine-tune the size and position of the predicted results. The approximate result is more reliable with bounding-box regression. The bounding box around the target becomes more compact as the target gets smaller, and also as the target gets bigger. The bounding-box regression reduces the probability of goal failure due to size changes in the target during monitoring. In order to balance bounding-box regression randomness and time cost, 10,000 samples are randomly generated for initialization.

### 4.2.3 Framework and Procedure

The essential steps of the proposed method's algorithm are shown in Algorithm 2. The bounding-box regression model and the tracker will be initialized in the first frame. The tracker will also use four correlation filters with deep and hand-crafted features to monitor the object. The pre-trained bounding-box regression model would then fine-tune the predicted position as the final predicted position. Finally, the long-short term correlation filters will be modified with the final expected result.

### 4.2.4 Experimental Results and Discussions

We use VGG19, which has been educated on ImageNet, for deep feature extraction. The HOG and CN features have been combined to form a single feature. Three features are used from conv3-4, conv4-4, and conv5-4, and the fusion features include those four features. The search scale is 1.8 times the input scale, with a learning rate of 0.001. The weights for conv3-4, conv4-4, conv5-4, and HOG + CN

---

**Algorithm 2:** Framework of the proposed method

---

**Input:**
    Initial object position $P_0$;
**Output:**
    Estimated object position $P_t = (x_t, y_t, w_t, h_t)$;
    Learned correlation filters;
    Learned bounding-box regression model;
  1: Train a bounding-box regression model;
  2: **repeat**
  3:     Crop the searching window in frame $t$ centered at $(x_{t-1}, y_{t-1})$ and extract deep, HOG and CN features;
  4:     Compute confidence score for each channel by using $f_l$;
  5:     Estimate the new position $original(x_t, y_t, w_t, h_t)$ on response map set;
  6:     Adjust $original(x_t, y_t, w_t, h_t)$ by bounding box regression and obtain $final(x_t, y_t, w_t, h_t)$;
  7:     Crop new patch centered at $P_t = final(x_t, y_t, w_t, h_t)$ and extract deep, HOG and CN features with interpolation;
  8:     Update correlation filters by long-short-term update strategy;
  9: **until** End of the video sequence;

---

are respectively $1, 0.5, 0.25$, and $0.1$. The bounding-box regression produces 10,000 samples for bounding-box regression training, positive samples are presumed to have an overlap of greater than 0.6, and the first 1000 positive samples are selected.

The proposed method is compared to state-of-the-art approaches on the OTB-100. Experiments on the benchmark dataset of 50 daunting monitoring recordings, referred to as OTB-50, are also checked for completeness. The proposed method is implemented in MATLAB using the MatConvNet toolbox and runs at approximately 24 frames per second on 4 4.2 GHz Intel 7700 k cores and an NVIDIA 1080Ti GPU. The proposed tracker's main computational load is feature extraction and bounding-box regression training of the first frame. In the first frame, 10,000 samples are produced around the object for bounding-box training, with a time of 2.9579 s for bounding-box training and less than 0.0001 s for online bounding-box regression. Deep feature extraction and handcrafted feature extraction are two types of feature extraction. The processing time for deep and handcraft feature extraction is 0.03726 s and 0.0094 s, respectively. To ensure the reliability of experiments for all tracking images, we use a similar dataset standard and the same parameter settings for all of them.

**Evaluation on OTB** OTB is a popular tracking benchmarks benchmark dataset that consists of 100 fully marked videos with different interferences. The problems are divided into 11 types. The evaluation is based on two methods: error of the center position and area-under-the-curve (AUC). To compare the proposed method with eight state-of-the-art trackers like DeepSRDCF [4], SRDCFdecon [16], HDT [17], CF2, CNN-SVM [3], MEEM, KCF, and SAMF-AT, one-pass evaluation (OPE) is used. These methods adopt different tracking structures and features. The experiment follows the protocol and uses the same parameter values for both sequences and sensitivity analysis. CF2 is another deep learning-based tracking algorithm to be aware of. For deep learning-based tracking methods, we choose CF2 as a baseline. tracking methods.

The target object is represented by the deep features of three layers of VGG19 that have been pre-trained on ImageNet, as well as the HOG + CN function. The weights of one-frame, three-frame, and five-frame update models are chosen as 0.8, 0.1, and 0.1 for the long-short-term update model, respectively. Bounding-box regression is used to fine-tune the location. Using the location accuracy rate and overlap success rate, Fig. 4.4 shows the findings under OPE for both the OTB-2013 and OTB-50 datasets.

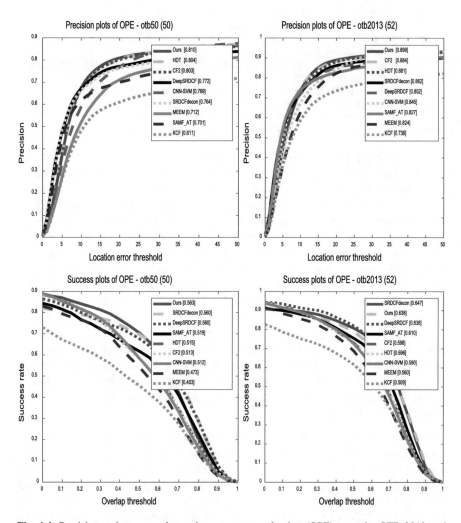

**Fig. 4.4** Precision and success plots using one-pass evaluation (OPE) over the OTB-2013 and OTB-50 benchmarks (the legend of position error precision shows threshold scores at 20 pixels, while the legend of overlap threshold shows the area-under-the-curve (AUC) score for each tracker)

It clearly shows that the proposed algorithm outperforms state-of-the-art real-time methods using OPE in terms of precision and area-under-the-curve (AUC) speeds, but not as well as non-real-time methods like ECO and MDNet. Place precision rate at 20 pixels, AUC rate, and tracking speeds are all quantitatively compared in Table 4.1. The efficiency of the process is demonstrated by the results for both OTB-50 (Benchmark I) and OTB-100 (Benchmark II). Table 4.1 also reveals that the proposed solution outperforms state-of-the-art real-time trackers in terms of precision and AUC rate. All of the efficiency metrics are lower than the OTB-100. Since OTB-50 has 50 more difficult videos to monitor, all of the output parameters are lower than those of OTB-100. Among the state-of-the-art non-real-time trackers, HDT and DeepSRDCF perform well in terms of both AUC and precision rate. The proposed method has a lower AUC rate than DeepSRDCF, but it has a higher precision rate and speed.

**Attribute-Based Evaluation**  The output of the OTB benchmark is also examined using 11 different video attributes (such as rapid motion, occlusion, and scale variation). The eight primary OPE video attributes in OTB-100 are shown in Fig. 4.5. The proposed approach performs better in the presence of context clutter and low resolution because deep, HOG, and CN features with semantics and spatial information better reflect the target object, while some other approaches only use deep, HOG, or CN features. CF2 only uses deep features, while KCF only uses HOG features. The combined deep, HOG, and CN features have the best representative ability, according to our findings.

The performance annotated in the OTB benchmark using 11 different video attributes (such as fast motion, occlusion, and variation of scale) is also analyzed. Figure 4.5 displays the eight primary OPE video attributes in OTB-100. In the case of background clutter and low resolution, the proposed approach performs better because deep, HOG, and CN features with semantics and spatial information will better represent the target object, whereas some other methods use only deep, HOG, or CN features. CF2 uses only deep features, and KCF uses HOG features only. The combined deep, HOG, and CN features have the best representative ability, according to our findings. The method performs well in terms of scale variance, and the bounding-box can be tighter around the objective, so bounding-box regression can better cope with scale changes. The approach is more reliable and stable in occlusion than CF2 since the long-short-term update model contains additional previous object functionality.

**Quantitative Evaluation**  For seven difficult sequences, Fig. 4.6 shows some of the tracking results of the top tracking methods, namely MDNet, KCF, MEEM, CF2, and the proposed process. The MEEM tracker works well for deformation and rotation sequences (*Trans* and *DragonBaby*), but not for background clutter and quick motion (*Soccer, MotorRolling*, and *Skating2*). This is because the color quantity feature is insufficient to handle cluttered backgrounds, and a larger search area is needed for fast motion (*emphSoccer, MotorRolling*, and *Skating*). The KCF tracker learns the kernel correlation filter and generates samples by moving the target object using the HOG function to find the maximum answer in the

**Table 4.1** Average precision plot and area success plot results on the OTB-50 (I) and OTB-100 (II) datasets (the first and second-best scores are highlighted in bold and italic, respectively)

|  |  | Ours | KCF | LCT | DSST | DeepSRDCF | CF2 | SRDCFdecon | HDT | MEEM | CNN-SVM |
|---|---|---|---|---|---|---|---|---|---|---|---|
| Pre.(%) | I | **81.0** | 61.1 | 69.1 | 62.5 | 77.2 | 80.3 | 76.4 | 80.4 | 71.2 | 76.9 |
|  | II | **85.2** | 69.3 | 76.2 | 69.3 | *85.1* | 83.7 | 82.5 | 84.8 | 78.1 | 81.4 |
| AUC(%) | I | **56.3** | 40.3 | 49.2 | 46.3 | 56.0 | 51.3 | 56.0 | 51.5 | 47.3 | 51.2 |
|  | II | 62.8 | 47.7 | 56.2 | 52.0 | **63.5** | 56.2 | 62.7 | 60.3 | 53.0 | 55.4 |
| Speed (FPS) |  | 24 | **172** | 24 | 24 | < 1 | 11 | 1 | 10 | 10 | 1 |

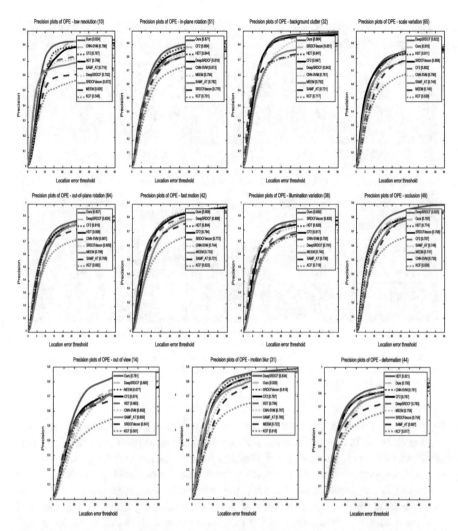

**Fig. 4.5** Over 11 tracking challenges, precision plots of occlusion, in-plane rotation, background clutter, scale variance, out-of-plane rotation, rapid motion, lighting variation, low resolution, out of focus, motion blur, and deformation. The scores are based on a 20-pixel threshold for each tracker

feature map. Since there is no multi-scale or re-detection module, it suits well with partial deformation and fast motion in video sequences (*SUV* and *Soccer*), but drifts when there is strong occlusion and rotation (*Skating2* and *MotorRolling*). The CF2 approach is based on KCF and chooses deep features to train three filters to calculate the function map. It performs well in rapid motion, context clutter, and occlusion conditions (*DragonBaby*, *Soccer*, and *Skating2*). However, since its bounding-box is loosely bound around the object, it has a lower overlap threshold rate than other tracking methods. The MDNet method works well in

──── Ours ──── MDNet ──── KCF ──── MEEN ──── CF2

**Fig. 4.6** Qualitative evaluation of the proposed method, MDNet, KCF, MEEM, and CF2 on seven challenging sequences (the video sequences are *Skating2-1*, *Trans*, *Soccer*, *SUV*, *MotorRolling*, *Singer1* and *DragonBaby*).)

the cases of deformation, rotation, and quick motion (*Trans*, *MotorRolling*, and *Skating2*), but it is less successful in the cases of occlusion and background clutter (*SUV* and *Soccer*), because rapid changes in appearance and long occlusion of the object appearance occur, preventing the tracker from tracking the object. The following is an explanation for why the suggested approach works well. The model is represented by a number of features, including deep, HOG, and CN features. Color, semantics, and spatial information are used to provide more object descriptions and are more effective than using a single function. The findings show that developing models with multiple features is more stable and accurate. The proposed approach performs well in deformations, rotations, and context clutter (*MotorRolling*, *Skating2*, *Soccer*, *DragonBaby*, and *Singer1*). For *MotorRolling* and *DragonBaby*, our system successfully achieved a position error threshold rate of 97.6% and 94.7%, respectively. Second, bounding-box regression will increase the threshold rate of overlap by tightening the expected bounding-box around the item. Third, the revised model combines the advantages of the short-term model for dealing with rapid deformation with the advantages of the long-term model for dealing with occlusion, effectively improving the proposed tracking method's robustness and efficiency. For seven difficult sequences, Fig. 4.6 shows some of the tracking results of the top tracking methods, namely MDNet, KCF, MEEM,

CF2, and the proposed process. The MEEM tracker works well for deformation and rotation sequences (*Trans* and *DragonBaby*), but not for background clutter and quick motion (*Soccer*, *MotorRolling*, and *Skating2*). This is because the color quantity feature is insufficient to handle cluttered backgrounds, and a larger search area is needed for fast motion (*emphSoccer*, *MotorRolling*, and *Skating*). The KCF tracker learns the kernel correlation filter and generates samples by moving the target object using the HOG function to find the maximum answer in the feature map. Since there is no multi-scale or re-detection module, it suits well with partial deformation and fast motion in video sequences (*SUV* and *Soccer*), but drifts when there is strong occlusion and rotation (*Skating2* and *MotorRolling*). The CF2 approach is based on KCF and chooses deep features to train three filters to calculate the function map. It performs well in rapid motion, context clutter, and occlusion conditions (*DragonBaby*, *Soccer*, and *Skating2*). However, since its bounding-box is loosely bound around the object, it has a lower overlap threshold rate than other tracking methods. The MDNet method works well in the cases of deformation, rotation, and quick motion (*Trans*, *MotorRolling*, and *Skating2*), but it is less successful in the cases of occlusion and background clutter (*SUV* and *Soccer*), because rapid changes in appearance and long occlusion of the object appearance occur, preventing the tracker from tracking the object.

**Analysis of Fusion Features** Comparative experiments are conducted on both OTB-2013 and OTB100 to demonstrate the efficacy of the proposed method's hierarchical function. We begin by assessing the impact of various features on monitoring outcomes. As shown in Table 4.2, VGG19 outperforms HOG+CN by 6.7% in terms of discrimination ability, allowing it to efficiently identify targets in complex environments. Using deep features and handicraft features together will improve the ability to discriminate against features. The final experimental results also show that multi-level features outperform single features in terms of tracking precision.

To show how the relative importance of various features influences the final result. Experiments in different weight settings are carried out on OTB-2013. The weight of the deep function in the object tracking area is the normal setting of 1, 0.5, and 0.25 for conv5-3, conv4-3, and conv3-3. To illustrate the effect of different weight features, we set the weight of the deep feature and modified the weight of the HOG+CN handcraft feature. As shown in Table 4.3 when the weight of HOG+CN is 0.1, the results show that the precision rate is 89.9%, which is higher than other weight settings.

**Table 4.2** Different features used in our method. Precision rates at 20 pixels for OTB-2013 are shown

|          | HOG+CN | VGG19 | HOG+CN+VGG19 |
|----------|--------|-------|--------------|
| Pre. (%) | 81.5   | 88.2  | 89.9         |

**Table 4.3** Different feature weights used in our method. Precision rates at 20 pixels for OTB-2013 are shown

|            | 1:0.5: 0.25:0.05 | 1:0.5: 0.25:0.1 | 1:0.5: 0.25:0.25 | 1:0.5: 0.25:0.5 | 1:0.5: 0.25:1 |
|------------|------------------|-----------------|------------------|-----------------|---------------|
| Pre. (%)   | 89.1             | 89.9            | 89.5             | 88.7            | 87.8          |

**Fig. 4.7** Performance evaluation with and without bounding-box regression in *Liquor*, *Carscale*, and *Dudek* video sequences (red and green denote boxes without and with bounding-box regression, respectively)

**Analysis of Bounding-Box Regression** To assess the effectiveness of the proposed approach with bounding-box regression, the output on the benchmark with 100 sequences is compared with and without using the bounding-box. According to Fig. 4.7, bounding-box regression is more efficient in most cases than when it is not used. Bounding-box regression will fine-tune the result to make it tighter around the object if there is enough scale variance. If the bounding box is not close enough, other useless information will be added to the tracking model, reducing the model's robustness and precision. As a result, a tighter bounding box around the object will minimize unnecessary data while still increasing model accuracy. In a tighter bounding box, the search area is more accurate, and tracking speed can be increased. Furthermore, since the bounding-box regression is trained with ground truth in the first frame, it can adjust the location when the tracking model misses the object. The overlap threshold rate with the bounding-box regression model is significantly improved using our system, as shown in Table 4.4. The proposed approach raises the AUC rates on both datasets by 2.3% and 1.9%, respectively, according to the experimental results. We also achieve precision rates of 89.9 and 85.2% using bounding box regression.

**Analysis of Long-Short-Term Update Strategy** To test the efficacy of the proposed long-short-term upgrade strategy, the performance of different update models

**Table 4.4** Bounding-box regression analysis On OTB-2013 (I) AND OTB-100 (II)

|  | I-Prc. | I-AUC | II-Prc. | II-AUC |
|---|---|---|---|---|
| Without | 87.3 | 62.4 | 83.6 | 60.7 |
| With | 89.9 | 64.7 | 85.2 | 62.8 |

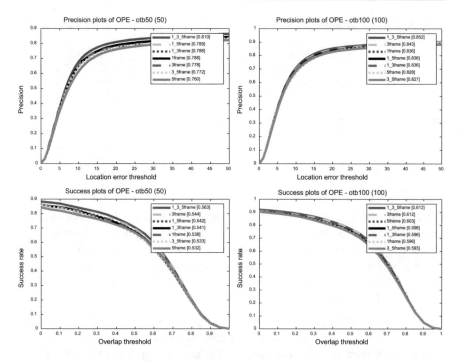

**Fig. 4.8** Performance evaluation using different update models. All single frames (1frame, 3frame and 5frame), combination of two of these frames (1_3frame, 1_5frame, 3_5frame), and all three update models together (1_3_5frame) are used on both OTB-50 and OTB-100

on OTB-100 is shown in Fig. 4.8. Testing has been completed with each individual model update (one-frame, three-frame, and five-frame), and then each model (one-frame and three-frame, one-frame and five-frame, three-frame and five-frame) has been merged and checked. Finally, a mix of all three versions is being considered for upgrading. There are six methods with different methods for both OTB-50 and OTB-100, as shown in Fig. 4.8. Combining only one or two update models for OTB-100 and OTB-50 object tracking is ineffective, while combining all three models outperforms other frame update models. The integrated model is more robust for object tracking and has both short and long memory for model updating. Figure 4.8 also reveals that the three-frame update model outperforms the one-frame and five-frame update models since the three-frame update model has more long- and short-term memories than the other two single update models.

**Evaluation on VOT2015** VOT [18] is a dedicated dataset with 60 video sequences and six object tracking field attributes for each sequence. It adopts a system that

**Table 4.5**  Comparisons with state-of-the-art tracking approaches)on VOT2015

|      | Ours  | DeepSRDCF | MEEM  | SAMF  | DSST  | KCF   | DeepSRDCF | Struck |
|------|-------|-----------|-------|-------|-------|-------|-----------|--------|
| AEO  | **0.313** | 0.299 | 0.221 | 0.202 | 0.172 | 0.171 | 0.288 | 0.141 |

**Table 4.6**  Evaluation results of trackers on TC128. We achieve improvement on both precision and success rates

|          | Ours  | KCF  | DSST | DeepSRDCF | SAMF | Struck | MEEM | SRDCF |
|----------|-------|------|------|-----------|------|--------|------|-------|
| Pre.(%)  | **67.1** | 46.5 | 47.5 | 65.8 | 56.1 | 40.9 | 62.2 | 62.2 |
| Suc.(%)  | **55.2** | 39.0 | 41.1 | 54.1 | 46.7 | 35.0 | 50.6 | 51.6 |

**Table 4.7**  Evaluation results of trackers on UAV123

|          | Ours  | KCF  | DSST | CSK  | SAMF | Struck | MEEM | SRDCF |
|----------|-------|------|------|------|------|--------|------|-------|
| Pre.(%)  | **68.6** | 52.3 | 58.6 | 48.8 | 59.2 | 40.9 | 62.2 | 67.6 |
| AUC(%)   | **48.3** | 33.1 | 35.6 | 31.1 | 39.6 | 38.1 | 39.2 | 46.4 |

implements a time penalty and relocation after the object is lost, preventing the object from being lost and subsequent tracking output being lost. At the same time, the tracking model's robustness is tested during the test using a random initial frame, a rotating object, and other adjustments. It primarily calculates the average estimated overlap to determine tracker performance (AEO). In comparison to state-of-the-art trackers, the findings are shown in Table 4.5.

**Evaluation on TC128** The TC128 [19] dataset differs from OTB and VOT. It contains 128 video sequences that monitor full-color objects such as people, vehicles, and other everyday items, some of which overlap with OTB-100. We put seven cutting-edge trackers to the test (SRDCF, DeepSRDCF, SAMF, DSST, Struck, KCF, MEEM) .The results are shown in Table 4.6.

**Evaluation on UAV123** 123 tracking sequences including vehicles and humans are in UAV123 [20]. We compare with 7 state-of-the-art trackers (SRDCF, CSK, SAMF, DSST, Struck, KCF, MEEM). The results are shown in Table 4.7. The bold values in Tables 4.5, 4.6 and 4.7 are results of the proposed trackers, which also show the best performance in both precision and success rate.

## 4.3  Context-Aware Correlation Filter Network

This section presents an end-to-end trainable discriminative context-aware correlation filter network, namely DCACFNet, which integrates context-aware correlation filter (CACF) into the fully-convolutional Siamese network. Firstly, the CACF is modeled as a differentiable layer in the DCACFNet architecture, which can back-propagate the localization error to the convolutional layers. Then, a novel channel attention module is embedded into the DCACFNet architecture to improve the target adaption of the whole network. Finally, this paper proposes a novel high-confidence update strategy to avoid model corruption under the challenges of occlusion and out-of-view.

### 4.3.1 Context-Aware Correlation Filter Network

**Context-Aware Correlation Filter** We briefly review the general DCF tracker. The DCF tracker relies more on the features extracted from the target area, which are enough robust to adapt to the appearance changes of the target. In successive video frames, the DCF can be used to predict the location of the target. Dense sampling around the target contributes to effective learning of the DCF. The DCF tracker forms the feature matrix $X_0$ with the circulant structure by concatenating the CNN features of which are from all possible translations in the search window of the tracking object. The DCF filter is solved by the optimization of the ridge regression problem.

$$\min_{w} \|X_0 w - y\|_2^2 + \lambda_1 \|w\|_2^2 \tag{4.11}$$

Here, the vector $w$ denotes the learned DCF, each row of the feature matrix $X_0$ is composed of the features extracted from the image patch $x_0'$ and its certain cyclic shift. The two-dimensional vectorized Gaussian image is denoted by the regression objective $y$. In the Fourier domain, this circulant feature matrix provides an efficient closed-form solution to the ridge regression problem of the DCF:

$$\widehat{w} = \frac{\hat{x}_0^* \odot \hat{y}}{\hat{x}_0^* \odot \hat{x}_0 + \lambda_1} \tag{4.12}$$

The context information around the tracking target has a great influence on the discriminative performance of the tracker. When the background around the tracking target has similar objects, the global context information is essential for successful tracking. Therefore, in the correlation analysis, global context information is used as a regularization item and introduced into the objective function. Similar to by the CACF method [21], the global context is added to our correlation filter for larger discriminative power. The context sampling strategy is usually important for the tracking performance. Our CACF adopts a simple and effective strategy to select context sample patches uniformly in the surrounding of the tracking target. Our CACF samples k context image patches $x_i'$ around the target image patch $x_0'$ of each frame. It is intuitive that various target distractors and diverse background clutter reflected in the context patches are likely to be a kind of hard negative samples. The correlation filter that we want to learn has different response for the target patch and context patches. In order to suppress various target distractors, the correlation filter has a high response and a close to zero response to the target patch and the context patch respectively.

$$\min_{w} \| X_0 w - y \|_2^2 + \lambda_1 \| w \|_2^2 + \lambda_2 \sum_{i=1}^{k} \| X_i w \|_2^2 \qquad (4.13)$$

Here, both $X_0$ and $X_i$ are their corresponding circulant feature matrix based on the extracted CNN features. Similar to the solution of the DCF in the Fourier domain, the closed-form solution for our CACF can be written as:

$$\widehat{w} = \frac{\hat{x}_0^* \odot \hat{y}}{\hat{x}_0^* \odot \hat{x}_0 + \lambda_1 + \lambda_2 \sum_{i=1}^{k} \hat{x}_i^* \odot \hat{x}_i} \qquad (4.14)$$

Here, $x_0$ represents the CNN feature of the image patch $x_0'$, i.e., $x_0 = \varphi(x_0')$, $\varphi(\cdot)$ means a feature transformation mapping of the convolutional layers in our network, the discrete Fourier transform of $x_0$ is denoted by the hat $\hat{x}$, $\hat{x}_0^*$ denotes the complex conjugate of the hat $\hat{x}$, and $\odot$ means the Hadamard product.

**DCACFNet Derivation with Back-Propagation** Previous CACF trackers often use manual features or convolutional features directly extracted from the convolutional network in the target classification field for video object tracking. The extraction of convolutional features and the training of CACF are independent of each other, which can't have the advantage of end-to-end training. Different from CACF using hand-crafted features, a novel end-to-end trainable Siamese network is designed to learn fine-grained representations suitable for a CACF that models CACF as a differentiable CACF layer after convolutional layer. With the fined-grained representations, the network is quite sufficient for accurate location. $z = \varphi(z', \theta)$ means the feature representation, where $z'$ means a search image and $\theta$ represents the parameters of the network. Then, the feature representations can be learned via the following objective function:

$$L = \| g(z') - y \|_2^2 + \gamma \| \theta \|_2^2 \qquad (4.15)$$

$$g(z') = Zw = F^{-1} (\hat{z} \odot \widehat{w}^*) \qquad (4.16)$$

Here, $Z$ denotes the circulant feature matrix of the search image patch $z'$, $F^{-1}$ represents the Inverse Discrete Fourier transform, and $w$ means the learned CACF based on the CNN features of the target image patch and the global context. The derivatives of the above objective function are then derived. In order to simplify the derivation process, this paper does not consider the common term about $\theta$. It can be seen from the objective function that $\frac{\partial L}{\partial x_0}$, $\frac{\partial L}{\partial x_i}$ and $\frac{\partial L}{\partial z}$ must be derived for end-to-end training. Since the intermediate variable in the derivative is a complex number type, the chain rule becomes complicated. Inspired by Mueller et al. [21], the partial derivative of Discrete Fourier transform, and Inverse Discrete Fourier transform can be written as:

$$\widehat{g} = F(g), \frac{\partial L}{\partial \widehat{g}^*} = F\left(\frac{\partial L}{\partial g}\right), \frac{\partial L}{\partial g} = F^{-1}\left(\frac{\partial L}{\partial \widehat{g}^*}\right) \tag{4.17}$$

For the back-propagation of the template branch,

$$\frac{\partial L}{\partial x_0} = F^{-1}\left(\frac{\partial L}{\partial \widehat{x}_0^*}\right) = F^{-1}\left(\frac{\partial L}{\partial \widehat{g}^*}\frac{\partial \widehat{g}^*}{\partial \widehat{w}}\frac{\partial \widehat{w}}{\partial \widehat{x}_0^*}\right) \tag{4.18}$$

$$\frac{\partial L}{\partial x_i} = F^{-1}\left(\frac{\partial L}{\partial \widehat{x}_i^*}\right) = F^{-1}\left(\frac{\partial L}{\partial \widehat{g}^*}\frac{\partial \widehat{g}^*}{\partial \widehat{w}}\frac{\partial \widehat{w}}{\partial \widehat{x}_i^*}\right) \tag{4.19}$$

For the back-propagation of the search branch,

$$\frac{\partial L}{\partial z} = F^{-1}\left(\frac{\partial L}{\partial \widehat{z}_i^*}\right) = F^{-1}\left(\frac{\partial L}{\partial \widehat{g}^*}\frac{\partial \widehat{g}^*}{\partial \widehat{z}_i^*}\right) \tag{4.20}$$

To get $\frac{\partial L}{\partial x_0}$, $\frac{\partial L}{\partial x_i}$ and $\frac{\partial L}{\partial z}$, this paper derives $\frac{\partial L}{\partial \widehat{g}^*}$, $\frac{\partial \widehat{g}^*}{\partial \widehat{w}}$, $\frac{\partial \widehat{g}^*}{\partial \widehat{z}^*}$, $\frac{\partial \widehat{w}}{\partial \widehat{x}_0^*}$ and $\frac{\partial \widehat{w}}{\partial \widehat{x}_i^*}$ as follows.

$$\vdots$$

$$\frac{\partial L}{\partial \widehat{g}^*} = F\left(\frac{\partial L}{\partial g}\right) = 2(\widehat{g} - \hat{y}) \tag{4.21}$$

$$\frac{\partial \widehat{g}^*}{\partial \widehat{w}} = \hat{z}^*_{...} \tag{4.22}$$

$$\frac{\partial \widehat{g}^*}{\partial \widehat{z}^*} = \widehat{w} \tag{4.23}$$

$$\vdots$$

$$\frac{\partial \widehat{w}}{\partial \widehat{x}_0^*} = \frac{\hat{y} - \hat{x}_0 \odot \widehat{w}}{\hat{x}_0^* \odot \hat{x}_0 + \lambda_1 + \lambda_2 \sum_{i=1}^{k} \hat{x}_i^* \odot \hat{x}_i} \tag{4.24}$$

$$\frac{\partial \widehat{w}}{\partial \widehat{x}_i^*} = \frac{-\lambda_2 \hat{x}_i \odot \widehat{w}}{\hat{x}_0^* \odot \hat{x}_0 + \lambda_1 + \lambda_2 \sum_{i=1}^{k} \hat{x}_i^* \odot \hat{x}_i} \tag{4.25}$$

When training the entire network, the localization loss is back-propagated layer by layer to learn convolutional features suitable for CACF tracker. Using the Hadamard product of the Fourier domain in the back-propagation of the CACF layer, the CACF tracker has the advantage of the fast computation. It can be applied to large-scale datasets for end-to-end training. CNN features suitable for the CACF tracker are extracted for real-time tracking after completing offline training, which improves the tracking performance of the tracking algorithm in complex scenes.

### 4.3.2   Channel Attention Mechanism

With the increasing of convolution feature channels, the convolution features of some channels may have redundancy, which seriously affects the feature representation ability of the deep network. Convolution features have different effects on different tracking target objects. A kind of convolution channel feature usually corresponds to a certain corresponding visual mode. In a specific tracking scene, some feature channels are more meaningful than others. Motivated by Jie et al. [22], we incorporate a novel channel attention trained using a shallow neural network to keep the target adaption of deep network under the appearance variation. The channel attention is used to explicitly model the relationship between different convolution feature channels, which selects important convolutional feature channels for different visual objects. The channel attention module has little effect on the tracking efficiency because of only involved in the temple branch during online tracking. As shown in Fig. 4.9, the channel attention consists of global average pooling and two fully-connected layers with a ReLU activation and a Sigmoid activation, respectively. One is used to reduce the channel space of 64 dimensions to 16 dimensions. The other is used to increase the channel space dimension to 64 dimensions. The global average pooling layer encodes global spatial information into a one-dimensional channel descriptor. The input of the channel attention module is $d$ channel convolutional features $X = [x_1, x_2, \cdots, x_d]$ with $x_i \in R^{W \times H}$, $W = H = 125, i = 1, 2, \cdots, d$. The output of the channel attention module is denoted by $\tilde{X} = [\tilde{x}_1, \tilde{x}_2, \cdots, \tilde{x}_d]$ with $\tilde{x}_i \in R^{W \times H}$, $W = H = 125, i = 1, 2, \cdots, d$. This can be achieved by executing the production of a set of channel parameter and the input.

$$\tilde{x}_i = \beta_i \cdot x_i \quad i = 1, 2, \cdots, d \tag{4.26}$$

Here $\beta_i$, represents the parameter of certain convolutional channel.

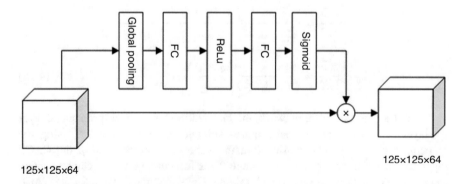

125×125×64

125×125×64

**Fig. 4.9** The channel attention architecture

### 4.3.3 Update with High Confidence Strategy

During the tracking process, the appearance of the target often changes because of the challenging of illumination variation, deformation and occlusion. In order to adapt to changes in the appearance of the target, the existing DCF trackers usually update the tracking model every frame without evaluating the tracking result. Such an update strategy improves the tracking effect to a certain extent. However, when the target is located inaccurately or partly occluded, the update strategy is not wise without considering the tracking result, which may make the total tracking process failed in the end.

In response to this problem, this paper designs a high-confidence update strategy that combines the peak value of the response map and the average peak-correlation energy (APCE) [23] to evaluate the tracking results. The high-confidence update strategy is used to determine whether to update the model or not. The high-confidence update strategy only updates the model when certain conditions are met, which can improve the speed of target tracking:

$$G = \max g\left(z'\right) \tag{4.27}$$

We calculated the peak value $G$ of the CACF response map at each frame and grouped them into a set $Q_G = G^{(2)}, G^{(3)}, \cdots, G^{(t)}$, which has always no more than 10 elements. The average of $Q_G$ is denoted by $\bar{G}$. The APCE reflects the fluctuation degree of the response maps, which can be defined as:

$$\text{APCE} = \frac{|g_{\max} - g_{\min}|^2}{\text{mean}\left(\sum_{w,h}\left(g_{w,h} - g_{\min}\right)^2\right)} \tag{4.28}$$

Similar to $G$, we calculated the APCE value of the CACF response map at each frame and grouped them into a set $Q_{APCE} = APCE^{(2)}, APCE^{(3)}, \cdots, APCE^{(t)}$, which has always no more than 10 elements. The average of $APCE_G$ is denoted by $\bar{APCE}$.

$$G \geq \alpha_1 \cdot \bar{G} \tag{4.29}$$

$$\hat{w}^t = (1 - \beta)\hat{w}^{t-1} + \beta\hat{w} \tag{4.30}$$

Here, $\alpha_1$ and $\alpha_2$ mean the control parameters. During the tracking process, it is high-confidence at the current frame. Then, the model should be updated with a fixed learning rate $\beta$.

$$\widehat{w}^t = (1 - \beta)\hat{w}^{t-1} + \beta\hat{w} \tag{4.31}$$

The peak and the fluctuation degree of the response map can convey t whether the tracking result is reliable. When the detected target closely matches the correct

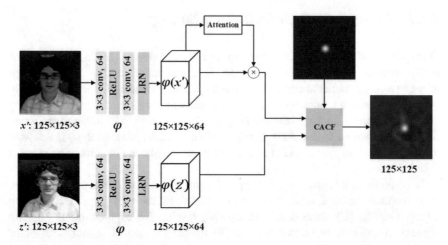

**Fig. 4.10**  The overall DCACFNet architecture

target, the ideal tracking result should have only one sharp peak and be smooth in all other regions. The sharper the correlation peak, the better the predicting accuracy is. Otherwise, the entire response map will fluctuate sharply, which is significantly different from the normal response map.

### 4.3.4  Framework and Procedure

The overall DCACFNet architecture is shown in Fig. 4.10. Different from SiamFC, the proposed DCACFNet architecture is asymmetric. In contrast to the search branch, the temple branch adds the channel attention module [24] after the convolutional feature transform. The outputs of these branches are fed into the CACF layer to locate the tracking target. In order to detail the DCACFNet architecture, this section briefly reviews the context-aware correlation filter at first. We subsequently drive the back-propagation of the context-aware correlation filter layer, which conducts online learning during the forward propagation. Then, a novel channel attention module is introduced to be embedded in the DCACFNet architecture. At last, the high-confidence update strategy is given to improve the tracking performance under the challenging of occlusion. The detailed procedure is shown in Algotithm 3.

### 4.3.5  Experimental Results and Discussions

This section introduces the experimental details of our DCACFNet at first. Then we perform an experimental analysis on two challenging tracking datasets: OTB-

---

**Algorithm 3:** Discriminative context-aware correlation filter network for visual tracking

---

**Input:** the position $p_1$ and the scale $s_1$ of the initial target $x'_1$;
**Output:** the position $p_t$ and the scale $s_t$ of the initial target $x'_t$;
1: Extract the initial target $x'_1$ according to $p_1$ and $s_1$ ;
2: Extract the convolutional feature with the template branch of the Siamese network;
3: Initialize the filter $\hat{w}$ according to the formula (4.14);
4: **repeat**
5:  The candidate sample $x'_t$ is extracted according to the tracking result $x'_{t-1}$ of the previous frame;
6:  Extract the convolutional feature with the search branch of the Siamese network;
7:  Calculate the peak value $G$ and the average peak-correlation energy value $APCE$ according to the formula (4.27) and the formula (4.28);
8:  **if** $G \geqslant \alpha_1 \cdot \bar{G}$ and $APCE \geqslant \alpha_1 \cdot A\bar{P}CE$ **then**
9:   Extract the target image patch and four context image patch on the position $t$ of the current target $x'_t$;
10:   Extract the convolutional feature with the search branch of the Siamese network.;
11:   Calculate the filter $\hat{w}^t$ according to the formula (4.14);
12:   **if** $|Q_G| = 10$ **then**
13:    $Q_G \leftarrow Q_G \setminus \{\underset{t}{minG}\}$;
14:    $Q_G \leftarrow Q_G \cup \{G\}$;
15:   **end if**
16:   **if** $|Q_{APCE}| = 10$ **then**
17:    $Q_{APCE} \leftarrow Q_{APCE} \setminus \{\underset{t}{minAPCE}\}$;
18:    $Q_{APCE} \leftarrow Q_{APCE} \cup \{APCE\}$;
19:   **end if**
20:  **end if**
21: **until** End of video sequence;

---

2013 with 50 videos and OTB-2015 with 100 videos. The experimental results demonstrate that the end-to-end trainable discriminative context-aware correlation filter network can improve the tracking performance.

Our lightweight network uses VGG-like network as base network, which consists of the convolutional layers, the channel attention module and the CACF layer. Compared to conv1 from VGG, we adopt two convolutional layers ($3 \times 3 \times 64$, $3 \times 3 \times 64$ ) by removing the pooling layer. The outputs of the temple branch and the search branch are the size of $125 \times 125 \times 64$, which are fed into the CACF layer to improve localization accuracy. Our whole network is trained on the ILSVRC 2015 dataset [25], which includes more than 4000 sequences and a total of about two million labelled frames. For each sequence, two frames within the nearest 10 frames are randomly picked, which are cropped with double size of the target and then scaled to $125 \times 125 \times 3$. We utilize stochastic gradient descent (SGD) to train the network in an end-to-end way. We train the model for 40 epoch with the learning rate of $10^{-2}$ and the mini-batch size of 32.

In online tracking, the hyper-parameters in the CACF layer play a vital role in tracking performance. The regularization coefficients are set as $\lambda_1 = 0.0001$ and

$\lambda_2 = 0.1$. For the high-confidence update strategy, the model updating rate is set to 0.01, and two control parameters $\alpha_1$ and $\alpha_2$ are set to 0.3 and 0.4, respectively. Meanwhile, the gaussian spatial bandwidth is set to 0.1. Moreover, we adopt three scale layers and then set the scale step and the scaled penalty to 1.0275 and 0.9925. The proposed DCACFNet is implemented with the Pytorch framework. All experiments are executed on a PC with a GeForce RTX 1080Ti GPU of 12 GB RAM.

**Comparison on OTB-2013** We evaluate our tracker on the OTB-2013 and OTB-2015, which contain 50 and 100 tracking sequences, respectively. The evaluation metrics consist of precision rate and success rate. The precision rate refers to center location error, and the success rate means bounding box overlap ratio.

In OTB-2013 experiment, we test our tracker in comparison with recent state-of-the-art trackers, including UDT [26], SiamFC-tri [27], DCFNet [23], CFNet [28], Staple_CA [7], SiamFC, Staple, DSST. Figure 4.11 shows the precision and success plot, respectively. Compared with the other eight popular tracking algorithms, DCACFNet in this chapter ranks first in the two indicators of accuracy and success rate of the OTB-2013 dataset, achieving the scores of 89.2% and 66.6%, respectively. It clearly indicates that the proposed tracker, denoted by DCACFNet, achieves competitive performance among these compared trackers in two indications. Compared with the two end-to-end correlation tracking algorithms of DCFNet and CFNet, the proposed DCACFNet outperforms DCFNet and CFNet by 9.7 and 7.0% in the precision rate respectively, because the proposed DCACFNet fully unifies background information, target adaptation, and tracking result. At the same time, the proposed DCACFNet outperforms DCFNet and CFNet by 4.4 and 5.6% in the success rate, respectively. Compared with three siamese tracking algorithms of UDT, SiamFC-tri and SiamFC, the proposed DCACFNet with shallow convolutional feature outperforms them by 7.7%, 7.7% and 8.3% in the precision rate respectively when the proposed DCACFNet outperforms them by 4.7%, 5.1% and 5.9% in the success rate respectively.

**Comparison on OTB-2015** In the OTB-2015 experiment, we compare our tracker against recent state-of-the-art trackers, which include UDT, SiamFC-tri, DCFNet, CFNet, Staple_CA, SiamFC, Staple, DSST. Figure 4.12 shows the precision and success plot about these compared trackers, respectively. Compared with the other eight popular tracking algorithms, the proposed DCACFNet ranks first in both the precision and success rates of the OTB-2015 dataset, obtaining the scores of 85.1% and 63.9%, respectively. It can be seen that our DCACFNet provides the best tracking performance in terms of precision and success metric. In contrast to the integration of correlation filter and Siamese network, our tracker outperforms DCFNet and CFNet by 10.0 and 7.4% in the precision rate respectively because of the fully combination of context-aware correlation filtering, channel attention mechanism and high confidence update strategy, Meanwhile, our tracker outperforms DCFNet and CFNet by 5.9 and 5.0% in the success rate, respectively. Compared with three siamese tracking algorithms of UDT, SiamFC-tri and SiamFC, the proposed DCACFNet with shallow convolutional feature outperforms them by 9.1%,

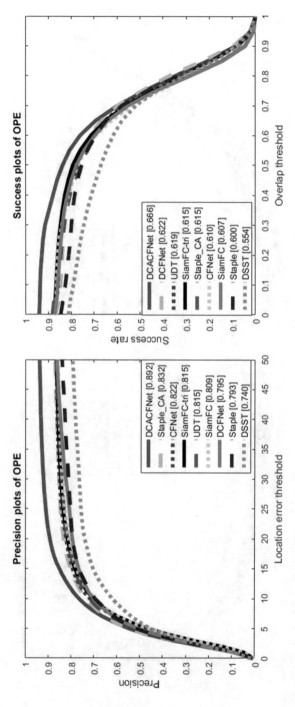

**Fig. 4.11** Experimental results on OTB-2013

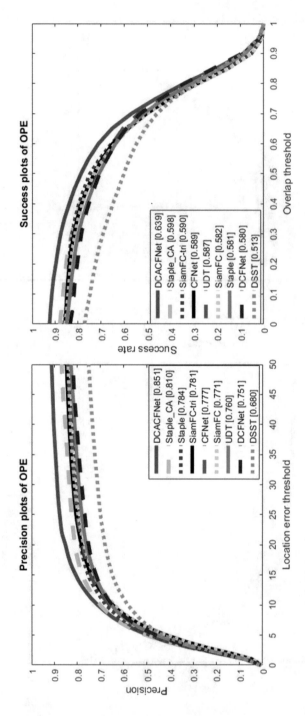

**Fig. 4.12** Experimental results on OTB-2015

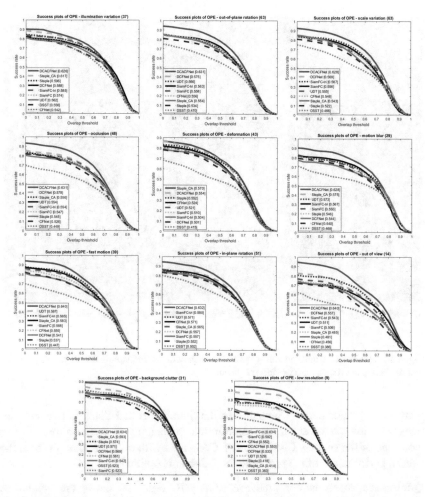

**Fig. 4.13**  Success plots obtained by the 9 state-of-the-art trackers about the 11 attributes annotated in OTB-2015

7.0% and 8.0% in the precision rate respectively when the proposed DCACFNet outperforms them by 5.2%, 4.9% and 5.7% in the success rate respectively.

**Attribute-Based Analysis**  In order to further analyze detailed performance, we report the results under 11 challenging attributes in OTB-2015, and the results are shown in Fig. 4.13. The results demonstrate that the tracking performance of our tracker is best under all challenging attributes except for deformation and low resolution. In particular, the success rate under motion blur, fast motion, and out-of-view increase by 8.4%, 9.9%, and 8.3% over the baseline DCFNet, respectively. For the deformation attribute, our tracker obtains a lower success score than the Staple and Staple_CA trackers, which benefit from the complementary of HOG

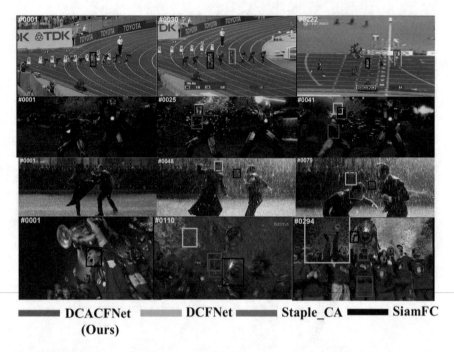

**Fig. 4.14** Qualitative results of our proposed tracker with three state-of-the-art trackers on the bolt, ironman, matrix and soccer video sequences

features and color name. Compared to the SiamFC-tri and SiamFC trackers, our tracker achieves a lower success score in the challenging of low resolution due to the usage of the shallow CNN features. Compared with other popular trackers, the overall performance of the proposed DCACFNet is optimal.

**Qualitative Analysis** For qualitative analysis, Fig. 4.14 shows the qualitative comparison with recent trackers under five challenging video sequences. As shown in Fig. 4.14, our DCACFNet is relative successful to track object under some challenging scenarios such as fast motion, motion blur and background clutter, while other trackers hardly cope with these challenges at the same time. When the target is severely deformed in the tracking scene, the proposed algorithm may not be able to accurately locate the target.

## 4.4  Auxiliary Relocation in SiamFC Framework

Visual object tracking is an online semi-supervised learning problem. The only training sample is from the state of the object at the first frame. How to construct the appearance model of the tracking object accurately, how to online update the appearance model to adapt to the changes of the object in the video, how to monitor the tracking process to relocate the object, how to introduce the prior knowledge of visual object tracking tracker to refine and improve the tracking results, and how to monitor the tracking process and detect the tracking failure when failures occur are the key points to be solved in visual object tracking. In this section, an auxiliary relocation branch is proposed to assist in object relocation and tracking. According to the prior assumptions of visual object tracking, some weights are involved in the auxiliary relocation branch, such as structure similarity weight, motion similarity weight, motion smoothness weight, and object saliency weight.

### 4.4.1  Auxiliary Relocation with Correlation Filters

For tracking tasks, especially for specific scenarios, there are some previous assumptions about tracking objects. For example, we always assume that the motion of the tracked object is smooth, which means that the state of the object does not change much between two adjacent frames. People tend to choose some conspicuous objects as tracking objects. In addition, the order of the objects can also help improve tracking results. Therefore, the purpose of the auxiliary relocation branch is to introduce some prior knowledge into AS-Siamfc and relocate the object when the tracker is running in an untrusted state. The auxiliary relocation branch and switch function (mentioned below) can be regarded as the fault detection and relocation part of AS-Siamfc. According to the above-mentioned previous assumptions, some weight maps are introduced into the structural auxiliary weight branch, such as structural similarity weights, motion similarity weight, motion smoothing weight, and object saliency weight. The detailed procedure is shown in Fig. 4.15.

For motion similarity weight sub-branch, we apply LucasKanade method(LK) [29] to calculate the optical flow $Op(i, i-1)$, between instance image $i$ and instance image $i-1$, and we also compute the optical flow $Op(i-1, i-2)$, between instance images $i-1$ and $i-2$. Then, according to the state of the object at instance image $i-1$, we select an area of optical flow $Op(i-1, i-2)$, and the Histograms of Oriented Optical Flow feature (HOF) [30] of this area is viewed as the motion characteristic of the object. Similarly, we also extract the $HOF$ of the optical flow $Op(i, i-1)$. Thus, the motion similarity weight can be calculated by the cross-correlation between the HOF of the selected area and optical flow $Op(i, i-1)$, as follows:

$$R_O = HOF(select(Op(i-1, i-2))) \circledast HOF(Op(i, i-1)) + b_o \quad (4.32)$$

where $R_O$ is the weight map of motion similarity weight subbranch, and it is the motion similarity weight used in this section. $(Op(i-1, i-2))$ represents the optical flow of the object calculated by instance image $i-1$ and instance image $i-2$. $HOF()$ means the extraction of the HOF feature. $b_o$ denotes the bias term of motion similarity weight sub-branch.

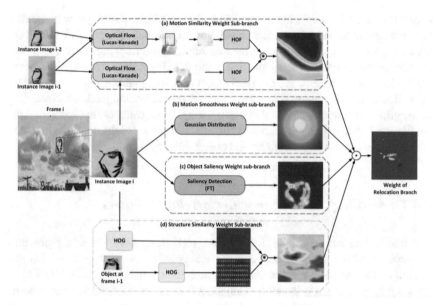

**Fig. 4.15** The procedure of the relocation branch. It can be divided into 4 sub-branches: (**a**) the motion similarity weight sub-branch, (**b**) the motion smoothness weight sub-branch, (**c**) the object saliency weight sub-branch and (**d**) the structure similarity weight sub-branch

For object saliency weight sub-branch, the Frequency Tuned salient region detection method (FT) [31] is applied to compute the weight map of the object saliency weight sub-branch, $R_S$ is as follows:

$$R_s(x, y) = \|I_\mu - I_{whc}(x, y)\| \tag{4.33}$$

where $I_\mu$ is the average value of all pixels in the instance image, and $I_{whc}$ denotes the smooth image of the instance image after Gaussian filtering. Thus, $I_{whc}(x, y)$ is the corresponding score of $I_{whc}$ at $(x, y)$.

For motion smoothness weight sub-branch, the traditional two-dimensional Gaussian distribution function, which is centered at $(x_c, y_c)$, is used to construct the weight map of motion smoothness weight sub-branch. $(x_c, y_c)$ can be obtained by the location of the object center in the previous frame. The two-dimensional Gaussian distribution function is as follow:

$$R_G(x, y) = \frac{1}{2\pi\sigma^2} e^{-\frac{(x-x_c)^2 + (y-y_c)^2}{2\sigma^2}} \tag{4.34}$$

where $\sigma$ is standard deviation of Gaussian distribution function, and $R_G$ is the weight map of motion smoothness weight subbranch.

For structure similarity weight, The Histograms of Oriented Gradients feature (HOG) [32] is applied to describe the structure information of the object. Firstly, we

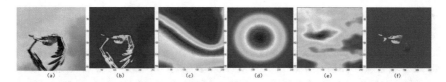

**Fig. 4.16** The visualization of the four weight sub-branches in auxiliary relocation branch. (**a**) is the original image, (**b**) is the object saliency weight, (**c**) is the motion similarity weight, (**d**) is the motion smoothness weight, (**e**) is the structure similarity weight, and (**f**) is the weight of auxiliary relocation branch

extract the HOG feature of both the instance image $i$, $I_x(i)$ and the object image of instance image $i - 1$, $I_0(i - 1)$. The object image of instance image $i - 1$ can be obtained by the state of the object at frame $i - 1$. Thus, the structure similarity weight can be calculated by the cross-correlation between the HOG feature of $I_0(i - 1)$ and $I_x(i)$ are as follows:

$$R_{st} = HOG(I_0(i - 1)) \circledast HOG(I_x(i)) + \boldsymbol{b_{st}} \qquad (4.35)$$

where $R_{st}$ is the weight map in structure similarity weight subbranch, and it is the structure similarity weight used In this section. $HOG()$ means the extraction of HOG feature, and $b_{st}$ denotes the bias term of structure similarity weight sub-branch. Thus the weight map of the auxiliary relocation branch can be calculated by Eq. 4.36 through the element-wise product.

$$R_r = R_O \odot R_G \odot R_S \odot R_{st} \qquad (4.36)$$

Figure 4.16 shows the weight maps of the object saliency weight, motion similarity weight, motion smoothness weight, structure similarity weight, and total weight map of auxiliary relocation. From Fig. 4.16, we find that the object saliency weight in Fig. 4.16b focuses on detecting the entire object, especially when the difference between object and background is obvious. The motion similarity weight in Fig. 4.16c pays more attention to the areas with similar objects. And this makes the response map of optical flow more suitable for tracking the moving rigid objects. At the same time, the motion smoothness weight in Fig. 4.16d estimates the probabilities of the object position in the instance image. It is consistent with the assumption that the motion of the object is smooth. Similar to the motion similarity weight, the structure similarity weight in Fig. 4.16e pays more attention to the areas with similar object structures. This may help the tracker deal with some tracking challenges, such as lighting changes, color variation, etc. More analyses about these three sub-branches can be found in Sect. 4.4.3. From Fig. 4.16f, We find that the weight map of the auxiliary relocation branch can outline the outline of the object and accurately estimate the position of the object center. Thus, we believe that the auxiliary relocation branch can optimize and relocate the objects when the proposed tracker operates in an untrusted state.

## 4.4.2 Switch Function for SiamFC Framework

Considering that the introduction of prior knowledge in AS-Siamfc may also bring noises, and sometimes, the prior knowledge itself is the noise that may affect tracking performance. Therefore, we should monitor the tracking process of the proposed tracker and ensure that it is included in the auxiliary tool to display prior knowledge. The relocation branch affects the response graph of the AS Siamese network. The object can be further optimized and relocated only when the tracker is running in an untrusted state. Therefore, in this section, a novel switching function based on the AS Siamese network response graph is proposed to monitor the tracking process and control the influence of the auxiliary relocation branch on the tracking performance. The proposed switch function is shown in Eq. 4.37.

$$s(R_A) = \varepsilon \left( \frac{\max(R_A) - avg(R_A)}{\max(R_A) - \min(R_A)} - S_t \right) \tag{4.37}$$

Where $R_A$ represents the response map of AS Siamese network. Thus, $\max(R_A)$, $avg(R_A)$ and $\min(R_A)$ are the maximum, average and minimum values of $R_A$. $\frac{\max(R_A) - avg(R_A)}{\max(R_A) - \min(R_A)}$ is the confidence percentage, which is used to assess the reliability of tracking process. $\varepsilon()$ denotes the unit step function and $S_t$ is the threshold. When the confidence percentage is over $S_t$, the switch function score is 1. Otherwise, the switch function score is 0. Thus, the final response map of AS-Siamfc can be calculated by Eq. 4.38, which is controlled by the switch function.

$$R_T = s(R_A)R_A + (1 + s(R_A))R_r \odot R_A \tag{4.38}$$

Where $R_T$ is the final response map of AS-Siamfc, $R_r$ and $R_A$ are the weight map of auxiliary relocation branch and the response map of AS network, respectively. From Eq. 4.38, we can see that when the confidence percentage is under the threshold $S_t$, we believe that the tracker runs under an untrusted state. The weight map of the auxiliary relocation branch helps to refine and relocate the object. Thus, the final response map $R_T$ is computed by an element-wise product, $R_T = R_r \odot R_A$. Otherwise, we think the tracker runs under a trusted state, and the final response map is equal to the response map of AS network, $R_T = R_A$. Another benefit of the proposed function is that we do not need to calculate the response map of the auxiliary relocation branch in every frame. Instead, we only compute the response maps of the auxiliary relocation branch when the tracker runs under an untrusted state. This may also increase the tracking speed and reducing the amount of calculation.

Figure 4.17 shows the relationship among response scores of $R_A$, scores of switch function, precision scores, and success scores in two different sequences. The horizontal axes are the indexes of frames, and the vertical axes are the corresponding scores. Figure 4.17a and e show plots of the maximum, minimum, and average values of $R_A$ of every frame. From these plots, we find that the average and

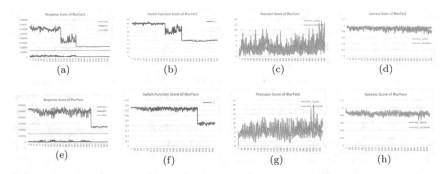

**Fig. 4.17** Visualization of the response scores, scores of the switch function, precision scores, and success scores on two sequences. (**a**) and (**e**) are the response scores of the proposed attention shake network. (**b**) and (**f**) show the values of confidence percentage in the switch function. (**c**) and (**g**) are the precision scores of Siamfc and AS-Siamfc. (**d**) and (**h**) are the success scores of Siamfc and AS-Siamfc

minimum values of $R_A$ in every frame do not change much. While the maximum values vary with the frames. In both Fig. 4.17a and e, we can see a significant decline in the maximum values of $R_A$. Figure 4.17b and f are the values of confidence percentage in switch function, which can be computed by $\frac{max(R_A)-avg(R_A)}{max(R_A)-min(R_A)}$. From these plots, we can also see the significant decline, which is consistent with the decline in Fig. 4.17a and e. By comparing the plots, Fig. 4.17a and b, Fig. 4.17e and f, the confidence percentage represents the ratio of the distance between the peak value and mean value of $R_A$ to the distance between the peak value and the valley value of $R_A$, and it can be applied to monitor tracking process and measure the confidence of the tracking results. When the confidence percentage is under a certain threshold, the maximum value of $R_A$ is low, which means the tracker is hard to tell the object from the background, and the tracker runs under an untrusted state. By comparing the precision and success scores of Siamfc and AS-Siamfc in Fig. 4.17c and d, Fig. 4.17g and h, we find that the precision and success scores of AS-Siamfc with switch function and relocation branch become smoother and higher, which also means the switch function and auxiliary relocation branch could monitor the tracking process, detect the failure and relocate the object when the tracker runs under an untrusted state.

### 4.4.3 Framework and Procedure

From Fig. 4.15, we can see that the auxiliary relocation branch can be divided into four sub-branches: motion similarity weight sub-branch, motion smoothness weight sub-branch, object saliency weight sub-branch, and structure similarity weight subbranch. Firstly, we calculate the weight maps of these four subbranches, respectively. Then, in order to merge the weight maps obtained from the four sub-branches, we normalize the weight maps of these four sub-branches. Finally, the response maps are merged by an element-wise function. Thus, we obtain the weight map of the auxiliary relocation branch. Noticing that the auxiliary relocation only works on the instance images.

The tracking process can be summarized as follows: firstly, we feed the exemplar image, $I_z$ (also templet obtained from the first image) and instance image, $I_x$ (also candidate search image which is larger than exemplar image and represents the search area) into the proposed AS network to compute the response map $R_A$. Then, we calculate the score of the proposed switch function $S(R_A)$. If $S(R_A)$ is larger than 0, we believe that the tracker runs under a trusted state. Therefore, we could estimate the state of the object only by the response map $R_A$. If not, the tracker runs under an untrusted state. The weight map of auxiliary relocation branch $R_r$ which Eqs. 4.32–Eqs. 4.36 helps to refine and relocate object with $R_A$. Thus, the final response map $R_T$ is calculated by an element-wise product, Eqs. 4.37. Finally, we estimate the state of the object by the final response map RT and update the instance image of the next frame by the object's state.

### 4.4.4  Experimental Results and Discussions

In order to illustrate the feasibility and effectiveness of our proposed auxiliary relocation branch and switch function, some basic experiments and analyses are set and provided in this section.

We discuss the impacts of the prior assumptions of visual object tracking on Siamese network-based trackers. Furthermore, we also present some analyses and results of the proposed auxiliary relocation branch and switch function. According to the prior assumptions that the object's movement is smooth, the object is obvious in a specific range, and the movement and structure of the object are consistent to a certain extent. We apply motion smoothness weight, object saliency weight, motion similarity weight, and structure similarity weight to fit the prior assumptions. All these methods are merged into the proposed auxiliary relocation branch.

Figure 4.18 shows the effects of saliency, optical flow, HOG feature, and the final response map of AS-Siamfc qualitatively. The first row of each sub-figure represents the original image. The second row of each sub-figure is the object saliency. The third and fourth rows of each sub-figure represent the object's optical flow and HOG feature, respectively. While the last row shows the final response map of AS-Siamfc. From Fig. 4.18, we can see that each method in the auxiliary relocation branch has its applicable video sequences and scenarios. As shown in Fig. 4.18, both saliency detection and optical flow could outline the object in some simple sequences, or the difference between object and background is large. Since the helmet in Fig. 4.18b is more prominent than the background, the saliency detection method is more suitable to locate the object than optical flow. On the contrary, Fig. 4.18c shows that optical flow is good at dealing with background clutter sequences which the saliency detection method cannot handle. Figure 4.18d and f show the sequences

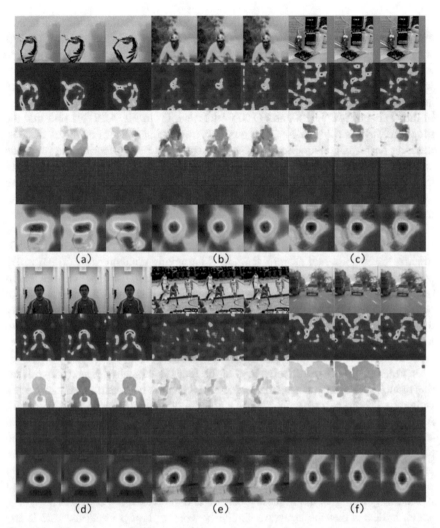

**Fig. 4.18** The saliency, optical flow, HOG feature and response map of proposed tracker for 6 sequences in OTB50 and OTB100

which are not applicable to the saliency detection method and optical flow. However, the structure (the HOG feature) of the objects in these two sequences does not change much. Figure 4.18e shows a complex sequence. In this sequence, the object's motion is not regular, the object is not very salient, and many other people have a similar structure with the object in this sequence. Thus, in this sequence, the saliency detection method, optical flow, and HOG feature are hard to estimate the object's location. However, with the help of motion smoothness weight, we can still estimate the object's state.

In order to further explore the impact of the proposed auxiliary relocation branch and switch function, Fig. 4.19 shows the precision and success plots of trackers with and without auxiliary relocation branch and switch function. Siamfc_R and Siamfc represent the Siamfc trackers with and without auxiliary relocation branch, respectively. While AS-Siamfc and AS-Siamf_W are the proposed trackers with and without auxiliary relocation branch, respectively. All these trackers are tested in the OTB-2013, OTB100, and OTB50 datasets. From Fig. 4.19, we find that the proposed AS-Siamfc tracker (with auxiliary relocation branch) achieves the best tracking performance among all these four trackers. By comparing the precision and success plots of AS-Siamfc and AS-Siamfc_W, we find that 2.87 and 6.80% increase the precision score and success score of AS-Siamfc on average. Comparing the precision and success plots of Siamfc_R and Siamfc, we can also find slight improvements. These experiments validate the effectiveness and availability of the proposed auxiliary relocation branch.

Table 4.8 also provides the precision and success scores of AS-Siamfc, AS-Siamfc_W, Siamfc, and Siamfc_R under 11 tracking challenges in OTB100. By comparing the precision and success scores of these four trackers, we can see that in most cases, the performances of the trackers with auxiliary relocation branches are better than those trackers without auxiliary relocation branches. Thus, we can say that the proposed auxiliary relocation branch, along with the switch function, could monitor the tracking process, refine and relocate objects when the tracker runs under an untrusted state and improve tracking performance.

In order to discuss the effectiveness of the four sub-branches in auxiliary relocation branch specifically, the performances of AS-Siamfc without motion smoothness weight (AS-Siamfc_msm), AS-Siamfc without motion similarity (AS-Siamfc_msi), AS-Siamfc without object saliency weight (AS-Siamfc_os), and AS-Siamfc without structure similarity (AS-Siamfc_ss) are shown in the Fig. 4.20 along with the performance without the whole auxiliary relocation branch (AS-Siamfc_W) and the proposed tracker ASSiamfc. From all the precision and success plots in Fig. 4.20, we can see that AS-Siamfc_ss shows the worst performance except AS-Siamfc_W, and AS-Siamfc_msm gets the highest precision and success score except AS-Siamfc, which indicates that the structure similarity weight plays a important role in the auxiliary relocation branch.

Furthermore, we also show the effectiveness of the threshold of switch function in the OTB100 dataset in Fig. 4.21. The first two figures in Fig. 4.21 are the precision and success plots of OPE respectively. The numbers in the brackets in legend indicate the corresponding thresholds applied in AS-Siamfc. Notice that the thresholds of AS-Siamfc and AS-Siamfc_W are 0.6 and 0. The third figure is the trend map of precision and success score. The abscissa of this figure is thresholds, while the ordinate is the corresponding precision and success scores. From Fig. 4.21 shows that when the threshold is less than 0.5, the precision and success score plots rise steadily and reach the peaks at 0.6. Then, the plots begin to plunge. The precision and scores may even lower than AS-Siamfc_W when the threshold is over 0.7. We believe the reason is that when the threshold is over 0.7, the performance of AS-Siamfc is more dependent on the auxiliary relocation branch

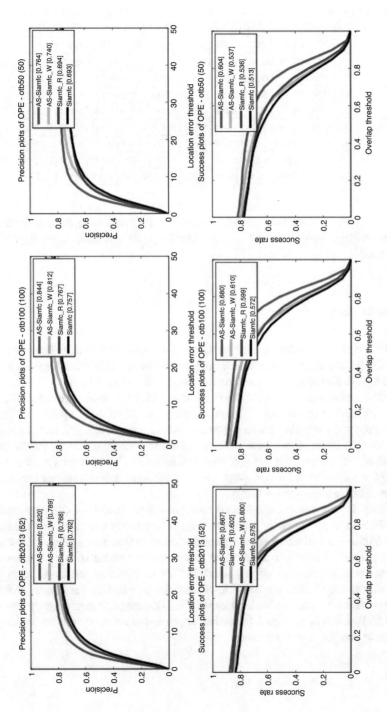

**Fig. 4.19** The precision and success plots of OPE in OTB-2013, OTB100 and OTB50

**Table 4.8** The precision and success scores of 11 tracking challenges in OTB100. For each tracker, the precision scores are in the first row, and the success scores are in the following row

| | | IV | SV | OCC | DEF | MB | FM | IPR | OPR | OV | BC | LR |
|---|---|---|---|---|---|---|---|---|---|---|---|---|
| Siamfc_R | Pre | 0.745 | 0.761 | 0.685 | 0.715 | 0.733 | 0.750 | 0.771 | 0.757 | 0.626 | 0.662 | 0.700 |
| | Suc | 0.584 | 0.590 | 0.542 | 0.545 | 0.603 | 0.602 | 0.594 | 0.577 | 0.500 | 0.514 | 0.537 |
| Siamfc | Pre | 0.746 | 0.751 | 0.667 | 0.694 | 0.721 | 0.732 | 0.752 | 0.733 | 0.621 | 0.669 | 0.751 |
| | Suc | 0.567 | 0.562 | 0.514 | 0.509 | 0.570 | 0.567 | 0.560 | 0.539 | 0.481 | 0.500 | 0.541 |
| AS-Siamfc | Pre | 0.791 | 0.837 | 0.784 | 0.824 | 0.810 | 0.812 | 0.835 | 0.833 | 0.708 | 0.753 | 0.705 |
| | Suc | 0.631 | 0.675 | 0.633 | 0.657 | 0.685 | 0.677 | 0.668 | 0.669 | 0.569 | 0.599 | 0.561 |
| AS-Siamfc_W | Pre | 0.760 | 0.806 | 0.739 | 0.797 | 0.786 | 0.774 | 0.800 | 0.798 | 0.664 | 0.726 | 0.693 |
| | Suc | 0.563 | 0.602 | 0.566 | 0.589 | 0.625 | 0.610 | 0.597 | 0.599 | 0.500 | 0.599 | 0.493 |

than on AS network. Thus, the auxiliary relocation branch may bring some noise and wrong knowledge, which leads to the error of AS-Siamfc and reduces the tracking performance.

## 4.5  Summary

In this section, three correlation filter tracking algorithms based on deep features are proposed. All three algorithms take advantage of the better discriminative power of deep features to perform robust tracking in complex environments.

The first method uses a combination of long and short term correlation filter updates, which can effectively balance the long and short term updates of the tracking model during the tracking process, while using HOG, CN and Deep features to fuse features and sum them according to a certain ratio to obtain the fused features for the representation of the tracking target. As the fused features can complement each other's shortcomings, the tracking algorithm can further improve the discriminative ability of the target.

The second method is a content-aware correlation filter-based tracking algorithm that combines depth features for robust tracking of targets in complex environments. Firstly the individual channels are weighted according to the tracking target features based on a channel attention mechanism to obtain discriminative depth features. A content-aware correlation filter network is then designed to further accurately distinguish the target from the tracking context through feature perception of the tracking environment and the tracking target. Finally, a model update strategy based on high confidence is designed to further improve the accuracy of the tracking algorithm in complex environments.

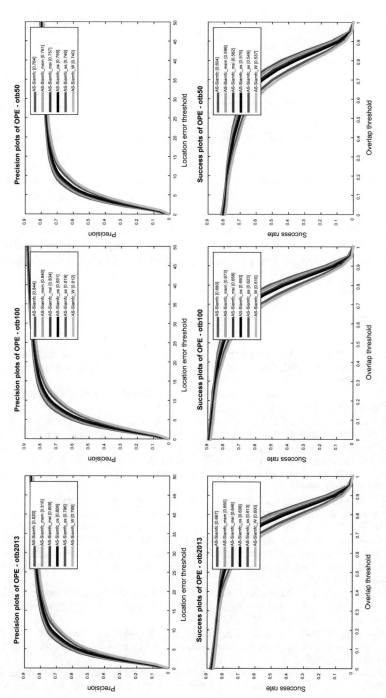

**Fig. 4.20** The precision and success plots of OPE in OTB2013, OTB100 and OTB50

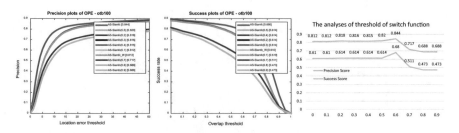

**Fig. 4.21** The analyses of the threshold of switch function in OTB100

The third method performs an auxiliary repositioning by means of a correlation filter, which improves the target tracking accuracy of the current frame by making a second judgment on the algorithm's prediction results, if the target is found to be missing or the accuracy is below a threshold. A switching function based on the SiamFC framework is also designed to further reduce the gap between the auxiliary repositioning and the target change to avoid target tracking failure due to relocation.

# References

1. Bolme, D.S., Beveridge, J.R., Draper, B.A., Lui, Y.M.: Visual object tracking using adaptive correlation filters. In: IEEE Conference on Computer Vision and Pattern Recognition, pp. 2544–2550 (2010)
2. Danelljan, M., Häger, G., Khan, F., Felsberg, M.: Accurate scale estimation for robust visual tracking. In: British Machine Vision Conference (2014)
3. Hong, Z., Chen, Z., Wang, C., Mei, X., Prokhorov, D., Tao, D.: Multi-store tracker (muster): A cognitive psychology inspired approach to object tracking. In: IEEE Conference on Computer Vision and Pattern Recognition, pp. 749–758 (2015)
4. Danelljan, M., Hager, G., Shahbaz Khan, F., Felsberg, M.: Convolutional features for correlation filter based visual tracking. In: IEEE International Conference on Computer Vision Workshops, pp. 58–66 (2015)
5. Kiani Galoogahi, H., Fagg, A., Lucey, S.: Learning background-aware correlation filters for visual tracking. In: IEEE International Conference on Computer Vision, pp. 1135–1143 (2017)
6. Zuo, W., Wu, X., Lin, L., Zhang, L., Yang, M. H.: Learning support correlation filters for visual tracking. IEEE Trans. Pattern Anal. Mach. Intell. **41**(5), 1158–1172 (2018)
7. Bertinetto, L., Valmadre, J., Golodetz, S., Miksik, O., Torr, P.H.: Staple: Complementary learners for real-time tracking. In: IEEE Conference on Computer Vision and Pattern Recognition, pp. 1401–1409 (2016)
8. Lukezic, A., Vojir, T., ˇCehovin Zajc, L., Matas, J., Kristan, M.: Discriminative correlation filter with channel and spatial reliability. In: IEEE Conference on Computer Vision and Pattern Recognition, pp. 6309–6318 (2017)
9. Danelljan, M., Robinson, A., Khan, F.S., Felsberg, M.: Beyond correlation filters: Learning continuous convolution operators for visual tracking. In: European Conference on Computer Vision, pp. 472–488 (2016)
10. Danelljan, M., Bhat, G., Shahbaz Khan, F., Felsberg, M.: Eco: Efficient convolution operators for tracking. In: IEEE Conference on Computer Vision and Pattern Recognition, pp. 6638–6646 (2017)

11. Ma, C., Huang, J.B., Yang, X., Yang, M.H.: Hierarchical convolutional features for visual tracking. In: IEEE International Conference on Computer Vision, pp. 3074–3082 (2015)
12. Dalal, N., Triggs, B.: Histograms of oriented gradients for human detection. In: IEEE International Conference on Computer Vision, pp. 886–893 (2005)
13. Danelljan, M., Shahbaz Khan, F., Felsberg, M., Van de Weijer, J.: Adaptive color attributes for real-time visual tracking. In: IEEE Conference on Computer Vision and Pattern Recognition, pp. 1090–1097 (2014)
14. Henriques, J.F., Caseiro, R., Martins, P., Batista, J.: High-speed tracking with kernelized correlation filters. IEEE Trans. Pattern Anal. Mach. Intell. **37**(3), 583–596 (2014)
15. Felzenszwalb, P.F., Girshick, R.B., McAllester, D., Ramanan, D.: Object detection with discriminatively trained part-based models. IEEE Trans. Pattern Anal. Mach. Intell. **32**(9), 1627–1645 (2009)
16. Danelljan, M., Hager, G., Shahbaz Khan, F., Felsberg, M.: Adaptive decontamination of the training set: A unified formulation for discriminative visual tracking. In: IEEE Conference on Computer Vision and Pattern Recognition, pp. 1430–1438 (2016)
17. Qi, Y., Zhang, S., Qin, L., Yao, H., Huang, Q., Lim, J., Yang, M.H.: Hedged deep tracking. In: IEEE Conference on Computer Vision and Pattern Recognition, pp. 4303–4311 (2016)
18. Kristan, M., Matas, J., Leonardis, A., et al.: The visual object tracking vot2015 challenge results. In: IEEE International Conference on Computer Vision Workshops, pp. 564–586 (2015)
19. Liang, P., Blasch, E., Ling, H.: Encoding color information for visual tracking: Algorithms and benchmark. IEEE Trans. Image Process. **24**(12): 5630–5644 (2015)
20. Mueller, M., Smith, N., Ghanem, B.: A benchmark and simulator for uav tracking. In: European Conference on Computer Vision, pp. 445–461 (2015)
21. Mueller, M., Smith, N., Ghanem, B.: Context-aware correlation filter tracking. In: IEEE Conference on Computer Vision and Pattern Recognition, pp. 1396–1404 (2017)
22. Jie, H., Shen, l., Albanine, Samuel, Sun G., Wu E.: Squeeze-and-excitation networks. IEEE Trans. Pattern Anal. Mach. Intell. **42**(8), 2011–2023 (2020)
23. Wang, M., Liu, Y., Huang, Z.: Large margin object tracking with circulant feature maps. In: IEEE Conference on Computer Vision and Pattern Recognition, pp. 4021–4029 (2017)
24. Hu, J., Shen, L., Sun, G.: Squeeze-and-excitation networks. IEEE Conference on Computer Vision and Pattern Recognition, pp. 7132–7141 (2018)
25. Russakovsky, O., Deng, J., Su, H., Krause, J., Satheesh, S., Ma, S., Fei-Fei, L.:. Imagenet large scale visual recognition challenge. Int. J. Comput. Vision **115**(3), 211–252 (2015)
26. Wang, N., Song, Y., Ma, C., Zhou, W., Liu, W., Li, H.: Unsupervised deep tracking. In: IEEE Conference on Computer Vision and Pattern Recognition, pp. 1308–1317 (2019)
27. Dong, X., Shen, J.: Triplet loss in siamese network for object tracking. In: Proceedings of the European Conference on Computer Vision, pp. 459–474 (2018)
28. Valmadre, J., Bertinetto, L., Henriques, J., Vedaldi, A., Torr, P.H.: End-to-end representation learning for correlation filter based tracking. IEEE Conference on Computer Vision and Pattern Recognition, pp. 2805–2813 (2017)
29. Jean-Yves,B.: Pyramidal implementation of the affine Lucas Kanade feature tracker description of the algorithm. Intel Corp. **5**(1–10), 4 (2001)
30. Rizwan, C., Avinash, R., Gregory, H., Rene, V., Avinash, R., Gregory, H., Rene,V.: Histograms of oriented optical flow and Binet-Cauchy kernels on nonlinear dynamical systems for the recognition of human actions. In: IEEE Conference on Computer Vision and Pattern Recognition, pp. 1932–1939 (2009)
31. Radhakrishna, A., Sheila, H., Francisco, E. ,Sabine, S.: Frequency-tuned salient region detection. In: IEEE Conference on Computer Vision and Pattern Recognition, pp. 1597–1604 (2009)
32. Navneet, D., Bill, T.: Histograms of oriented gradients for human detection. In: IEEE Computer Society Conference on Computer Vision and Pattern Recognition, pp. 886–893 (2005)

# Chapter 5
# Deep Learning Based Visual Object Tracking

With the development of deep learning, more and more deep learning methods are applied to visual object tracking. This chapter mainly introduces three deep learning methods, including the Siamese network, generative adversarial network, and reinforcement learning. We enhance the performance of visual object tracking methods by improving those methods.

## 5.1 Introduction

With the rapid development of deep learning in recent years, deep learning models have been widely used in the computer vision field. Their powerful learning and discrimination abilities have surpassed the traditional methods with state-of-the-art performance. For object tracking, deep learning based methods design tracking framework through deep network models and perform supervised or semi-supervised pre-training through massive samples to obtain robust tracking models [1]. Afterward, deep reinforcement learning and Siamese network have also been introduced into object tracking. Deep reinforcement learning-based methods [2, 3] can effectively transfer the training knowledge to the tracking environments and quickly adapt to the new scenes through self-learning. To accelerate the tracking process, Siamese network [4, 5] uses template matching and non-update model strategies to reduce feature calculation and model update cost. However, the existing methods mainly balance speed and accuracy by selecting different deep models without optimizing deep features. Meanwhile, complex models require massive, diverse training samples. At the same time, most tracking methods do not have data processing or only use geometric transformation to increase sample diversity, limiting the robustness of the model.

Danelljan et al.(SRDCFdecon) found that samples may have information that can lower the tracker performance. In order to address this problem, they designed a training method that optimizes both the model parameters and the sample weights, and, unlike binary decision making, uses a continuous representation of the parameter weights, which effectively reduces the weights of the contaminated samples and increases the weights of the correct samples. To ensure the validity of the weights, the sample weights can be recalculated in each frame to correct the incorrect contaminated sample weights. Based on SRDCFdecon, DeepSRDCF chose the depth features based on neural networks instead of the original artificial features for tracking targets based on the SRDCF. By comparing the discriminative power of the depth features extracted from different convolutional layers in the neural network, it is found that the depth features extracted from shallow convolutional layers have better discriminative power than those extracted from deep convolutional layers, which can reduce the amount of network computation and accelerate the tracking speed. To further improve the speed of the algorithm, PCA was also used to reduce the dimensionality of the features in the first convolutional layer, further reducing the computational effort of the network.

## 5.2   Attention Shake Siamese Based Visual Object Tracking

Siamese network is highly regarded in the visual object tracking field because of its unique advantages of pairwise input and pairwise training. It can measure the similarity between two image patches, which coincides with the principle of the matching-based tracking algorithm. In this section, a variant Siamese network-based tracker is proposed to introduce an attention module into a traditional Siamese network. A novel attention shake layer is proposed to replace the max-pooling layer in the Siamese network. This layer could introduce and train two different kinds of attention modules simultaneously, which means the proposed attention shake layer could also help improve the expression power of the Siamese network without increasing the depth of the network.

### 5.2.1   Attention Mechanisms in Siamese Network

The Siamese network based trackers treat visual object tracking as a cross-correlation problem and compute the response map from the Siamese network-based deep model. They usually have two branches for the pairwise input. One branch is to learn the presentation of the object $z'$ in a semantic embedding space $\phi()$, and the other branch shows the presentation of the search area $x'$. Thus the response map can be calculated by $f(z', x') = \Phi(z') \circledast \Phi(x') + \mathbf{b}$, where $\mathbf{b}$ is bias term and $\circledast$ denotes the cross-correlation operation. The goal is to match the maximum value in the response map to the object location.

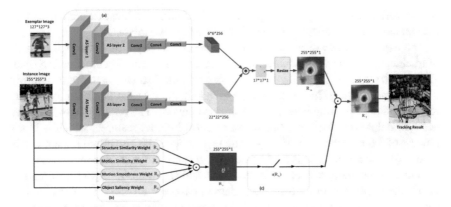

**Fig. 5.1** The main framework of the proposed AS-Siamfc. It basically consists of 3 parts: (**a**) the attention shake network with proposed attention shake layer. (**b**) the auxiliary relocation branch which contains structure similarity weight, motion similarity weight, motion smoothness weight and object saliency weight. (**c**) the switch function which is used to control the four weights in relocation branch

In this section, we describe the architecture of the proposed tracker. As shown in Fig. 5.1, the architecture of AS-Siamfc can be mainly divided into three parts: attention shake network, relocation branch, and switch function. Moreover, at the right side of Fig. 5.1, a weight-based fusion method controlled by switch function is proposed to introduce the prior knowledge of visual object tracking into the proposed tracker and calculate the final response map, $R_T$. $\odot$ and $\circledast$ in Fig. 5.1 denote element-wise product and cross-correlation operation respectively.

For the part of the attention shake network Fig. 5.1a, a novel attention shake layer is proposed to replace the max-pooling layer in the AlexNet based Siamese network. This proposed attention layer could combine two different attention modules and improve the expression power. For the part of relocation branch Fig. 5.1b, many weight maps, such as structure similarity weight, motion similarity weight, motion smoothness weight, and object saliency weight, are applied to introduce some prior knowledge into AS-Siamfc. These types of prior knowledge could refine and relocate objects when the proposed tracker runs under an untrusted state. For the switch function part Fig. 5.1c, by observing the relationship between the score of the response map of AS network and the success rate of AS-Siamfc, we design a switch function to monitor the tracking process online and control the effect of auxiliary relocation branch on tracking results.

The whole process can be summarized as follows: firstly, we feed the exemplar image, $I_z$ (also templet obtained from the first image) and instance image, $I_x$ (also candidate search image which is more significant than exemplar image and represents the search area) into the proposed AS network and obtain the response map. Then, the switch function is used to monitor the tracking process according to the response map. If the tracker runs under a trusted state, the tracking results can be obtained directly according to the response maps. Otherwise, the response map of

AS network is updated by the weight map of the auxiliary relocation branch through the element-wise product to refine and relocate the tracking results.

The expression power of the Siamese network directly affects the performance of tracking, and attention modules are proved to be effective in classification tasks. Thus, we try to introduce attention modules into the Siamese network to improve the expression power. In this section, a novel attention shake layer is proposed to replace the max-pooling layer in the Siamese network. The pooling layer in a deep network helps to reduce the dimension of convolutional features, which is like a process of feature selection. Max pooling layer selects the maximum impact within an area (the max value). This could reduce the error of the estimated mean caused by the error of parameters in convolution layers and retain more helpful information. While the average pooling layer considers the average effect of all elements in a specific area (the mean value). Thus, the average pooling layer pays more attention to the integrity of information and helps to reduce the estimated variance caused by the constraints of neighborhood size. Considering the analyses above, the proposed AS layer can have the advantages of both the max-pooling layer and average pooling layer at the same time.

As shown in Fig. 5.2, the AS layer can be mainly divided into two parts: the attention part and the shake part. In the attention part, there are two modified Squeeze and Excitation blocks. (SE block) [6] based attention modules: the max-attention module (left side of Fig. 5.2a) and the average-attention module (right side of Fig. 5.2a). Unlike the traditional SE block, the modified SE blocks in this section are applied to refine further the feature map of max pooling and average pooling. The architectures of the max-attention module and average-attention module can be found in Fig. 5.2a. The max-pooling and average pooling are used as the spatial attention in AS layer. After the max-pooling layer (or average pooling layer), another global pooling layer is used to transfer the feature map of max-pooling (or average pooling) from $((H - 3)/2 + 1) * ((H - 3)/2 + 1) * C$ to $1 * 1 * C$, where H, W and C denote the height, width and channel of convolution feature map $X$. Then two fully convolutional layers are used to reduce and then increase the number of channels with a penalty coefficient $r$, respectively. Finally, the channel attention weight can be calculated by a sigmoid function. The feature map of max-attention, $AT_{max}$, and average-attention, $AT_{avg}$, can be obtained by Eqs. 5.1 and 5.2.

$$AT_{max}(X) = sig(W_{m1}(W_{m0}(maxpool(X)))) \otimes maxpool(X) \qquad (5.1)$$

$$AT_{avg}(X) = sig(W_{a1}(W_{a0}(avgpool(X)))) \otimes avgpool(X) \qquad (5.2)$$

where $W_{m0}$ and $W_{a0}$ are the operations of the first fully connected layers of max-attention and average-attention, which try to reduce the channels from C to C/r. While, $W_{m1}$ and $W_{m2}$ are the operations of the second fully connected layers of max-attention and average attention, which try to raise the channels from C/r back to C. $sig()$ denotes the sigmoid function, and $\otimes$ is the channel-wise product.

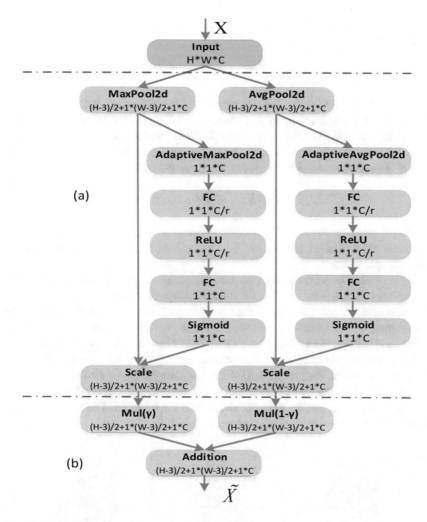

**Fig. 5.2** The architecture of the proposed attention shake layer. It can be divided into two parts: (**a**) the attention part and (**b**) the shake part

## 5.2.2   Shake-Shake Mechanism in Siamese Network

In order to make the proposed attention shake network contain the advantages of both max-attention and average-attention, the shake-shake model [7] is introduced into the AS layer. As shown in Fig. 5.2b, the shake part in AS layer combines the feature map of max-attention and average-attention by a weighted sum. One benefit of the shake part is that the weight coefficient is dynamic in the training process, which could cause the attention part to adjust its parameters dynamically and prevent over-fitting problems. The feature map of the AS layer can be computed by Eq. 5.3.

$$M_{AS}(X) = \hat{X} = \gamma * AT_{max}(X) + (1 - \gamma) * AT_{avg}(X) \tag{5.3}$$

where $M_{AS}(X)$ denotes the feature map of AS layer, and $\gamma$ denotes the weight coefficient. In the training process, $\gamma$ varies according to uniform distribution from 0 to 1. In the tracking process, $\gamma$ is set to be a fixed scalar, like 0.5. Since the proposed attention shake network is based on the Siamese network, the response map of the attention shake network can be calculated by Eq. 5.4.

$$f(I_z, I_x) = g(\varphi(I_z), \varphi(I_x)) = \varphi(I_z) \circledast \varphi(I_x) + \mathbf{b} \tag{5.4}$$

where $\varphi()$ denotes the attention shake network, $\circledast$ denotes the cross-correlation operation and $\mathbf{b}$ denotes a bias term. $I_z$ and $I_x$ are the exemplar image and instance image, respectively.

Figure 5.3b shows the response maps of Siamfc [8] and the proposed AS-Siamfc, respectively. Figure 5.3b and c are the response maps of instance images. In order to show the effect of the attention shake layer persuasively, the response maps of the whole frame are shown in Fig. 5.3e and f. By comparing the response maps between Siamfc and the proposed AS-Siamfc, we find that Siamfc only focuses on the center part of an object and cannot cover the whole object. While AS-Siamfc could focus on the whole object. Furthermore, AS-Siamfc makes the object area of the response map redder and the background area bluer, which means the proposed method could increase the discrimination between object and background. The attention shake layer could improve the expression power of the Siamese network.

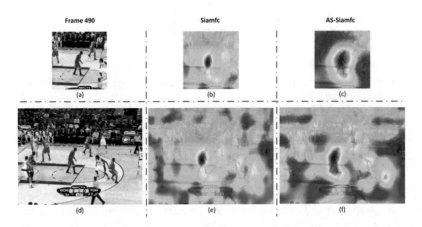

**Fig. 5.3** The response maps of instance image and the whole image, using Siamfc and AS-Siamfc. (**a**) and (**d**) show the instance image of Frame 490 and the whole image respectively. (**b**) and (**e**) are the response map of Siamfc. (**c**) and (**f**) are the response map of AS-Siamfc

## 5.2.3  Framework and Procedure

Similar to Siamfc [8], the proposed AS-Siamfc can be divided into the offline training process and online tracking process. During the training process, we try to optimize the parameters of the proposed AS network by reducing the loss of the whole dataset. While, in the tracking process, the pre-trained AS network is used to calculate $R_A$ and obtain the final response map $R_T$ along with the weight map of the auxiliary relocation branch $R_r$. The state of the object can be estimated by searching the index of peak value in $R_T$.

We adopt the logistic loss as the loss function for the training process and train the proposed AS network on positive and negative pairs. The obtaining of positive and negative pairs is similar to Siamfc [8]. The loss function of a single response map is shown in Eq. 5.5.

$$L(I_y, v_{x,z}) = \frac{1}{|D|} \sum_{u \in D} \log(1 + e^{-l_y[u]v_{x,z}[u]}) \tag{5.5}$$

where $l_y$ is the set that contains all the labels of a response map, and $v_{x,z}$, $z$ is the set that contains all the real values of a response map. Thus, $l_y[u]$ and $v_{x,z}[u]$ represent the $u - th$ label and real value of a response map. The loss function of a response map is the mean value of logistic losses of all elements in the response map. $D$ is the set of the index in a response map, and |D| is the number of indexes in D. For each index $u$ in a response map, the label $l_y[u]$ can be obtained by Eq. 5.6.

$$l_y[u] = I(\|u - c\| - r \le 0) - I(\|u - c\| - r \ge 0) \tag{5.6}$$

Where $c$ is the center of the object, and $r$ is the radius. $I(*)$ denotes the indicate function. When $*$ is true, $I(*) = 1$, otherwise, $I(*) = 0$. Thus, when the distance between $u$ and $c$ is longer than the radius $r$, the label $l_y[u] = 1$, otherwise, $l_y[u] = 1$. Furthermore, the parameter $\theta$ of AS network can be optimized by minimizing the mean value of all response maps in the dataset with Stochastic Gradient Descent (SGD). The equation is shown in Eq. 5.7.

$$\theta = \arg\min_{\theta} \frac{\sum_{(I_z, I_x, I_y) \in Da} L(l_y, f(I_z, I_x; \theta))}{|Da|} \tag{5.7}$$

Where $Da$ and $|Da|$ represent the dataset and the number of the dataset used to train the proposed AS network, $(I_z, I_x, I_y)$ is a training sample in the dataset. $I_z$, $I_x$, and $I_y$ are the exemplar image, instance image, and label of training data, respectively.

For the tracking process, we try to estimate the state of the object through the response map $R_A$, obtained by the pre-trained AS network and the weight map of the auxiliary relocation branch Rr. The pseudo-code is shown in Algorithm 4.

---

**Algorithm 4:** Pseudo code of AS-Siamfc

---

**Input:** The exemplar image, $I_z$; The initial object state, $X_G$; The pretrained AS
network,Threshold, $s_t$; Number of frames, $N_f$.
**Output:** The states of the object $X_t, t \in \{1, 2, ., N_f\}$.

  1: Calculating the feature map of exemplar image by feeding $I_z$ into The AS network;
  2: Initializing the object state, $X_1 = X_G$;
  3: **for** $i \leftarrow 2$ to $N_f$ **do**
  4:     Calculating the instance image $I_x$, according to $X_{t-1}$;
  5:     Feeding the instance image $I_x$ into AS network and computing the response map;
  6:     Resizing the response map to $(255 * 255 * 1)$ and obtaining $R_A$;
  7:     Computing the score of switch function $S(R_A)$;
  8:     **if** $S(R_A \geq 0)$ **then**
  9:        Estimating the location of the object through $R_A$;
10:        Updating the state of the object $X_t$;
11:     **else**
12:        Calculating the response map of auxiliary relocation branch, $R_r$;
13:        Computing the final response map, $R_T$;
14:        Estimating the location of the object through $R_T$;
15:        Updating the state of the object $X_t$;
16:     **end if**

---

17: **end for**
18: **return** $X_t, t \in \{1, 2, ., N_f\}$

---

## 5.2.4   *Experimental Results and Discussions*

In this section, we show some details about the settings and implementation of the
proposed AS-Siamfc tracker. All the experiments run on a remote server with 64G
memory and one GeForce GTX Titan X. The proposed AS network is trained on
GOT-10K [9] benchmark, which contains 10,000 video sequences and 1.5 million
manually labelled boxes. Unlike some other training datasets, the tracking objects
in this dataset belong to more than 560 categories, which is helpful to improve
the classification ability of AS-Siamfc. During the training process, the weight
coefficient $\gamma$ in the attention shake layer varies randomly from 0 to 1. While, in
the tracking process, $\gamma$ is set to be 0.5. Moreover, the widely used benchmarks,
OTB-2013 [10], OTB100 [11], and OTB50, along with their evaluation criteria, are
applied in this section to test the performance of the proposed AS-Siamfc tracker.
OTB50 is composed of 50 hard-to-track sequences selected from the OTB100. The
proposed tracker could track objects in real-time. The average tracking speed of
AS-Siamfc on the OTB100 dataset is 70.625 fps, which is slightly slower than
Siamfc [8], which is 84 fps. Besides, some state-of-the-art trackers are used for
the comparison experiments, such as Siamfc [8], SAMF [12], DSST [13], Struck
[14], TLD [15], CSK [16], ASLA [17], OAB [18] and IVT [19].

**Some Analyses of the Attention Shake Method**   In this section, we show some
results and analyses of different attention shake methods. In order to discuss the
influence of the pooling layer on the Siamese network, the results of the Siamese

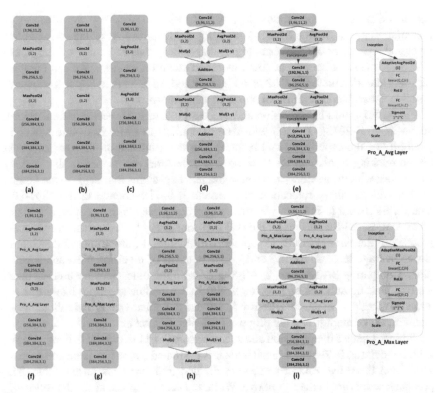

**Fig. 5.4** Nine kinds of attention shake network architectures for comparison. (**a**) Siamfc_R. (**b**) SA3. (**c**) Sap. (**d**) Sap_s. (**e**) SA1. (**f**) SA2_a. (**g**) SA2_m. (**h**) SA2_s. (**i**) AS-Siamfc

networks with different pooling layers are also shown in this section. Firstly, we design 9 kinds of Siamese network architectures for comparison. These 9 kinds of designed networks contain different pooling layers and attention shake methods. Secondly, we present the precision and success plots of these 9 networks in OTB100.

As shown in Fig. 5.4, there are 9 kinds of Siamese network architectures that are designed for comparison. The Pro_A_Avg layer and Pro_A_Max layer at the right side of Fig. 5.4 are the proposed max-attention module and average-attention module, respectively. Figure 5.4a is the backbone architecture of Siamfc network, and ASSiamfc in Fig. 5.4i is the proposed AS-Siamfc network. The others are some possible variants of this network. In order to discuss the influences of pooling layers in the Siamese network, we also construct two networks SA3 in Fig. 5.4b and Sap in Fig. 5.4c by replacing the max-pooling layers in Fig. 5.4a with convolutional layers and average pooling layers respectively. Besides, we also combine the max-pooling layers and average pooling layers with a shake module and construct the Sap_s network in Fig. 5.4d. In order to analyze the proposed max-attention module and average-attention module Separately, we construct the SA2_a network, which only contains the average-attention module, and the SA2_m network, which only contains a max-attention module in Fig. 5.4f and g respectively. We also design a spatial attention model, SA1, by merging the feature map of the max-pooling layer and average pooling layer in Fig. 5.4e. Noticing that SA3, Sap_s, SA2_a, and SA2_m can also be viewed as some modified attention methods, we can compare different attention methods. SA2_s in Fig. 5.4h and AS-Siamfc in Fig. 5.4i show two possible network architectures of attention shake network.

Figure 5.5 shows the precision and success plots of the 9 network architectures above in OTB-2013, OTB100 and OTB50 dataset. In order to ensure the comparability of the experiment and better reflect the influence of different networks on the tracking results, all the 9 network architectures are applied in the tracking framework with the auxiliary relocation branch. Especially, Siamfc_R is the Siamfc tracker with auxiliary relocation branch, and it is also trained in the GOT-10K dataset. As shown in Fig. 5.5, we can see that comparing with the other 8 network architectures, AS-Siamfc shows the best performance of both precision and success plots in all the three datasets. Compared with Siamfc_R, the proposed AS-Siamfc has an average increase of 6.63 and 7.13% in terms of precision plots and success plots. Comparing SA2_s, Sap_s, AS-Siamfc with the other network architectures, we find that the network architectures with shake module are more likely to have good tracking performance. This also illustrates the effectiveness and rationality of attention shake module and the proposed AS-Siamfc tracker.

Table 5.1 shows the precision and success scores of 11 tracking challenges in the OTB100 dataset. In Table 5.1, each tracker is evaluated by the precision and success score, and these two sets of scores are divided into two rows in the Table. The precision scores are in the row above. While the success scores are in the following row. IV, SV, OCC, DEF, MB, FM, IPR, OPR, OV, BC, and LR in Table 5.1 represent illumination variation, scale variation, occlusion, deformation, motion blur, fast motion, in-plane rotation, out-of-plane rotation, out-of-view, background clutters and low resolution respectively. By comparing the precision and success scores of Siamfc_R, SA3, Sap, and Sap_s, we can get some empirical conclusions about the influence of pooling layers on the Siamese network. It is that comparing with Sap and SA3, the Siamese network with max-pooling layers can obtain relatively better results. However, the performance of the designed Sap_s, which contains the shake module, is better than Siamfc_R in the tracking challenge of out-of-plane, scale variation, deformation, motion blur, in-plane rotation, etc. This also presents the shake module that could improve the expression power of the Siamese network. Generally, the attention shake-based backbone network architectures, SA2_s and AS-Siamfc, can rank in the top three of the 9 network architectures in all tracking challenges. This illustrates the effectiveness of attention shake-based network architectures. Comparing with the other network architectures, the proposed AS-Siamfc tracker shows a better performance in all tracking challenges.

In order to analyze the effectiveness of the shake part in the attention shake layer, we also designed four different training and tracking methods for the proposed tracker. The first one is training with random weight coefficients of the shake part but tracking with a fixed weight coefficient. It is also known as AS-Siamfc_W, which is applied In this section. The second one is training with random weight coefficients

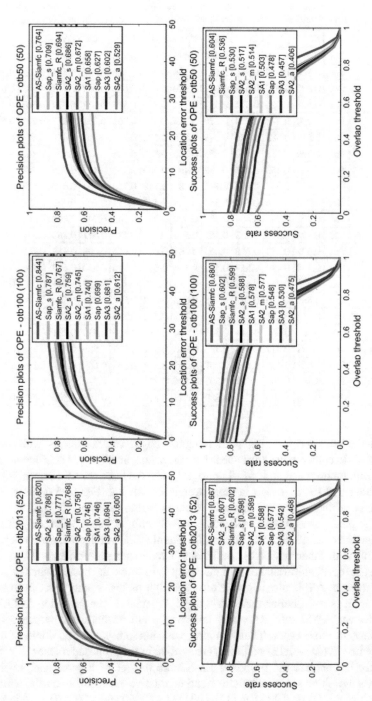

**Fig. 5.5** The precision and success plots of OPE in OTB-2013, OTB100 and OTB50

**Table 5.1** The precision and success scores of 11 tracking challenges in OTB100. For each tracker, the precision scores are in the first row, and the success scores are in the following row

|            |      | IV    | SV    | OCC   | DEF   | MB    | FM    | IPR   | OPR   | OV    | BC    | LR    |
|------------|------|-------|-------|-------|-------|-------|-------|-------|-------|-------|-------|-------|
| SA1        | Pre. | 0.713 | 0.720 | 0.630 | 0.702 | 0.675 | 0.698 | 0.738 | 0.721 | 0.561 | 0.681 | 0.708 |
|            | Suc. | 0.562 | 0.556 | 0.506 | 0.537 | 0.556 | 0.569 | 0.566 | 0.551 | 0.451 | 0.534 | 0.535 |
| Sap        | Pre. | 0.670 | 0.674 | 0.648 | 0.671 | 0.680 | 0.670 | 0.696 | 0.697 | 0.477 | 0.642 | 0.631 |
|            | Suc. | 0.523 | 0.525 | 0.516 | 0.524 | 0.556 | 0.545 | 0.537 | 0.537 | 0.374 | 0.503 | 0.460 |
| Sap_s      | Pre. | 0.750 | 0.773 | 0.714 | 0.770 | 0.743 | 0.742 | 0.761 | 0.783 | 0.617 | 0.727 | 0.671 |
|            | Suc. | 0.571 | 0.585 | 0.556 | 0.578 | 0.598 | 0.592 | 0.572 | 0.590 | 0.487 | 0.554 | 0.479 |
| SA2_a      | Pre. | 0.529 | 0.586 | 0.520 | 0.635 | 0.606 | 0.562 | 0.588 | 0.602 | 0.403 | 0.461 | 0.490 |
|            | Suc. | 0.417 | 0.453 | 0.409 | 0.482 | 0.496 | 0.455 | 0.457 | 0.459 | 0.309 | 0.362 | 0.354 |
| SA2_m      | Pre. | 0.675 | 0.747 | 0.672 | 0.723 | 0.687 | 0.730 | 0.750 | 0.753 | 0.610 | 0.618 | 0.697 |
|            | Suc. | 0.528 | 0.574 | 0.531 | 0.553 | 0.568 | 0.583 | 0.571 | 0.569 | 0.476 | 0.476 | 0.526 |
| SA2_s      | Pre. | 0.702 | 0.743 | 0.684 | 0.735 | 0.693 | 0.711 | 0.788 | 0.748 | 0.603 | 0.667 | 0.686 |
|            | Suc. | 0.541 | 0.569 | 0.543 | 0.561 | 0.564 | 0.566 | 0.572 | 0.571 | 0.464 | 0.518 | 0.498 |
| SA3        | Pre. | 0.601 | 0.633 | 0.658 | 0.663 | 0.608 | 0.643 | 0.684 | 0.698 | 0.453 | 0.645 | 0.587 |
|            | Suc. | 0.474 | 0.489 | 0.517 | 0.512 | 0.490 | 0.512 | 0.519 | 0.530 | 0.358 | 0.497 | 0.434 |
| Siamfc_R   | Pre. | 0.745 | 0.761 | 0.685 | 0.715 | 0.733 | 0.750 | 0.771 | 0.757 | 0.626 | 0.662 | 0.700 |
|            | Suc. | 0.584 | 0.590 | 0.542 | 0.545 | 0.603 | 0.602 | 0.594 | 0.577 | 0.500 | 0.514 | 0.537 |
| Siamfc     | Pre. | 0.746 | 0.751 | 0.667 | 0.694 | 0.721 | 0.732 | 0.752 | 0.733 | 0.621 | 0.669 | 0.751 |
|            | Suc. | 0.567 | 0.562 | 0.514 | 0.509 | 0.570 | 0.567 | 0.560 | 0.539 | 0.481 | 0.500 | 0.541 |
| AS-Siamfc  | Pre. | 0.791 | 0.837 | 0.784 | 0.824 | 0.810 | 0.812 | 0.835 | 0.833 | 0.708 | 0.753 | 0.705 |
|            | Suc. | 0.631 | 0.675 | 0.633 | 0.657 | 0.685 | 0.677 | 0.668 | 0.669 | 0.569 | 0.599 | 0.561 |
| AS-Siamfc_W | Pre. | 0.760 | 0.806 | 0.739 | 0.797 | 0.786 | 0.774 | 0.800 | 0.798 | 0.664 | 0.726 | 0.693 |
|            | Suc. | 0.563 | 0.602 | 0.566 | 0.589 | 0.625 | 0.610 | 0.597 | 0.599 | 0.500 | 0.599 | 0.493 |

of the shake part and tracking with random weight coefficients as well (AS-Siamfc_RR). In contrast, the third one is training with a fixed weight coefficient, but tracking with random weights (AS-Siamfc_SR), and the last one, AS-Siamfc_SS, is both training and tracking with a fixed weight coefficient. Figure 5.6 shows the performance of these four training and tracking methods. From Fig. 5.6, we can see that the precision and success scores of AS-Siamfc_W and AS-Siamfc_RR are higher than those of AS-Siamfc_SR and AS-Siamfc_SS, which means the trackers which train with random weight coefficients have better performance. Thus, the shake part in the attention shake layer may help to improve the performance of AS-Siamfc. Though, ASSiamfc_RR may also get high precision and success scores. Sometimes, it is even better than AS-Siamfc_W, such as the precision in OTB-2013. However, AS-Siamfc_RR seems less robust, and ASSiamfc_W shows better performance in most cases. Thus, training with random weight coefficients and tracking with a fixed weight coefficient are applied in the proposed tracker.

In order to compare the proposed AS-Siamfc tracker with some state-of-the-art trackers, we show some quantitative and qualitative experiments on the widely used benchmarks, OTB-2013 [10], OTB100 [11], OTB50 and VOT2018 [20] in this

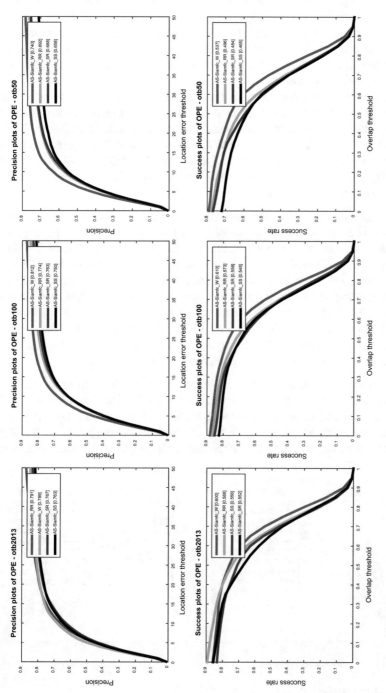

**Fig. 5.6** The precision and success plots of OPE in OTB2013, OTB100 and OTB50

section. Firstly, we show the precision and success plots of One-Pass Evaluation (OPE) in benchmark OTB-2013, OTB100 and OTB50, along with the Accuracy-Robustness plots (AR plots) in VOT2018. The performances of the proposed tracker under 10 tracking challenges are also analysed in this section. Secondly, we provide the tracking bounding boxes of 10 sequences to show the qualitative analyses of the proposed AS-Siamfc tracker.

We provide some quantitative analyses in this section. We also selected some state-of-the-art trackers including some Siamese network based trackers for comparison which is conducted on the widely used benchmark, OTB-2013, OTB100 and OTB50. Two metrics, precision and Area Under Curve (AUC), are used to rank these trackers. Firstly, we show the comparison results of OTB-2013, OTB100 and OTB50 respectively. Then, we analyse the performance of the proposed AS-Siamfc tracker under 10 tracking challenges.

**Experiments on OTB-2013 Dataset**  OTB-2013 is one of the widely used benchmarks with 52 fully annotated sequences. In order to facilitate the comparison test, the author also provides two evaluation criteria and a toolkit. Figure 5.7 shows the precision and success plots of One-Pass Evaluation (OPE) in the OTB-2013 dataset. From Fig. 5.7, we can see that our proposed AS-Siamfc tracker achieves the best tracking performance against the other comparative trackers at the average speed of 70.625 fps. The precision score and success score are 0.820 and 0.667, respectively. Comparing with the Siamfc tracker, the performance of the proposed AS-Siamfc tracker exceeds the performance of the Siamfc tracker 0.058 and 0.092 on the precision score and success score, respectively.

**Experiments on OTB100 Dataset**  In order to increase the number of sequences of the OTB-2013 dataset and to evaluate the visual object trackers more accurately, Wu et. al. [11] add some fully annotated sequences into the OTB-2013 dataset to construct the OTB100 dataset. Thus, the OTB100 dataset expends the OTB-2013 dataset from 52 sequences to 100 sequences. Similarly, the evaluation criteria and

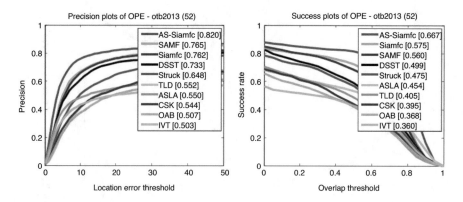

**Fig. 5.7**  The precision and success plots of OPE in OTB-2013

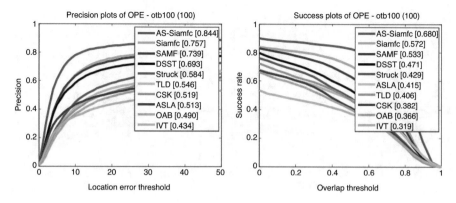

**Fig. 5.8** The precision and success plots of OPE in OTB100

toolkits in the OTB-2013 dataset are also applicable in OTB100. Figure 5.8 shows the precision and success plots of OPE in the OTB100 dataset. From Fig. 5.8, we can see that the precision score and success score of the proposed AS-Siamfc are 0.844 and 0.680, which are also the highest scores. The proposed tracker's precision score and success score are 0.087 and 0.108 larger than that of Siamfc. By comparing the scores of AS-Siamfc tracker in OTB-2013 and OTB100, we find that the scores of ASSiamfc in OTB100 are average 1.85% higher than that in OTB-2013. We believe the reason is that the number of sequences in the OTB-2013 dataset is relatively small, which will have a great impact on the overall precision and success scores if the tracking performances of a certain sequence are not good. On the contrary, there are more sequences in OTB100, and the distribution of the sequences in OTB100 is relatively uniform. Thus, the tracking results of a single video sequence have little influence on the overall precision and success scores. This also illustrates the effectiveness and applicability of the proposed AS-Siamfc tracker.

**Experiments on OTB50 Dataset** OTB50 is composed of 50 hard-to-track sequences selected from the OTB100. It is one of the widely used benchmarks with 50 fully annotated sequences. The toolkit proposed in OTB-2013 [10] can also apply in the OTB50 dataset. Figure 5.9 shows the precision and success plots of OPE in the OTB50 dataset. As shown in Fig. 5.9, our performance of the proposed tracker is better than the other state-of-the-art trackers. The precision score and success score are 0.764 and 0.604, respectively. Comparing with the Siamfc tracker, the performance of the proposed AS-Siamfc tracker exceeds the performance of the Siamfc tracker 0.071 and 0.091 on the precision score and success score, respectively.

**Experiments on VOT2018 Dataset** VOT2018[20] is also one of the widely used benchmarks, which contents 60 sequences, including many tiny, similar tracking objects. Figure 5.10 shows the mean AR plot and pooled AR plot for the experiment baseline of the VOT2018 dataset, respectively. According to the definition of

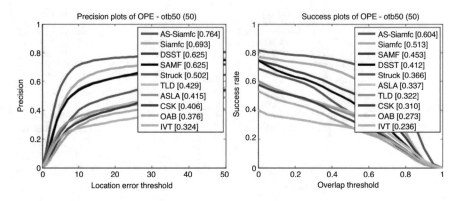

**Fig. 5.9** The precision and success plots of OPE in OTB50

AR plot in VOT2018 [20], the trackers located at the upper right quarter of the AR plot perform better than those located at the lower-left quarter. As shown in Fig. 5.10, though the proposed AS-Siamfc tracker has a low score on robustness, its accuracy score is the highest among the trackers for comparison. Generally, when comparing with some state-of-the-art trackers, AS-Siamfc could give a comparable performance in VOT2018, which illustrates the efficiency of the proposed tracker.

**Experiments of 10 Tracking Challenges in OTB100** In order to analyze the applicability of the proposed AS-Siamfc tracker in different sequences in detail. The sequences in the OTB100 dataset are divided into 11 tracking challenges, including illumination variation, out-of-plane rotation, scale variation, occlusion, deformation, motion blur, fast motion, in-plane rotation, out of view, background clutter, and low resolution. Figure 5.11 shows the precision and success plots of AS-Siamfc under these challenges along with some state-of-the-art trackers. In order to make the figure neat, we select ten challenges in Fig. 5.11 instead of all 11 challenges.

From Fig. 5.11, we can see that the proposed AS-SimaFC tracker performs better than the other trackers under all the ten tracking challenges. By comparing the performances of the proposed tracker and Simafc tacker, we find that the proposed tracker shows better performances under the challenges of out-of-plane rotation, scale variation, deformation, and fast motion, etc., especially the deformation. From Fig. 5.11d, we can see that our proposed tracker shows a good performance in the tracking challenge of occlusion, even though AS-Siamfc does not deliberately design a module to deal with this challenge. We believe the reason is the proposed switch function could indirectly detect the occurrence of occlusion to some extent, and using auxiliary relocation branch to refine the tracking results, since when occlusion occurs, the response map of AS Siamese network may get a low response score, which also means the tracker is running under an untrusted state. Indeed, there are also many occlusion-aware methods in visual object tracking and motion segmentation. Integrating these occlusion-aware methods in the proposed tracking

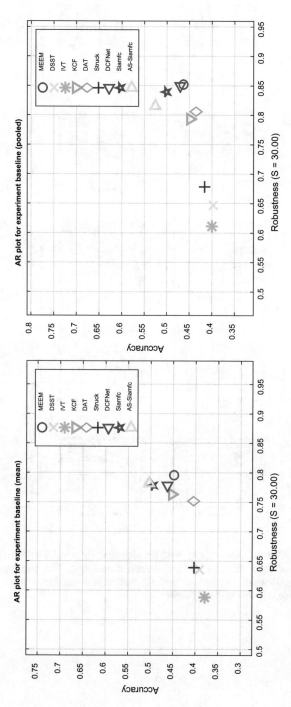

**Fig. 5.10** The AR plot for experiment baseline of VOT2018

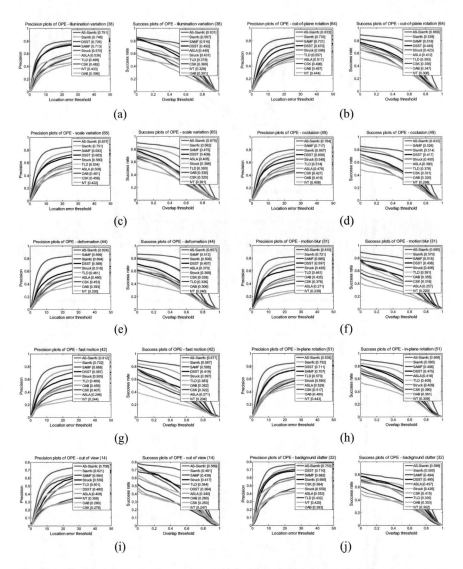

**Fig. 5.11** The precision and success plots of 10 tracking challenges in OTB100, using proposed tracker and 8 state-of-the-art trackers. (**a**) Illumination variation. (**b**) Out-of-plane rotation. (**c**) Scale variation. (**d**) Occlusion. (**e**) Deformation. (**f**) Motion blur. (**g**) Fast motion. (**h**) In-plane rotation. (**i**) Out of view. (**j**) Background clutter

**Fig. 5.12** Qualitative results of 10 typical video sequences in OTB-2013, OTB100 and OTB50, using the proposed tracker and 9 state-of-the-art trackers

framework to further improve tracking performance will be our future work. In Fig. 5.11e, the precision score and success score of AS-Siamfc are 0.13 and 0.148 higher than that of Siamfc and are 0.125 and 0.145 higher than that of SAMF tracker [12], which is also the second-ranking tracker in Fig. 5.11e. We believe this also proves that the proposed AS network and auxiliary relocation branch with switch function could improve the expression power of the Siamese network and provide good tracking performances.

In addition to the above-mentioned quantitative analysis experiments, we also show some tracking bounding boxes of the sequences in OTB-2013, OTB100, and OTB50 for qualitative analyses in this subsection.

As shown in Fig. 5.12, we select 10 typical video sequences in OTB-2013, OTB100 and OTB50. The names of these ten sequences are CarScale, Matrix, DragonBaby, Skiing, Jump, Diving, Girl2, FleetFace, Soccer, and David3 in order from left to right and from top to bottom. These ten sequences contain all the 11 tracking challenges (one sequence may contain multiple challenges). However, to show the advantages of the proposed AS-Siamfc tacker better, these sequences focus more on the challenges of deformation, scale variation, and fast motion. From the sequence CarScale, we can see that AS-Siamfc could better estimate the state of the object when the car runs from far to near and gradually larger. In the sequences of Diving and Jump, the athletes have obvious and fast deformations. Even so, the proposed tracker can still track the athletes well. Meanwhile, Matrix sequences, DragonBaby and Skiing show the challenge of fast motion, since the people in the fighting or skiing always move fast. The proposed tracker can also provide an accurate tracking performance. Generally, all the quantitative and qualitative experiments can prove the applicability and effectiveness of the proposed AS-Siamfc tracker.

## 5.3    Frequency-Aware Siamese Network Based Visual Object Tracking

We propose a quick and efficient tracker called FAF. Offline IoU modulation, online IoU predictor, online classifier, and update-modules are the four modules that make up the proposed tracker. The offline IoU modulation is independently pre-trained with large training datasets to learn the relationship between target scale and location during the offline training stage. The offline IoU modulation will direct the online IoU predictor with the IoU regression score for the online tracking point, and the classifier will provide the classification score. Based on the classification and regression ranking, the joint judgment strategy will provide an optimized goal scale and position information. The update module will then update the IoU predictor and classifier. ResNet18 is used as the backbone in the proposed process, and it is pre-trained on ImageNet [21]. We optimize the original backbone using feature decomposition and sample fusion methods to boost the backbone's discrimination ability.

### 5.3.1    Frequency-Aware Siamese Network

Fixed structures with fixed-scale convolutional layers are currently used in object tracking models. The shallow convolution features, on the other hand, contain the obvious features, while the deep convolution features contain the sophisticated semantic features. As a result, the features used in conventional convolution actually have information redundancy, which improves network estimation and reduces the network's capacity of distinguishing.

To solve this issue, we integrate frequency-aware functionality into object tracking in a novel way. Unlike other tracking methods that differentiate between the features of different convolution layers, we decompose the features of each convolution layer, as inspired by Zhang et al. [22]. High-frequency features and low-frequency features are divided among the features in a convolution layer, with high-frequency features containing semantic information. As shown in Fig. 5.13, low-frequency features combine high-frequency features with compressed low-frequency features to minimize network calculations and increase the network's ability to distinguish targets.

The regular features are divided into high-frequency and low-frequency features in Fig. 5.13. The convolution operation can be made more efficient by compressing the low-frequency component, processing the high-frequency and low-frequency sections, and sharing information between them. The low-frequency component is $(0.5h, 0.5w)$ in dimension, with a duration and width that is exactly half that of the high-frequency part $(h, w)$. Since the low-frequency portion is compressed, it effectively extends the receptive field in the original pixel space, which can help with recognition. We control the high and low-frequency feature segmentation ratio

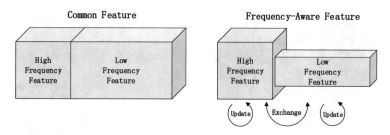

**Fig. 5.13** Frequency-aware feature

by setting the hyperparameter $\alpha$ as follows,

$$X \in \mathbb{R}^{c \times h \times w}$$

$$X^H \in \mathbb{R}^{(1-\alpha)c \times h \times w} \tag{5.8}$$

$$X^L \in \mathbb{R}^{\alpha c \times \frac{h}{2} \times \frac{w}{2}}$$

where $X$ means common feature, $w$, and $h$ are the width and height of the feature, $c$ is the channel number, and $X^H$ and $X^L$ is high-frequency and low-frequency features, respectively.

High-frequency and low-frequency features can update at their respective frequencies during the feature update process. Furthermore, the features exchange operation will update the high-frequency and low-frequency features information between frequencies. As a result, the high-frequency function encompasses the information mechanism as well as maps from low to high frequency and vice versa. The frequency-aware function has a wide receptive area of low frequency-feature charts, which is another benefit. It effectively doubles the receptive field as compared to the standard feature, allowing each frequency-aware feature to collect more contextual information and enhance recognition efficiency. This is the first time, as far as we know, that a frequency-aware feature-based Siamese network has been designed for object tracking.

## 5.3.2 Pre-training and Joint Update

**Pre-training** In recent years, large-scale deep learning has made breakthroughs, and they all have two things in common: The first step is to create more complex network structures. Larger training datasets are suggested as a second choice. Data augmentation approaches based on existing datasets are used to increase the data since the training dataset needs a lot of manual markings. Some models for object tracking problems use geometric transformations to increase data and improve the model's robustness. Current data augmentation methods, on the other hand,

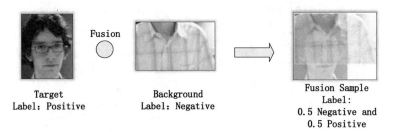

        Target                Background             Fusion Sample
  Label: Positive          Label: Negative           Label:

**Fig. 5.14** Training sample fusion when $\lambda = 0.5$

are based on the same class. The relationship between different classes is not considered, which cannot increase the diversity of the data and limit its performance.

To address this issue, we proposed a novel pre-training sample fusion approach that increased data diversity. Unlike the classification problem, the object tracking problem only has two classes: goal and context, and it is less concerned with the object's category. We improve the data by weighting the fused samples and sample labels, as suggested by Chen et al. [23]. The model will learn proximity relations through examples of different classes with such data augmentation.

To be more precise, we use a Gaussian distribution to produce candidate samples around the ground truth bounding box. Candidate samples are graded as positive or negative samples based on the intersection-over-union (IoU) overlap with the ground reality. We fuse the positive and negative samples to obtain fusion samples, as shown in Fig. 5.14. The size of the fusion sample is the maximum of the two images, unlike current methods that explicitly use the classified samples for model training. Information can be found in Algorithm 5.

---

**Algorithm 5:** Pre-training sample fusion

---

**Input:** the image $M$, the ground truth bound box $P(x, y, w, h)$, the number of fusion samples $N_{fus}$, the number of negative samples $N_{neg}$, the number of positive samples $N_{pos}$, and interpolation strength parameter $\alpha$.

1: Generate candidate samples around $P(x, y, w, h)$ using Gaussian distribution in $M$
2: Calculate IoU for all candidate samples with ground truth
3: Choose $N_{pos}$ positive samples when IoU > 0.7
4: Choose $N_{neg}$ negative samples when IoU < 0.3
5: **for** $n = 0$ to $N_{fus}$ **do**
6:     Random choose positive sample $(x_1, y_1)$ and negative sample $(x_2, y_2)$ from the corresponding sample set, respectively
7:     $\lambda = Beta(\alpha, \alpha)$
8:     $\tilde{x} = \lambda x_1 + (1.-\lambda)x_2$
9:     $\tilde{y} = \lambda y_1 + (1.-\lambda)y_2$
10:    Obtain fusion sample $(\tilde{x}, \tilde{y})$
11: **end for**
12: Obtain $N_{fus}$ fusion samples
13: Loss = $\lambda$*criterion(outputs, $y_1$) + $(1 - \lambda)$*criterion(outputs, $y_2$)

---

The $\alpha \in (0, \infty)$ controls the interpolation between feature-target pairs and generates weight $\lambda$ from Beta distribution. Finally, we measure the loss function separately for the labels of the two samples, then perform a weighted sum of the loss functions using the weight $\lambda$. The results of the experiment show that data fusion can significantly boost the model's robustness.

**Joint Update** The proposed strategy is motivated by the fact that tracking methods use classification confidence (CC) and regression confidence (RC) separately, which cannot represent the bounding box positioning accuracy. Since RC and CC are not mutually exclusive, current tracking methods can only solve high CC with high RC, but not the other three types: low CC with low RC, high CC with low RC, or low CC with high RC.

To solve this problem, a joint judgment strategy is designed based on [24]. The final prediction result has both higher classification and regression confidences through a joint analysis of classification and regression confidence. We assume the bounding box is a Gaussian distribution $P_\Theta(x) = \frac{1}{2\pi\sigma^2}e^{-\frac{(x-x_e)^2}{2\sigma^2}}$, and the ground truth bounding box is a Dirac delta distribution $P_D(x) = \delta(x - x_g)$. The KL divergence is used to measure the asymmetry of two probability distributions. The position problem is converted to minimize the KL divergence between $P_D(x)$ and $P_\Theta(x)$, the closer the KL divergence is to 0, the more similar the two probability distributions are, which is shown as follows:

$$\hat{\Theta} = \underset{\Theta}{argmin}\, D_{KL}(P_D(x)\|P_\Theta(x)) \tag{5.9}$$

where the KL divergence transforms the bounding box into a Gaussian distribution that is closer to the ground truth. Regression trust is defined as the IoU of the expected bounding box. The candidate bounding boxes within the threshold IoU will be averaged based on their neighbor bounding boxes to obtain the final bounding box, which will increase the bounding box's accuracy even more. As an example, consider the new $x1$ object location for the $i$th box $x1_i$.

$$x1_i := \frac{\sum_j x1_j/\sigma^2_{x1,j}}{\sum_j 1/\sigma^2_{x1,j}} \tag{5.10}$$

Where the final bounding box is obtained with a higher RC and CC. We can effectively solve the three situations described above by combining the RC and the CC. Furthermore, based on the predicted neighbor bounding boxes, a more accurate final bounding box will be created, which can reduce object loss due to interference information and improve the model's robustness in complex scenes.

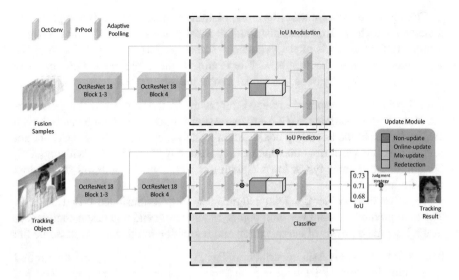

**Fig. 5.15** The framework of the proposed frequency-aware feature (FAF)

## 5.3.3   Framework and Procedure

The optimized ResNet18 obtains two-way frequency-aware features from fusion samples for the offline training level, as shown in Fig. 5.15, where the shallow layer feature contains position information and the deep layer feature contains semantic information, and the related features are used to learn the scale and position of the target. The conv and pooling layers are used to boost the features' discrimination ability. The IoU modulation is trained offline and without updates during online monitoring on massive video and image datasets.

The first frame of the object based on data fusion will be used to initialize the IoU predictor and the classifier module for the online tracking point. Unlike the offline level, the IoU predictor will get two-way features from IoU modulation: related frame guidance features and aim features from the current frame. The IoU predictor and classifier will then return the object's IoU and classification scores in the current frame. Finally, the proposed joint decision approach would make a final forecast based on scores and use the update module to update the IoU predictor and classifier.

## 5.3.4   Experimental Results and Discussions

The proposed method is written in Python and runs at 45 frames per second on a PC with a 4-core 4.2 GHz Intel 8700k CPU and two NVIDIA 2080 Ti GPUs with 11 GB of memory. The pre-training datasets are TrackingNet, OxUvA, and LaSOT, and the network parameters are the same for all assessment datasets. All hyperparameters are set in accordance with previous research. The following are the training parameters: We freeze all weights during preparation for the backbone network. The weight decay for the network is 0.00005, and the momentum is 0.9. We use the mean-squared error loss function and train for 40 epochs with 64 image pairs per batch. The ADAM optimizer is employed with an initial learning rate of $10^{-3}$ and using a factor 0.2 decay every epoch. The experiments are carefully designed based on the same protocols and parameters.

**Evaluation on OTB100**   The proposed FAF is first evaluated on a famous benchmark dataset OTB100 dataset. Eight state-of-the-art trackers are compared with the proposed method, including ECO, MDNet, ATOM [25], DeepSRDCF [26], CF2 [27], HDT [28], and KCF [29]. These methods include CF-based methods, deep learning-based methods, and reinforcement learning-based methods.

On the OTB100, the monitoring results of state-of-the-art approaches during one-pass evaluation (OPE). The proposed FAF has high precision and performance rates, as shown in Fig. 5.16. As compared to the state-of-the-art real-time tracker ATOM with 30 FPS, our tracker achieves precision and success rates of 90.1% and 67.3%, respectively, which are 1.9% and 1.4% higher than ATOM. KCF has a handcraft feature and can monitor at a rate of 160 frames per second. However,

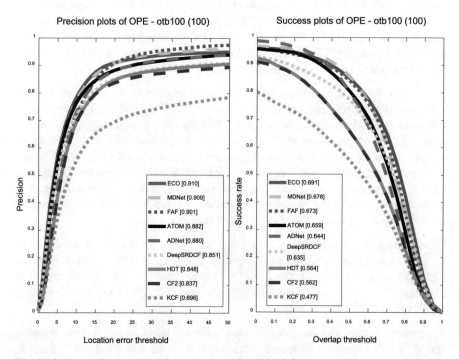

**Fig. 5.16**   The precision and success rate plots on the OTB100 dataset are performed using the one pass evaluation (OPE) method. The proposed method performs well compared to state-of-the-art methods

**Table 5.2** The accuracy and speed of the proposed method depend on $\alpha$. The best results are in bold

|      | 0     | 0.5   | 1         | 10    | $\infty$ |
|------|-------|-------|-----------|-------|----------|
| Pre. | 0.875 | 0.886 | **0.901** | 0.891 | 0.883    |
| Suc. | 0.654 | 0.660 | **0.673** | 0.664 | 0.659    |
| FPS  | **48**| 45    | 45        | 45    | **48**   |

**Table 5.3** Ablation results of the FAF on the OTB100, which shows the effectiveness of each component of the proposed method. The best results are in bold

|      | Baseline | I     | I+II  | I+II+III  |
|------|----------|-------|-------|-----------|
| Pre. | 0.882    | 0.887 | 0.893 | **0.901** |
| AUC  | 0.659    | 0.662 | 0.667 | **0.673** |
| FPS  | 30       | 30    | **45**| **45**    |

tracking accuracy suffers as a result of the poor discrimination ability. Both ECO and MDNet use deep models with optimization to improve tracking efficiency, but they are unable to meet real-time tracking requirements. In addition, our tracker outperforms them in both speed and accuracy in the following datasets experiments.

**Ablation Analysis** We compare different alpha values on the OTB100 dataset to see how alpha affects accuracy and speed. We only increase positive or negative samples, as shown in Table 5.2, and no mixup samples are obtained when alpha is 0 or $\infty$. Without a mixup phase, the tracker speed will be increased. When alpha = 1, the tracker performs better. On precision and AUC frequencies, it improves by 0.015 and 0.013 as compared to alpha = 0.5. When alpha = 1, samples are hard samples for mixup, which can help the qualified model be more resilient.

To demonstrate the effectiveness of each component in the proposed method FAF, ablation experiments are performed on OTB-2015. The baseline means the original model without any optimization, "**I**" means the baseline with pre-training sample fusion optimization, and "**I+II**" denotes the baseline with both pre-training sample fusion and frequency-aware feature optimizations. For the version of the full components, "**I+II+III**" denotes the complete model with all pre-training sample fusion, frequency-aware feature, and joint judgment strategy optimizations. The performances of all those variations are shown in Table 5.3, and every component can improve the performance of the proposed method.

**Pre-training Sample Fusion** Pre-training sample fusion increases the diversity of samples and improves the model's ability to learn proximity relations between groups, which can improve the model's discrimination ability without incurring additional costs. The findings show that precision and AUC rates have increased by 1.1% and 0.8%, respectively.

**Frequency-Aware Feature** The frequency-aware functionality boosts tracking speed by 1.5 times and increases precision and AUC rates by 2.0% and 2.2%, respectively. Since we decompose the layer function into high-frequency and low-frequency components, compress the redundant low-frequency component,

**Table 5.4** Comparison with state-of-the-art trackers on the VOT 2018 dataset. The results are presented in terms of expected average overlap (EAO), accuracy value (A), and robustness value (R). The best and second results are in red and blue, respectively

|     | SiamRPN++ | ATOM | UPDT | DaSiamRPN | DRT [30] | FAF |
|-----|-----------|------|------|-----------|----------|-----|
| EAO | 0.414 | 0.401 | 0.378 | 0.383 | 0.356 | 0.422 |
| R   | 0.234 | 0.204 | 0.184 | 0.276 | 0.201 | 0.179 |
| A   | 0.6 | 0.59 | 0.536 | 0.586 | 0.519 | 0.597 |
| FPS | 35 | 30 | – | 160 | – | 45 |

and splice it into multi-frequency components in a novel way. The frequency-aware feature will eliminate redundancies in low-frequency feature calculations and boost the proposed model's feature discrimination capacity without raising model complexity.

**Joint Update** Finally, the joint decision approach is proposed to achieve a more reliable goal location by taking into account both classification and regression outcomes. The precision and AUC rates have increased by 0.7% and 0.6%, respectively, as shown in Table 5.3.

**State-of-the-Art Comparison** We compare our tracker FAF with state-of-the-art methods on four challenging tracking datasets.

**VOT2018** VOT2018 consists of 60 test video sequences, with the overall output rating determined by failure rate (R), average overlap (A), and Expected Average Overlap (EAO). For contrast, we use short-term monitoring experiments with cutting-edge approaches. We equate our approach to the top five methods in the VOT2018 dataset, as shown in Table 5.4. Although maintaining a competitive A ranking, our system achieves the highest R and EAO ratings. Only SiamRPN++ achieves a 0.003 higher accuracy score than the proposed method among the top trackers. In comparison to ATOM, our approach improves EAO, R, and A scores by 2.1%, 2.5%, and 0.7%, respectively.

**GOT10K** GOT10K contains over 10,000 video sequences and over 1.5 million target frames, all of which are manually annotated. The dataset is divided into 563 target categories based on five categories: animals, man-made things, humans, natural scenery, and component. The model is trained using only the GOT10K dataset, and 180 test video sequences are used to evaluate FAF's output using five state-of-the-art methods. Table 5.5 shows the results. FAF has the highest AUC, precision (0.5), and precision (0.75) rates, with 0.581, 0.453, and 0.672. Compared with non-real-time methods ECO and MDNet, the proposed method achieves huge improvements in all three evaluation indexes.

**TrackingNet** TrackingNet splits the original 23 categories into 27 categories using the video sequences in Youtube-BB. The video sequence is automatically divided into 15 attributes and visually examined. Mark missed goal boxes with the DCF

**Table 5.5** Comparison with the state-of-the-art trackers on the GOT10K dataset. The results are presented in terms of precision (0.5), precision (0.75), and robustness value (R). The best and second results are in red and blue, respectively

|            | ATOM  | SiamFC | ECO   | MDNet | CCOT  | FAF   |
|------------|-------|--------|-------|-------|-------|-------|
| Pre.(0.5)  | 0.634 | 0.404  | 0.309 | 0.303 | 0.328 | 0.672 |
| Pre.(0.75) | 0.402 | 0.144  | 0.111 | 0.099 | 0.104 | 0.453 |
| AUC        | 0.556 | 0.374  | 0.316 | 0.299 | 0.325 | 0.581 |
| FPS        | 30    | 80     | 8     | 1     | 1     | 45    |

**Table 5.6** Comparison with state-of-the-art trackers on the TrackingNet dataset. The results are presented in terms of precision, normal.precision, and AUC. The best and second results are in red and blue, respectively

|           | ATOM  | GFS-DCF [31] | UDT [32] | C-RPN | CACF  | FAF   |
|-----------|-------|--------------|----------|-------|-------|-------|
| Pre.      | 0.648 | 0.566        | 0.557    | 0.619 | 0.536 | 0.667 |
| Norn.Pre. | 0.771 | 0.718        | 0.702    | 0.749 | 0.467 | 0.786 |
| AUC       | 0.703 | 0.609        | 0.611    | 0.669 | 0.608 | 0.727 |
| FPS       | 30    | 8            | 55       | 32    | 35    | 44    |

tracker. For the preparation, there are 12 chunks of 2511 sequences and one chunk of 511 sequences. The results are described in Table 5.6 in terms of precision, normalized precision, and AUC. C-RPN scores 0.619, 0.749, and 0.669 in terms of precision, normalized precision, and AUC, respectively. In terms of precision, the proposed method FAF outperforms the second method ATOM by 1.9%, 1.5%, and 2.4%, respectively. The proposed method FAF outperforms the second method ATOM with 1.9%, 1.5%, and 2.4% in terms of precision, normalized precision, and AUC rates, respectively.

**LaSOT** With an average video length of 2512 frames, LaSOT gathers 1400 sequences and 3.52 million frames from YouTube videos. It has 70 categories, each with 20 sequences; the training subset has 1120 videos with 2.83 million frames, and the test subset has 280 sequences with 690,000 frames. On a test dataset with 280 sequences, we compare the proposed approach to five state-of-the-art methods. Table 5.7 shows the findings in terms of normalized precision and success. With AUC and precision scores of 0.537 and 0.601, FAF is the best of the state-of-the-art methods. Compared with SiamRPN++, our method significantly improves the AUC and precision rates by 4.1% and 3.2%, respectively.

**Failure Case Analysis** The first row is the Singer2 sequence, and the second row is the Tran sequence, as shown in Fig. 5.17. On those two sequences, the proposed approach fails miserably. The goal and context are too close in the Singer2 series. The proposed approach fails to differentiate between them correctly, resulting in the target being missed. During the monitoring phase of the Tran sequence, the target's

**Table 5.7** Comparison with state-of-the-art trackers on the LaSOT dataset. The results are presented in terms of precision and AUC. The best and second results are in red and blue, respectively

|      | GradNet [33] | ATOM  | SiamRPN++ [4] | SPM [34] | C-RPN | FAF   |
|------|--------------|-------|---------------|----------|-------|-------|
| Pre. | 0.351        | 0.576 | 0.569         | 0.471    | 0.459 | 0.601 |
| AUC  | 0.365        | 0.515 | 0.496         | 0.485    | 0.455 | 0.537 |
| FPS  | 80           | 30    | 35            | 120      | 32    | 44    |

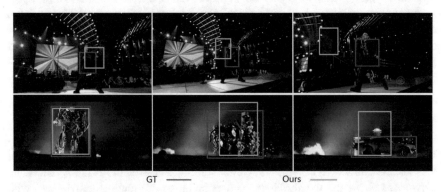

GT ——          Ours ——

**Fig. 5.17** Failure case analysis. The red and green bounding boxes are the ground truth and results of the proposed method, respectively

size and appearance changed dramatically. During the sudden and drastic shift of the target, our tracker does not correctly learn the target characteristics, resulting in the target being lost. We will try to design a size-aware module and use handcraft features to solve those problems in future work.

## 5.4  Improved Generative Adversarial Network Based Visual Object Tracking

Accuracy and speed are two indicators of the tracking algorithm. However, it is difficult for many tracking algorithms based on deep networks to strike a balance between these two indicators. MDNet [35] and VITAL[36] are typical detection and tracking algorithms that apply deep learning technology. They have achieved excellent tracking accuracy on mainstream benchmark datasets, but the running speed of these algorithms cannot meet real-time requirements. In this section, we propose an improved real-time visual tracking algorithm based on the MDNet model using adversarial learning to obtain a more balanced result in accuracy and tracking speed.

### 5.4.1  Improved Adversarial Learning Strategy

The Generative Adversarial Network[37] was proposed in 2014. It is a neural network model that includes a generative network G (generator) and a discriminant network D (discriminator). Generating adversarial networks does not require a large amount of labelled data in advance and can train models on unlabelled datasets. Specifically, the generator G obtains the noise vector z from the distribution $P_z(z)$ as input and output G(z). The discriminator D takes G(z) or real data x as input and outputs the classification probability. In model training, the generator and discriminator will update their parameters to minimize the loss, which is a minimax process. The objective function of GAN is defined as:

$$L = \min_{G} \max_{D} V(D, G) = E_{(x \sim p_{data}(x)}[\log D(x)] +$$

$$E_{(z \sim p_z(z)}[\log(1 - D(G(z)))]$$

(5.11)

Inspired by Song et al. [36], we introduce $G$ between the feature extraction and the classifier, as shown in Fig. 5.19. Define the characteristic of the input generating network as $F$. We use the introduced $G$ to generate a deformation matrix $G(F)$ with the same scale. These deformation matrices act on the feature map to represent the change in the target's appearance to enhance the data. Under the action of adversarial learning, $G$ will gradually identify the matrices that may cause the classifier to judge errors, which means that the template learned by $G$ can identify features with strong discriminative power. The matrix identifies the discriminative feature as $T$. Since the existence of $G$ continuously interferes with $D$, $D$ will not overfit the discriminative features of a specific frame.

Sample imbalance is a very common situation in actual scenarios and has a significant impact on the model's performance. In this section, sample imbalance means that the number of simple samples is much larger than the number of hard samples. Specifically, simple samples are those that are easy to identify. In fact, only a part of these samples is enough in the training process, which is of little significance to model training. Too many simple samples will dominate the training direction. There are many ways to deal with sample imbalance, such as undersampling, oversampling, and threshold adjustment. Focus loss focuses on solving the serious imbalance between positive and negative samples in one-stage target detection. This function reduces the weight of a large number of negative samples in training. We combine the focus loss idea with the objective function of the adversarial generative network and introduce modulation factors $\lambda_1$ and $\lambda_2$ to adjust the loss weights of positive and negative samples. We define the objective function as:

$$L_{GAN} = \min_{G} \max_{D} E_{(F,T) \sim P(F,T)}[\lambda_1 \cdot \log D(T \cdot F)]$$

$$+ E_{F \sim P(F)}[\lambda_2 \cdot \log(1 - D(G(F) \cdot F))]$$

(5.12)

$\lambda_1 = (1 - D(T \cdot F))^2$ and $\lambda_2 = D((G(F) \cdot F))^2$ are the modulating factors to balance the loss of training samples. In the section, we consider the loss of sample information generated by the generator, that is, the loss of Euclidean distance between the features generated by the adversarial learning and the real samples' features to ensure that the generated features are similar to the real features. The information loss is defined as:

$$L_{INF} = |G(F) \cdot F - F| \tag{5.13}$$

so we reformulate the objective function as:

$$L = L_{GAN} + \alpha L_{INF} \tag{5.14}$$

In order to adapt to changes in the target state and better deal with model drift, our update strategy is to use long-term and short-term updates to maintain the robustness and stability of the model. The long-term update refers to updating the network within a fixed period of time, while the short-term update refers to updating the network when the target score is below a fixed threshold. Therefore, we use the target score to judge whether the target state is stable and adaptively update the network. First, set $t_0 = 5$ as the detection period of the target state, and then calculate the evaluation index C of the target state in the target detection period. A large number of experiments have proved that as the target state tends to be stable, the smaller the C value, the more unstable the target state. The calculation formula of C is defined as:

$$C = \frac{1}{t_0} \sum_{i=1}^{t_0} (S_{t-i} - \hat{S})^2 \tag{5.15}$$

according to the above formula, $S_i$ is the score obtained by tracking the target in the $i_{th}$ frame, $\hat{S}$ is the average score obtained from the target during the detection of the current frame. When the state of the moving target is less than the fixed threshold $C_0$, it means that the state of the moving target is stable, and the network model does not need to be updated frequently. When the state of the moving target is greater than the fixed threshold $C_0$, it means that the state of the moving target has changed significantly, and the model needs to be trained in time update. When $C_0$ is set to be less than 0.6, the model update frequency is fast, and the model is easy to drift. When $C_0$ is greater than 0.6, the accuracy of the tracking result is significantly reduced, so we set $C_0 = 0.6$.

## 5.4.2   Precise ROI Pooling for Faster Feature Extraction

Fast-RCNN [38] uses RoIPooling to improve the speed of feature extraction, but this technique requires two quantization operations and cannot effectively locate

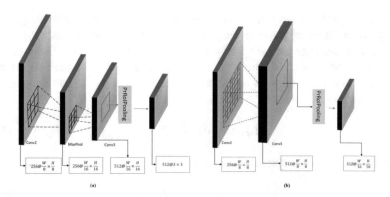

**Fig. 5.18** The schematic diagram of network model modification. (**a**) Original VGG-M network. (**b**) Improved network

the target. In order to solve this problem, RoIWrap Pooling and RoIAlign Pooling respectively reduce the number of quantization operations and completely remove the quantization operations, but there are limitations. RT-MDNet [1] proposed Adaptive RoIAlign so that the value of dividing the sub-region N is not a fixed value. However, this method has the limitation for target localization at the high precision area.

This work adds the Precise ROI Pooling(PrRoIPooling) [39] layer to the tracking-by-detection framework [36]. Figure 5.18 is an example of using the PrRoIPooling layer to extract candidate targets from the feature map. This work uses a PrRoIPooling layer after the Conv3 layer of the MDNet network to extract a fixed-size feature map for each candidate box. And delete the Maxpooling layer behind the second convolutional layer of the MDNet network model, and use the hole convolution with the rate $r = 3$ in the third convolutional layer to improve the receptive field of the model to obtain a high-resolution and rich feature mapping of semantic information and the improvement of the representation ability of feature maps. The comparison between the modified network model and the original VGG-M network model is shown in Fig. 5.18.

The feature aggregation algorithm based on PrRROIPooling avoids any quantization operation of coordinates. Given a feature graph F, let $(i, j)$ be the coordinates on the feature graph and $w_{i,j}$ be the pixel values corresponding to the feature graph $(i, j)$. According to the bilinear interpolation method, discrete feature maps can be considered as continuous at any continuous coordinate $(x, y)$:

$$f(x, y) = \sum_{i,j} IC(x, y, i, j) \times w_{i,j} \tag{5.16}$$

$$IC(x, y, i, j) = max(0, 1 - |x - i|) \times max(0, 1 - |y - j|) \tag{5.17}$$

where $IC(x, y, i, j)$ is the interpolation coefficient, calculate the product of the offset of each successive x and y direction, and express the bin of the candidate region as $bin = \{(x_1, y_1), (x_2, y_2)\}$, the coordinates of the upper left and lower right corners of the rectangular box are $(x_1, y_1)$, $(x_2, y_2)$.

$$Proipooling = \frac{\int_{y_1}^{y_2} \int_{x_1}^{x_2} f(x, y)dxdy}{(x_2 - x_1) \times (y_2 - y_1)} \tag{5.18}$$

The PrRoIPooling uses bilinear interpolation to map discrete feature map data to continuous space, then utilizes double integration and then averages to achieve pooling as shown in Eq. 5.18, which can extract more accurate targets and candidate targets from the feature map. Compared with the RoI Align method, PrRoIPooling solves the problem that the value of N (the number of divided subregions) is difficult to adapt. According to the above formula, the coordinates of $Proipooling(bin, f)$ for bin region are continuously differentiable, and the partial derivative of $Proipooling(bin, f)$ to $x_1$ is as follows:

$$\frac{\partial Proipooling(bin, F)}{\partial x_1} = \frac{Proipooling(bin, F)}{x_2 - x_1} - \frac{\int_{y_1}^{y_2} f(x, y)dy}{(x_2 - x_1) \times (y_2 - y_1)} \tag{5.19}$$

### 5.4.3   Framework and Procedure

The architecture of our network is illustrated in Fig. 5.19. Our network structure is based on the MDNet [35] network structure improvement and receives a $107 \times 107$ RGB input to get a fixed size feature map after convolution. It mainly includes

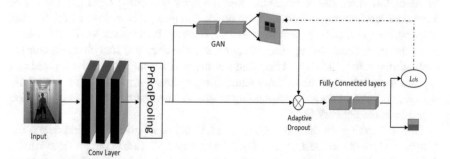

**Fig. 5.19** The network architecture of our proposed algorithm. The network is composed of three convolutional layers for extracting a shared feature map, the PrRoIPooling layer for obtaining specific features and pooling to a fixed size, the generation network for enhancing positive samples, and three fully connected layers for binary classification

three convolutional layers (con1–3), a PrRoIPooling layer for extracting features of each ROI, and three fully connected layers (fc4–fc6). Simultaneously, we introduced a generative network between the last convolutional layer and the first fully connected layer to enhance the positive samples in the feature space. Specifically, the convolution method of the third convolution layer is changed to dilated convolution to increase the convolution field so that each convolution output contains a larger range of information.

---

**Algorithm 6:** Real-time object tracking based on improved adversarial learning

---

**Input:** The pre-trained network model, the position $b_1$ and scale $s_1$ of the initial target $x_1$.
**Output:** The position $b_t$ and scale $s_t$ of the current target $x_t$.
 1: Initialize the parameters of the last fully connected layer, establish long-term training
    sample set $T_{long}$ and short-term training sample set $T_{short}$.
 2: Train a bounding box regression model
 3: Extract positive sample $S_1^+$ and negative sample $S_1^-$ to train the classifier.
 4: **for** $t = 2$ to $N_f$ **do**
 5:    The candidate sample $x_t$ is extracted according to the tracking result $x_{t-1}$ of the
      previous frame.
 6:    **if** $f(x_t^*) > 0.5$ **then**
 7:       Extract the positive sample $S_t^+$ and negative sample $S_t^-$ of the current frame $x_t$, and
        update the training sample set $T_{long}$ and $T_{short}$.
 8:    **end if**
 9:    **if** $C > C_0$ ‖ t mod 10 == 0 **then**
10:       Use the training sample $T_{long}$ and $T_{short}$ to update the network parameters.
11:    **end if**
12: **end for**

---

Model initialization. The model is initialized in two steps in series. In the first stage, the positive and negative samples in the training dataset are used to pre-train the network model offline. In the second stage, samples are sampled from the first frame of the video image sequence, and the fully connected layer parameters of the model are fine-tuned online. In the online training process, firstly initialize the discriminator D randomly, and then use the tracking benchmark VOT [20], which annotates each frame for lighting changes, motion changes, size changes, camera motion, occlusion, etc. By adding feature maps, G's goal is to make a matrix to capture these changes. Select annotated image pairs before and after a specific change, and obtain their corresponding features. Then calculate the loss function to pre-train the network G.

Online tracking. In this process, network G is not involved. We first delete the generator G, then sample around the predicted target position in the previous frame, then put the samples into the network for forwarding propagation, and finally obtain the predicted target position according to the discriminator D.

Model update. When the tracking failure is detected, the short-term update is performed in the same way as in MDNet to update the network, and the target state evaluation index $C_0$ is used to assist the network model for long-term tracking.

## 5.4.4  Experimental Results and Discussions

In this section, we conduct ablation studies from two perspectives: (1) We investigate the use of PrRoIPooling to obtain more accurate feature extraction results. (2) To demonstrate the effectiveness of our proposed objective function. Then we compare our tracker with state-of-the-art trackers on the benchmark datasets OTB-2013 and OTB-2015 for performance evaluation. Our implementation is based on PyTorch and runs on a PC with an i9-9900K CPU and a GeForce RTX 2080ti GPU.

We use a similar network architecture as in [35] to develop our baseline tracker. We trained our model on ImageNetVid [40], which is a large-scale video dataset for object detection for offline pretraining of the model. For online pretraining, we train D first and then G. Specifically, when training D, after feature F is extracted, F is input into G to generate a deformation matrix. The deformation matrix is applied to F and sent to classifier D for classifier learning. Since G is random in the initial state, initially G generates a random deformation matrix based on F. After D training, given the input picture, randomly generated multiple deformation matrices to interfere with the features of the input picture, then use D to discriminate the features of the interference map, choose the matrix with the largest loss, and set this matrix to T in the Eq. 5.14. The learning rate for training G and D are $10^{-3}$ and $10^{-4}$. During online tracking, the pre-trained network is fine-tuned on the first frame of each test video. Furthermore, calculate C according to formula Eq. 5.15, and compare C with a fixed threshold to assist in the long-term update of the network model.

**Ablation Studies**  We perform several ablation studies to demonstrate the effectiveness of individual components in our tracking algorithm.

**Performance Evaluation of ProRoIPooling**  This work introduces the PrRoIPooling technique to extract more accurate and investigate how the PrRoIPooling technique contributes to the quality of our tracking algorithm. In this experiment, we use RoIAlign, AdaptiveRoIAlign, and PrRoIPooling for feature extraction. We present several options to extract target representations in Fig. 5.20, which depend on the choice among RoIAlign, Adaptive RoIAlign, and PrRoIPooling. The success rate and Precision rate of the tracking algorithm based on PrROIPooling are 65.2% and 89.0%, respectively. The results show that the PrRoIPooling layer we introduced makes a meaningful contribution to tracking performance improvement.

**Performance Evaluation of Improved Objective Function**  In order to verify the effectiveness of the introduction of the adversarial learning module, the baseline algorithm is implemented using the standard cross-entropy loss without introducing the adversarial learning module. Second, we introduce the adversarial learning module on the Baseline algorithm to train the network. Finally, we use the improved objective function to train the network. Experiment with the above three methods and the results are shown in Fig. 5.21. The success rate and accuracy of the algorithm using the adversarial learning module and the improved objective function

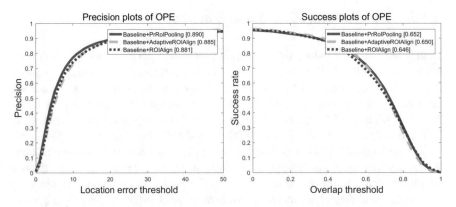

**Fig. 5.20** The result of comparison between using different regional feature aggregation algorithms

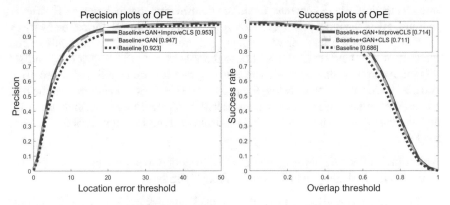

**Fig. 5.21** The precision and success plots on the OTB-2013 dataset using the one-pass evaluation

to train the network are 71.4% and 95.3%, respectively, compared with the other two algorithms Compared with the best tracking performance, the introduction of the adversarial learning module to train the network can suppress the most discriminative features in a single video frame and utilize the most robust features in the video sequence.

Experiment results show that the proposed objective function, PrROIPooling, and GAN are helpful to improve the experimental performance.

We follow the standard benchmark protocols on the OTB-2013 and OTB-2015 datasets. We use the one-pass evaluation (OPE) with precision and success plot metrics. The two plots are generated by computing ratios of successfully tracked frames at a set of different thresholds in the two metrics. The precision metric measures the center pixel distance between the predicted locations and the ground truth annotations. The threshold distance is set as 20 pixels. The success plot metric

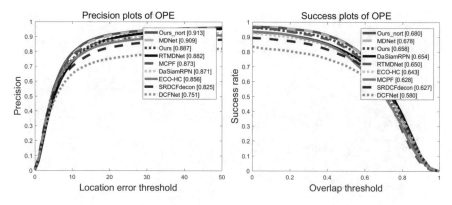

**Fig. 5.22**  The precision and success plots of OPE in OTB-2015

is used to measure the overlap between the predicted bounding box and the ground truth annotations.

**Evaluation on OTB-2015 Dataset**  OTB-2015 [11] is a popular tracking benchmark that contains 100 sequences. The evaluation is based on two metrics: success and precision plot. The precision plot shows the percentage of frames that the tracking results are within 20 pixels from the target. The success plot shows the ratios of successful frames when the threshold varies from 0 to 1, where a successful frame means its overlap is larger than the given threshold. The area under curve (AUC) of the success plot is used to rank the tracking algorithm. The one-pass evaluation (OPE) is employed to compare our algorithm with several state-of-the-art models: ECO [41], VITAL [36], MDNet [35], DaSiamRPN [42], RTMDNet [1], ECO-HC [41], SRDCFdecon [43], DCFNet [44], SINT [45], Staple [46], KCF [47], DLSSVM [48], DSST [13]. For presentation clarity, we only show the top 10 trackers.

Figure 5.22 is a comparison of the tracking results of the success rate and precision rate of each algorithm on the OTB-2015 dataset. Ours_nort algorithm is a non-real-time implementation of the algorithm in this section introduces an adversarial learning module based on the MDNet algorithm. As shown in Fig. 5.22, the success rate and precision rate of the Ours_nort algorithm are 68.0% and 91.3%, which are 0.2% and 0.4% higher than the MDNet algorithm in success rate and precision rate, respectively. The success rate and precision rate of the real-time target tracking algorithm we proposed are 65.8% and 88.7%, respectively, which are 0.8% and 0.5% higher than the RTMDNet algorithm. The mask generated by adversarial learning can capture the changes in the appearance of moving targets and maintain robust features over a long time sequence. Compared with the ECO-HC, MCPF, SRDCFdecon, and DCFNet algorithms, the success rate is 1.5%, 3.0%, 3.1%, 7.8% higher, and the accuracy is 3.1%, 1.4%, 6.2%, 13.6% higher. The tracking performance of the real-time target tracking algorithm based on improved adversarial learning is significantly improved. In order to further verify the

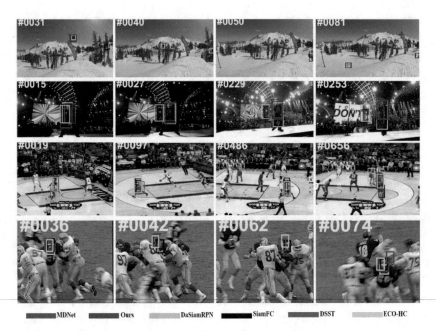

**Fig. 5.23** The qualitative results of our proposed tracker with five state-of-the-art trackers in different video sequences

performance of the proposed algorithm, the proposed algorithm and MDNet [35], DaSiamRPN [42], SiamFC [8], DSST [13], ECO-HC [41] are qualitatively analyzed on OTB-2015 dataset. Figure 5.23 shows the qualitative results of the tracker proposed in this section and the other five advanced trackers on five different video sequences on the OTB-2015 dataset. As shown in Fig. 5.23, our proposed algorithm and MDNet algorithm can accurately locate the tracked target in challenging scenes such as size change, deformation, plane rotation, background confusion, and motion blur, while other trackers have difficulty coping with these complex changes at the same time.

**Evaluation on OTB-2013 Dataset** The experimental comparison results of the target tracking algorithm proposed in this section and other algorithms on the OTB-2013 dataset on the success rate and accuracy are shown in Fig. 5.24. On the OTB-2013 dataset, the success rate and accuracy of the Ours_nort algorithm are 71.4% and 95.3%, respectively, which are 0.6 and 0.5% higher than the MDNet algorithm in success rate and accuracy, respectively. The success rate and accuracy of the real-time target tracking algorithm proposed in this section are 68.0% and 91.8%, respectively. Compared with the MCPF, CCOT, SINT, and DCFNet algorithms, the tracking performance is significantly improved.

In this section, a real-time object tracking model based on adversarial learning is proposed. Initially, this algorithm accelerates the feature extraction procedure and extracts a more precise representation of targets by introducing PrRoIPooling. In

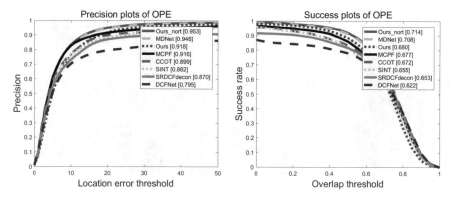

**Fig. 5.24**  The precision and success plots of OPE in OTB-2013

addition, GAN is introduced into the multi-domain learning tracking algorithm to enhance sample diversity and prevent model overfitting. Meanwhile, this algorithm uses the improved objective function to reduce the impact of easy negative samples. The proposed algorithm is evaluated on the public visual tracking benchmark datasets, and our method performs favorably against state-of-the-art approaches. Especially, extensive experiments prove that the proposed method can effectively real-time track vehicles in complex scenes.

## 5.5   Improved Policy-Based Reinforcement Learning Based Visual Object Tracking

In this section, we propose a robust RL-based tracker AEVRNet. The tracking framework is shown in Fig. 5.25, which is divided into three stages: (1) off-line supervised training, (2) off-line RL training, and (3) online tracking. For the first stage, an initial model is trained with supervised learning based on non-convex optimization, and we obtain the supervised trained model. For the second stage, non-convex optimization, regression, and adaptive exploration methods train the supervised trained model and obtain an online tracking model. The offline training process is based on ALOV300 [49] dataset, which is the same as ADNet. For the third stage, with the background and bounding box of the previous frame, our tracker will predict the location and scale of the object in the current frame by adaptive exploration, and the tracker will be updated continuously. The model structure and the tracking problem definition based on reinforcement learning will be introduced in the following.

**Problem Definition**  Considering object tracking as a sequential decision problem, we achieve reinforcement learning by introducing the Markov decision process (MDP) to define the tracking problem. MDP consists of four major entities: action,

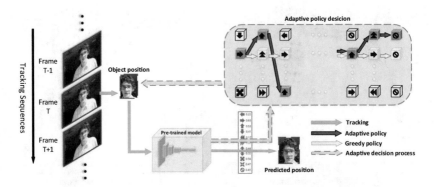

**Fig. 5.25** The online tracking framework of our proposed tracker AEVRNet. Assume default greedy search yields the policy plan along the direction of light blue arrows. The red arrows show the adaptive exploration policy decision

state, state transition function, reward, and the four entities can be specified as follows. Action is defined by the change of bounding boxes involving 11 object move actions (i.e., left, right, up, down, double left, double right, double up, and double down), scale changes (scale up and scale down), and stop. Each action is encoded by one 11-dimensional vector with a one-hot form. The information within the bounding box describes the state. The state transition function is formulated with horizontal and vertical change. According to the prediction action, the tracker will move the target bounding box according to a new position. Different from the existing RL-based trackers using simple strategies to build action space, we innovatively design an adaptive exploration strategy combined with temporal and spatial information to enhance the exploration of our tracker, which can successfully escape local optima.

**Tracking Model Structure** In the proposed tracking framework, we follow the famous object tracking model structure. As shown in Fig. 5.25 the backbone structure is designed with three convolutional layers of VGG-M and two fully-connected layers with ReLU activation. The last layer is connected to a vector consisting of action probabilities and confidence scores. In order to further improve the training convergence speed and model accuracy of RL-trackers training methods, we innovatively propose non-convex optimized SVRG as backward propagation to relieve local optima problem for tracking problem. Moreover, an action-reward loss function is designed with regression to train AEVRNet, which honors Intersection Over Union (IoU) between the estimation and ground truth bounding boxes. Unlike existing RL-based trackers using classification, regression is more sensitive to the target states, such as the width and height of the target. The model can learn more scale change information and reduce target loss caused by extra interference information, which can further improve the accuracy of the proposed tracker. The main contributions and details are described as follows.

### 5.5.1 Non-Convex Optimized Variance Reduced Backward Propagation

Supervised learning for object tracking problem can be formulated into composite optimization problem:

$$\min_{x \in \mathbb{R}} F(x) \triangleq f(x) + g(x) \qquad (5.20)$$

where $f(x)$ is a smooth function and $g(x)$ is referred to as regularizer. Currently, majority of tracking problems are solved by SGD method with the backward propagation as Eq. 5.21, where $\theta$ is model parameter, $B$ denotes mini-batch, $g$ is regularier, $\eta$ is learning rate, and $t$ refers to update iteration.

$$\theta_{t+1} = \theta_t - \eta_t [\frac{1}{B} \sum_{i=1}^{B} \nabla f_i(\theta_t) + \nabla g(\theta_t)]. \qquad (5.21)$$

However, SGD usually takes much time to converge because of the large variance of $\nabla f_i(\theta_t)$ during random sampling [50]. In order to improve the accuracy and efficiency of our proposed AEVRNet, a non-convex SVRG backward propagation is introduced instead of SGD as shown in Eq. 5.23.

Supposing the current training epoch is $s$, and we will develop a snapshot for the model parameters obtained from the last training epoch $\theta^{s-1}$. Given the current sampled data $i$, the previous gradient $\nabla f_i(\theta^{s-1})$ is calculated based on the snapshot model parameters and the average gradient $\hat{\mu}$ across all data in one epoch is calculated with the snapshot model parameters. The difference between them is used to adjust the currently calculated gradient, thus reducing model updating variance, shown in Eq. 5.24.

$$\theta_{t+1} = \theta_t - \eta_t \cdot [\hat{\mu} + \frac{1}{B} \sum_{i=1}^{B} (\nabla f_i(\theta_t^s) - \nabla f_i(\theta^{s-1})) + \nabla g(\theta_t^s)]. \qquad (5.22)$$

Furthermore, visual tracking is a non-convex problem and the backward propagation without non-convex optimization may severely suffer local optima and cause tracking failure. Therefore, we conduct non-convex optimization with stochastic process to alleviate premature convergence to local optima and the details are shown in Algorithm 7.

Same as supervised learning, non-convex optimized SVRG backward propagation is also introduced into RL training process to alleviate convergence to local optima. Inspired by [51], the period gradient will adjust current calculated gradient and reducing model updating variance. When solving policy gradient problem, Algorithm 7 will be subjected to bias and a correction term $\omega$ is employed during gradient projection. This term $\omega$ is calculated by $\omega(\tau \mid \theta_t, \hat{\theta}) = \frac{p(\tau|\hat{\theta})}{p(\tau|\theta_t)}$ with importance weighting from policy snapshot. The details are shown in Algorithm 8.

---

**Algorithm 7:** Non-convex SVRG optimization for supervised learning training process

---

**Input:** a set of images $D_N$, number of epochs $S$, epoch size $m$, step size $\eta$, initial parameter $\boldsymbol{\theta}_m^0 := \hat{\boldsymbol{\theta}}^0$.

1: **for** $s = 0$ to $S - 1$ **do**
2:      $\boldsymbol{\theta}_0^{s+1} := \hat{\boldsymbol{\theta}}^s = \hat{\boldsymbol{\theta}}_m^s$
3:      $\hat{\mu} = \nabla f(\hat{\boldsymbol{\theta}}^s)$
4:      **for** $t = 0$ to $m - 1$ **do**
5:          $x_B \sim U(D_N)$
6:          $v_t^{s+1} = \hat{\mu} + \frac{1}{B} \sum_{i=0}^{B-1} (\nabla f_i(x \mid \boldsymbol{\theta}_t^{s+1}) - \nabla f_i(x \mid \hat{\boldsymbol{\theta}}^s))$
7:          $\boldsymbol{\theta}_{t+1}^{s+1} = \boldsymbol{\theta}_t^{s+1} + \eta v_t^{s+1}$
8:      **end for**
9: **end for**
10: **return** $\boldsymbol{\theta}_t^s$ for a random pair $(s, t) \in \{[0, S - 1] \times [0, m - 1]\}$

---

As far as we know, it is the first time introducing SVRG backward propagation into object tracking. In particular, we innovatively designed non-convex optimized SVRG backward propagation for both supervised learning and RL visual tracking process, as shown in Fig. 5.26.

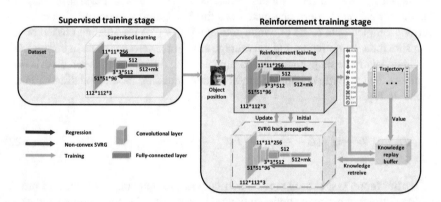

**Fig. 5.26** The pre-training process of our proposed method AEVRNet. The pipeline starts from image database, and then, goes through supervised learning training, and next, experiences fine-tuning with RL. The forward propagation is conducted based on regression loss function. The backward propagation is accomplished with non-convex SVRG method

---

**Algorithm 8:** Non-convex SVRG optimization for policy gradient tracking training process

---

**Input:** a set of images $D_N$, number of epochs $S$, epoch size $m$, step size $\eta$, batch size $N$, mini-batch size $B$, gradient estimator $g$, initial parameter $\boldsymbol{\theta}_m^0 := \hat{\boldsymbol{\theta}}^0$.

1: **for** $s = 0$ to $S - 1$ **do**
2: $\quad \boldsymbol{\theta}_0^{s+1} := \hat{\boldsymbol{\theta}}^s = \hat{\boldsymbol{\theta}}_m^s$
3: $\quad$ Sample $N$ trajectories $\{\tau_i\}$
4: $\quad \hat{\mu} = \hat{\nabla}_N J(\hat{\boldsymbol{\theta}}^s)$
5: $\quad$ **for** $t = 0$ to $m - 1$ **do**
6: $\qquad$ Sample $B$ trajectories $\{\tau_i\}$ from $p(. \mid \hat{\boldsymbol{\theta}}_t^{s+1})$
7: $\qquad c_t^{s+1} = \frac{1}{B} \sum\limits_{i=0}^{B-1} (\nabla f(\tau_i \mid \boldsymbol{\theta}_t^{s+1}) -$
$\qquad \omega(\tau_i \mid \boldsymbol{\theta}_t^{s+1}, \hat{\boldsymbol{\theta}}^s) \nabla f(\tau_i \mid \hat{\boldsymbol{\theta}}^s))$
8: $\qquad v_t^{s+1} = \hat{\mu} + c_t^{s+1}$
9: $\qquad \boldsymbol{\theta}_{t+1}^{s+1} = \boldsymbol{\theta}_t^{s+1} + \eta v_t^{s+1}$
10: $\quad$ **end for**
11: **end for**
12: **return** $\boldsymbol{\theta}_t^s$ for a random pair $(s, t) \in \{[0, S-1] \times [0, m-1]\}$

---

## 5.5.2  ε-Greedy Strategy for Action Space Exploration

RL-based object tracking methods usually suffer the issue of local optima due to limited action space. When the model reaches a local optimum, the limited action space prevents the model from jumping out of the local optima and causes tracking failure. However, existing RL-based trackers try to solve this problem with a simple action space searching strategy, which may still be stuck in local optima. Hence, we propose an adaptive exploration method that employs Spatio-temporal information to optimize action space search and jump out of local optima to find a better solution. This method expends the action space with Spatio-temporal information and improves tracking performance by leveraging the balance between exploitation and exploration. The adaptive exploration strategy is formulated with policy gradient and combinatorial upper confidence bound (CUCB) [52] to expand the action space with spatio-temporal information and then the action obtained by adaptive exploration strategy will fine-tune deep neural network to jump out of local optima and find a better solution.

Our adaptive exploration combines exploration actions into a sequential exploitation process as shown in Fig. 5.25. Generally, stochasticity can expand the action search space, and can jump out of local optima. However, random perturbation may only jump out of local optima without finding a better solution, which increases the risk of target losing due to stochasticity perturbation. To address this issue, the prior spatio-temporal knowledge of action explorations is adopted to improve the quality of action space search. While introducing stochasticity makes the model can jump out of local optima, it can also constrain stochasticity through the spatio-temporal

---

**Algorithm 9:** Adaptive exploration for policy search

---

**Input:** arbitrarily initialized $\theta$, frame number $T$, current frame $t_0$, step size $\eta$, episode length $\tau$, update interval $k$, action set $A$, and episode set $\emptyset$.

1: **for** $t = t_0$ to $t_\tau$ by $k$ **do**
2:     **if** $t_0 > T$ **then**
3:        $a_t = \arg\max\limits_a Q_t(a)$
4:     **else**
5:        $a_t \sim CUCB[A_t]$
6:     **end if**
7: **end for**
8: **for** each episode $\{s_{t_0}, a_{t_0}, r_{t_1}, \ldots, s_{t_{\tau-1}}, a_{t_{\tau-1}}, r_{t_\tau}\} \sim \pi_\theta$ **do**
9:     **for** $t = t_0$ to $t_\tau$ **do**
10:        $\theta \leftarrow \theta + \eta \nabla_\theta \log \pi_\theta(s_t, a_t) Q^{\pi_\theta}(s_t, a_t)$
11:     **end for**
12: **end for**
13: **return** $\theta$

---

information of previous tracking results to ensure that the model can find a better solution. The optimization process is summarized in Algorithm 9.

The adaptive exploration is initialized with the default greedy method. When a new frame comes, the tracking model will calculate the score for each action. Given the score set, the action with maximum score will be chosen for optimal policy solution and bounding box projection (shown by Eq. 5.23). After initialization, the tracking process will be warmed up with several frames.

$$A_t = \arg\max_a Q_t(a) \tag{5.23}$$

where $Q_t(a)$ denotes the score of an action and $t$ is current frame number.

After warming up period, the action space search strategy will be replaced by CUCB, and $X$ means the warm up stage flag, which is shown as Eq. 5.24, and the designed CUCB is shown as Algorithm 10.

---

**Algorithm 10:** Combinatorial upper confidence bound

---

**Input:** action $i$, the total number of times action $i$ is played in action memory $M_i$, the mean of all outcomes scores of action $i$ observed in action memory $\hat{\mu}_i$.

1: For each action $i$, play $A_i$ and update variables $M_i$ and $\hat{\mu}_i$.
2: **while** true **do**
3:     $t \leftarrow t + 1$
4:     For each action $i$, set $\bar{\mu}_i = \hat{\mu}_i + \sqrt{\frac{3 \ln t}{2 M_i}}$
5:     $A_t = \arg\max\limits_a (Q_t(a_i) + \bar{\mu}_i)$
6:     Play action $A_t$ and update all $M_i$ and $\hat{\mu}_i$
7: **end while**

---

During the tracking process, the frame number $T$ is an important hyper parameter and is used to control the beginning of adaptive exploration. When $T$ is not smaller than a specific number, adaptive exploration system is activated. Otherwise, default greedy-search is activated. We test $T$ with different values on OTB-2013, which is detailed in experiment section, and the tracker performs better when $T=30$. The tracking failure score is used for cost function and optimal hyper parameter is achieved after several iterations.

$$A_t = \begin{cases} CUCB(a), & \text{if } T \geq 30 \\ \arg\max_a Q_t(a), & \text{otherwise.} \end{cases} \tag{5.24}$$

### 5.5.3   Regression Based Reward Function

The first stage is to pre-train tracker with supervised learning. The existing RL-based trackers, like ADNet or ACT, formulate action-reward function with classification setting. This formulation requires the location of the target to be converted into a marked training sample. However, spatial continuous information is lost during this conversion. To preserve this important information, we propose a regression training method for forward propagation to train the proposed model. We innovatively designed a regression based action-reward loss function for RL-based tracker. Instead of discrete binary reward function, a continuous function is developed to map IoU with reward, as shown in Eq. 5.26, and then, reward contains more detailed information of target.

The training dataset consists of image patches $\{p_j\}$, action labels $\{o_j^{(act)}\}$, and regression value $\{r_j^{(reg)}\}$. During training, the action dynamics vector $\{d_j\}$ is set to zero. The ground truth patch position, size and image, are provided. A sample patch $p_j$ is generated around the ground truth with Gaussian importance sampling and its corresponding action $o_j^{(act)}$ is assigned by,

$$o_j^{(act)} = \arg\max_a IoU(\bar{f}(p_j, a), G) \tag{5.25}$$

where $\bar{f}(p_j, a)$ denotes the patch moved from $p_j$ by action $a$ and $G$ means the ground truth patch. In order to make full use of the object information, the corresponding action regression value $r_j^{(reg)}$ to $p_j$ is innovatively defined as follows,

$$r_j^{(reg)} = IoU(p_j, G). \tag{5.26}$$

Different from the existing RL-based trackers using the classification method to train the tracker, which is not sensitive to the target deformation and leading to target loss. We propose and define a regression based action-reward loss function, which is more sensitive to aspects of the target states, e.g., the width and height of the target and reduce tracking failure due to target deformation.

A training batch consists of the randomly training samples $\{(p_j, o_j^{act}, r_j^{reg})\}_{j=1}^m$. The proposed network ($W_{SL}$) minimizes the multi-task loss function by non-convex optimized SVRG. The multi-task loss function is defined by minimizing the following loss $L_{SL}$,

$$L_{SL} = \frac{1}{m} \sum_{j=1}^m L_1(o_j^{(act)}, \hat{o}_j^{(act)}) + \frac{1}{m} \sum_{j=1}^m L_2(r_j^{(reg)}, \hat{r}_j^{(reg)}) \qquad (5.27)$$

where $m$ denotes the size of patch batch, $L_1$ denotes the cross-entropy loss, $L_2$ denotes the squared loss, and $\hat{o}_j^{(act)}$ and $\hat{r}_j^{(reg)}$ denote the predicted action and corresponding action regression IoU value, respectively.

The second stage is to pre-train tracker with RL. The network is fine-tuned by policy gradient approach and uses the same parameters of $W_{SL}$ as the initial network parameters. The tracking process has sequential states $s_{t,l}$, the corresponding action $a_{t,l}$ and the reward function $r(s_{t,l})$. $a_{t,l}$ is defined by,

$$a_{t,l} = \arg\max_a p(a|s_{t,l}; W_{RL}) \qquad (5.28)$$

where $p(a|s_{t,l})$ means conditional action probability and the reward function $r(s_{t,l})$ is as follows,

$$r(s_{t,l}) = \begin{cases} 1, & if \quad IoU(b_T, G) > 0.7 \\ -1, & otherwise \end{cases} \qquad (5.29)$$

where $b_T$ means the terminal patch position.

Same as other trackers, we use the first six layers of the network to training. The parameters $(w_1, \ldots, w_6)$ in $W_{RL}$ are updated by non-convex optimized SVRG to maximize the tracking scores as follows,

$$\Delta W_{RL} \propto \sum_{l=1}^L \sum_{t=1}^{T_l} \frac{\delta \log p(a_{t,l}|s_{t,l}; W_{RL})}{\delta W_{RL}} Z_{t,l} \qquad (5.30)$$

where $Z_{t,l} = r(s_{t,l})$ means the reward, $L$ is training frames, and $T_l$ is steps during the $l - th$ frame.

### 5.5.4 Framework and Procedure

After the first and second pre-training stages, the pre-trained tracker will track and be updated during online visual tracking for the third stage. For each frame, our method chooses the position with maximum score given by adaptive exploration strategy as the estimated object position. Then tracker will be updated with samples by Gaussian sampling around the predicted location. We only fine-tune the fc layers $w_4, \ldots, w_7$ instead of all layers, for the fc layers would have the video specific knowledge while convolutional layers would have generic tracking information. The tracking framework is shown in Algorithm 11.

---

**Algorithm 11:** Framework of our proposed method for online tracking

---

**Input:** initial object position $P_0$.
**Output:** estimated object position $P_t = (x_t, y_t, w_t, h_t)$;
1: Generate samples in the first frame to update all fully-connected layers in network;
2: **repeat**
3:   Extract features from $(x_{t-1}, y_{t-1})$;
4:   **repeat**
5:     Compute scores for 11 actions and choose action with adaptive policy exploration;
6:     Move the bounding box with the selected action and add the selected into the action sequence;
7:     Extract features from the bounding box;
8:   **until** The selected action is a stop action;
9:   Compute score of the bounding box;
10:  **if** score<-0.5 **then**
11:    Use re-detection module to find a position with a higher score around the bounding box;
12:  **end if**
13:  Update the network by the predicted position $P_t = (x_t, y_t, w_t, h_t)$ and action sequence;
14: **until** End of video sequence;

---

## 5.5.5 Experimental Results and Discussions

Our proposed AEVRNet is implemented in MATLAB 2017b with MatConvNet toolbox, which runs on a PC with a 4-cores 4.2 GHz Intel 7700k CPU and an NVIDIA 2080Ti GPU with 11G memory. During off-line training, we used ALOV300 as the training dataset, which is same with ADNet. At the stage of online tracking, only fully-connected layers are fine-tuned. Concerning sample generation, 150 negative and 200 positive samples are generated from the first frame. After the first frame, 15 negative and 20 positive samples are generated when tracking is successful, and 512 samples are generated in the re-detection model when tracking fails. In terms of adaptive exploration, $T$ is set to 30, which means the CUCB strategy starts at the 31st frame.

**Evaluation on OTB** Our proposed method is evaluated with OTB dataset which is a popular benchmark dataset. The tracking performance is also compared of another 9 state-of-the-art trackers, including ECO, MDNet, ADNet, DeepSRDCF, CF2, HDT, SRDCFdecon, MEEM, and KCF. These methods can be classified into

CF based methods, deep learning based methods, and RL-based methods. The experiments are carefully designed based on the same protocols and the same parameters.

The selected OTB datasets include OTB-50, OTB-100, and OTB-2013. Figure 5.27 shows the tracking results of all trackers under one-pass evaluation(OPE) on these datasets. The performance of our proposed method is shown in Fig. 5.27, exhibits high precision and success rate, and the state-of-the-art trackers are beaten. The precision of our tracker is 88.6%, 90.9%, and 95.3% on OTB-50, OTB-100, and OTB-2013, receptively. It is shown that the proposed method yields higher precision than ECO and MDNet in OTB-2013. In terms of OTB-50 and OTB-100, the precision of our method is comparable with ECO and MDNet. In addition, compared with ADNet, our method runs significantly faster and accurately.

**Quantitative Evaluation** OTB divides the video sequences into 11 attributes (e.g., fast motion, occlusion, scale variation and illumination variation) and those attributes in OTB benchmark are also analyzed. Figure 5.28 lists the results from all trackers based on eight main video attributes of OPE in OTB-100. Our method AEVRNet still better performs on illumination variation, low resolution, and background clutter. Compared with ADNet, AEVRNet outperforms in scale variation, in-plane rotation by 2.6% and 4.1%, receptively. As our method use regression instead of classification method, which is more sensitive to aspects of the target states, e.g., the width and height of the target. Compared with ECO and MDNet, our proposed AEVRNet uses adaptive exploration to enhance larger action space and have chance to jump out of local optima. Meanwhile, the performance of the proposed method in fast motion slightly lower than some state-of-the-art trackers. This result is relevant to feature extraction of deep neural network. Since we use less layers in our constructed network to accelerate tracking, which lower the discriminative ability of feature.

**Qualitative Evaluation** Figure 5.29 shows tracking results of several top tracking methods: MDNet, KCF, ADNet, CF2, together with our proposed method on seven challenging sequences. CF2 performs well in rotation and deformation conditions (*Diving* and *MotorRolling*), but misses the object when fast motion and large-scale variation occur (*Biker*, *Bird2*, and *Matrix*), because it has no re-detection module. KCF uses only HOG feature to represent the object, as a result, it can track fast but cannot fully describe the object, which leads to object missing. It also fails to track the object when heavy occlusion and background clutter occur (*Bird2*, *MotorRolling*, and *Matrix*). ADNet based on RL performs well in rotation and scale variation conditions (*Diving*, *Walking2*, and *MotorRolling*). However, for fast motion and heavy occlusion conditions, it may miss the object (*Biker*, *Matrix*, and *Bird2*) as its greedy strategy may not jump out of local optima. MDNet performs well in rotation, fast motion and occlusion conditions (*MotorRolling*, *Bird2*, and *Diving*) with multi-domain theory, but when background clutter and large-scale variation situations occur (*Biker*, *CarScale*, and *Matrix*), its performance is less

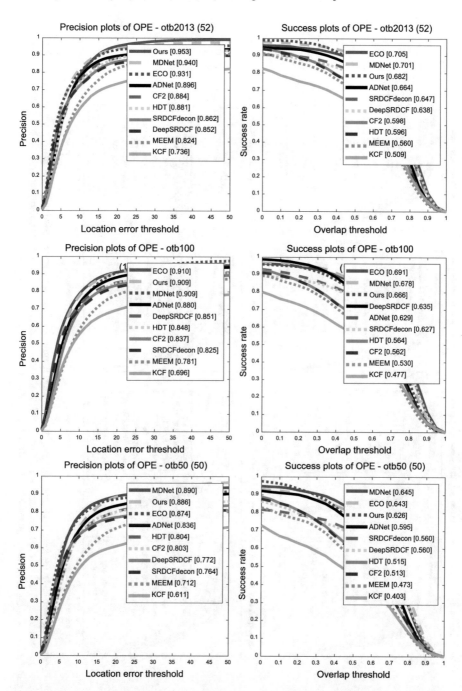

**Fig. 5.27** Precision and success plots using the one-pass evaluation(OPE) over OTB-100, OTB-50, and OTB-2013 benchmarks. The legend of location error precision contains threshold score at 20 pixels for each tracker. The performance of AEVRNet is favorably against the state-of-the-art trackers

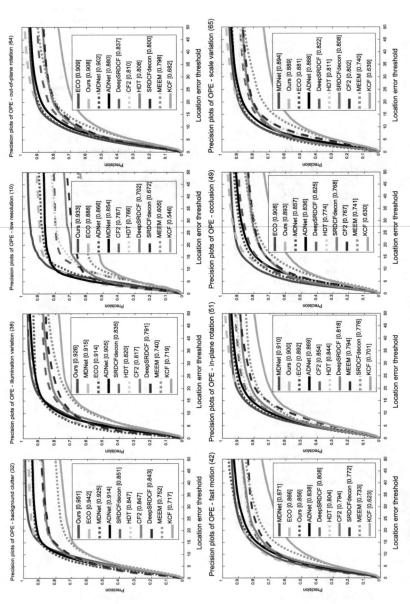

**Fig. 5.28** Precision plots over eight tracking challenges of background clutter, illumination variation, scale variation, out-of-plane rotation, low resolution, occlusion, in-plane rotation, and fast motion. The scores are obtained with a threshold of 20 pixels for each tracker. Our proposed method AEVRNet performs favorably against the state-of-the-art trackers on these eight challenging attributes

**Fig. 5.29** Qualitative evaluation of our method, MDNet, KCF, ADNet, and CF2 on seven challenging sequences, *Biker, Bird2, CarScale, Diving, Walking, MotorRolling*, and *Matrix*

accurate because the tracker cannot follow the object well under fast appearance changes.

The proposed method performs well for two main reasons. Firstly, the regression training method is more coupled to tracking problem. Different from the existing RL-based trackers using the classification method to train the tracker, which is not sensitive to the target deformation and leading to target loss. Our proposed method pays more attention to learn the target states, e.g., the width and height of the target. The results show that our proposed AEVRNet performs well in deformations, rotations, and scale variation conditions (*CarScale, Walking2, Diving*, and *MotorRolling*). Especially for *CarScale*, our method adjusts almost perfectly to the scale variation of the ground truth, much better than other methods. Secondly, the adaptive exploration method can enable the proposed tracker to expand the action space and jump out of local optima. Furthermore, the results show that our method performs well in occlusion, background clutter, and fast motion (*Biker, Bird2*, and *Matrix*). It performs better than ADNet in all aforementioned seven challenging sequences.

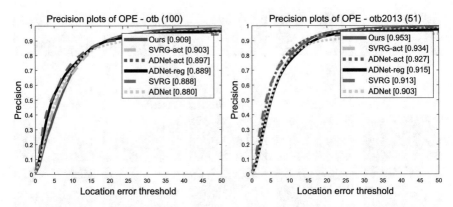

**Fig. 5.30** Precision plots of different component of our proposed AEVRNet on OTB-100 and OTB-2013, which shows the improvement of each component of AEVRNet

**Ablation Analysis** To further analyze the contribution of each component in the model, we evaluate different variations of our method on OTB-100 and OTB-2013. Here, ADNet is used as a baseline. "SVRG" denotes the case that the proposed method is only with non-SVRG to do offline training and online tracking. "SVRG-Action" denotes the case that the proposed method used both non-SVRG and adaptive exploration for object tracking. "Ours" denotes the case that the proposed method used all of non-SVRG, adaptive exploration and regression based training.

The performances of all those variations is shown in Fig. 5.30. It is obtained that every single component can improve performance of the proposed method. For adaptive exploration combines temporal and spatial relations to solve the problem of RL-based visual tracking during online tracking, which can enhance exploration and successfully escapes local optima. The results show that it gains 2.9 and 5.0% improvements on two datasets. The regression reduces information loss and improves the robustness of the proposed method.

**Non-convex Optimized Stochastic Variance Reduced Gradient Backward Propagation** We analyze the impact of the proposed non-convex SVRG and trains 120 epochs, which is the same as the ADnet settings. From Table 5.8 we can find that non-convex optimized SVRG (non-SVRG) can converge fast with a lower loss on training and test datasets by 0.017 and 0.027, respectively. Because non-SVRG uses the optimal solution of the current epoch of training to initial the

**Table 5.8** The training loss and test error of pre-training for our proposed method. The non-SVRG method performs better than SGD method, which convergences faster with lower loss and error

| Epoch | | 1 | 30 | 60 | 90 | 120 |
|---|---|---|---|---|---|---|
| Training loss | SGD | 1.753 | 1.578 | 1.569 | 1.562 | 1.558 |
| | non-SVRG | 1.748 | 1.559 | 1.550 | 1.545 | 1.541 |
| Test error | SGD | 0.543 | 0.436 | 0.429 | 0.423 | 0.419 |
| | non-SVRG | 0.540 | 0.407 | 0.401 | 0.396 | 0.392 |

parameter of next epoch. Compared with SGD using the random parameter as the initial parameter, the model training can be accelerated. The online tracking results are shown in Fig. 5.30, the non-SVRG can improve the baseline's precision by 0.8 and 0.6% on two datasets. The It is mainly benefited from the robust model trained by non-SVRG can convergence faster with lower loss and improves the accuracy of the proposed method.

**Adaptive Exploration Based on CUCB**   We also analyze the impact of the hyper parameter $T$ in adaptive exploration. The hyper parameter $T$ is tested on OTB-2013 by different values from 0 to 50, and the proposed method performs better when $T$ is 30 as shown in Table 5.9. That means when the tracker is robust to the object, the adaptive exploration can enhance the exploration ability better. Adaptive exploration combines temporal and spatial information to solve action space selection, which can enhance exploration and successfully escapes local optima. The results show that it gains 2.3 and 3.1% improvements on two datasets shown in Fig. 5.30. As shown in Fig. 5.31, the adaptive exploration can effectively alleviate target loss in occlusion and blur.

**Table 5.9**  The average precision results on OTB-2013 dataset. The best scores are highlighted in bold. Our proposed method performs best when T=30

|           | T=0   | T=10  | T=20  | T=30      | T=40  | T=50  |
|-----------|-------|-------|-------|-----------|-------|-------|
| Precision | 0.920 | 0.926 | 0.935 | **0.953** | 0.941 | 0.933 |

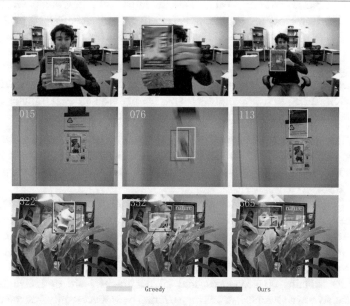

**Fig. 5.31**  Performance evaluation using greedy and our adaptive exploration method in *ClifBar*, *BlurOwl* and *Tiger2* video sequences. Yellow and red bounding boxes denote greedy and our adaptive exploration, respectively

**Fig. 5.32** Performance evaluation using regression and classification methods in *Biker*, *Bird1* and *Girl2* video sequences. Red and green bounding boxes denote regression and classification methods, respectively

**Regression Based Training** We analyze the impact of regression based training. Figure 5.32 shows that the regression is sensitive to different aspects of the target states, e.g., the width and height of the target, which can help tracker predict position more accurate around the tracking object. Figure 5.30 shows that it gains 0.6 and 2.0% improvements on two datasets, since our model is sensitive to aspects of the target states, e.g., the width and height of the target and reduces interference information passed to tracker. Furthermore, the regression based training can also reduce re-detection frequency by 30% on average when blur occurs.

**Evaluation on Other Datasets** In order to further analyze the effectiveness of the proposed method, we choose four famous datasets. For each dataset, we select representative state-of-the-art tracking methods to compare with the proposed method, respectively.

NFS [53] includes 100 sequences with 240 fps high frame rate. Most of those sequences are more than 5000 frames, we evaluate on the 240 fps version of the dataset with 8 state-of-the-art trackers. Table 5.10 shows success plot over 100 videos, reporting AUC scores in the legend. The proposed method significantly outperforms CCOT with a relative improvement of 4%.

VOT16 contains 60 sequences, and all the trackers are evaluated by EAO (Expected Average Overlap), A (average overlap over successfully tracked frames), and R (failure rate). Our method performs better than CREST, which is RL-based. Because CREST has limit exploration ability, which shows that adaptive exploration for action space is crucial for robust tracking. SiamFC and SA-Siam ignore background information resulting in low robustness. The results in Table 5.11

**Table 5.10** Comparison with the state-of-the-art trackers on the NFS dataset. The results are presented in terms of AUC. The best scores are highlighted in bold

| | Ours | ECO | BACF [53] | ADNet | CCOT | FCNT [54] | DeepSRDCF | DaSiamRPN [42] | MDNet | MKCF [55] |
|---|---|---|---|---|---|---|---|---|---|---|
| AUC | **0.532** | 0.470 | 0.342 | 0.461 | 0.492 | 0.393 | 0.353 | 0.395 | 0.425 | 0.499 |

**Table 5.11** Comparison with the state-of-the-art trackers on the VOT 2016 dataset. The results are presented in terms of expected average overlap (EAO), accuracy value (A), and robustness value (R). The best scores are highlighted in bold

|       | Ours  | CCOT  | MDNet | SiamFC | CREST | DSLT [56] | SA-Siam [57] | VITAL | Meta-Tracker [58] | RTINet [59] |
|-------|-------|-------|-------|--------|-------|-----------|--------------|-------|-------------------|-------------|
| EAO   | **0.342** | 0.331 | 0.257 | 0.277  | 0.283 | 0.332     | 0.291        | 0.323 | 0.314             | 0.298       |
| R     | **0.8**   | 0.85  | 1.204 | 1.382  | 1.083 | 0.93      | 1.08         | 0.97  | 0.934             | 1.07        |
| A     | **0.52**  | 0.523 | 0.533 | 0.549  | 0.524 | 0.525     | 0.54         | 0.531 | 0.521             | 0.57        |

**Table 5.12** Precision and success plots of our proposed method on TC128 and UAV123. The best scores are highlighted in bold

|        |      | Ours     | ECO      | ADNet | SiamRPN | DRL-IS |
|--------|------|----------|----------|-------|---------|--------|
| TC128  | Suc. | 0.603    | **0.605** | 0.574 | 0.578   | 0.599  |
|        | Pre. | 0.821    | **0.825** | 0.783 | 0.799   | 0.818  |
| UAV123 | Suc. | **0.531** | 0.525    | 0.502 | 0.527   | –      |
|        | Pre. | **0.752** | 0.741    | 0.716 | 0.748   | –      |

shows the efficiency of the proposed method with an EAO score of 0.342 and achieves the best A and R scores among those trackers.

TC128 contains 128 challenging colorful tracking sequences. The same evaluation setting is developed for TC128 and other datasets. 4 state-of-the-art methods (ECO, ADNet, DRL-IS, and SiamRPN) are compared with our proposed method. ECO achieves a precision rate of 85.2% and our proposed method outperforms ADNet with an improvement of 3.8% shown in Table 5.12.

UAV123 includes 123 tracking sequences and most of them are vehicles, which is harder to track while facing occlusion and out of view problems. Our method is compared with 12 state-of-the art methods, the obtained precision is shown in Table 5.12. Our tracker outperforms ECO and achieves precision of 75.2%.

## 5.6   Summary

In this section, four target tracking algorithms based on Siamese networks, generative adversarial networks and reinforcement learning are introduced to improve the tracking accuracy and speed of target tracking algorithms in complex environments using the latest deep learning techniques.

The first and second methods optimise the Siamese network in terms of attention mechanisms and frequency domain features respectively, to improve the tracking algorithm's ability to discriminate between targets. The first method designs an attention mechanism based on the Siamese network, and weights the features in the Siamese network according to their importance to the current tracking target by the Shake-Shake method, so that the weighted depth features have better discriminative ability. The second method reduces the feature size and speeds up the computation by compressing the low frequency domain features through weighting and optimising the frequency domain features. At the same time, in order to improve the model update efficiency, a joint model update strategy based on target classification and target scale change is designed, which can effectively reduce the model online update overhead and improve the online tracking speed of the tracking algorithm.

The third approach is based on adversarial generative network technology, which adds an adversarial learning generation strategy to the original algorithm, allowing for the generation of samples that better match the target, enhancing the robustness of the model in tracking in complex environments. In order to improve the feature discrimination capability, Precise ROI Pooling layer is used to process the depth features and obtain more location information between targets, further improving the accuracy of the algorithm in target tracking in complex environments.

The fourth method is a policy-based deep reinforcement learning target tracker. Considering that the model will be trapped in the local optimal solution and cannot jump out of it, this method adopts the $\epsilon$-Greedy approach to select the sub-optimal solution with a certain probability, giving the model the ability to jump out of the local optimal solution and obtain a more robust tracking effect. To further accelerate the model training speed, the gradient calculation is carried out using non-convex optimized variance reduced backward, which improves the computational speed while maintaining the accuracy of the model. Finally, a regression-based payoff function is designed to further improve the tracking accuracy in target-scale prediction.

# References

1. Ilchae, J., Jeany, S., Mooyeol, B., Bohyung, H.: Real-Time MDNet. In: European Conference on Computer Vision, pp. 83–98 (2018)
2. Chen, B., Wang, D., Li, P., Wang, S., Lu, H.: Real-time'Actor-Critic'Tracking. In: European Conference on Computer Vision, pp. 318–334 (2018)
3. Yun, S., Choi, J., Yoo, Y., Yun, K., Young Choi, J.: Action-decision networks for visual tracking with deep reinforcement learning. In: IEEE Conference on Computer Vision and Pattern Recognition, pp. 2711–2720 (2017)
4. Li, B., Wu, W., Wang, Q., Zhang, F., Xing, J., Yan, J.: Siamrpn++: Evolution of siamese visual tracking with very deep networks. In: Proceedings of the IEEE/CVF Conference on Computer Vision and Pattern Recognition, pp. 4282–4291 (2019)
5. Fan, H., Ling, H.: Siamese cascaded region proposal networks for real-time visual tracking. In: IEEE Conference on Computer Vision and Pattern Recognition, pp. 7952–7961 (2019)
6. Jie, H., Li, S., Gang, S.: Squeeze-and-excitation networks. In: IEEE Conference on Computer Vision and Pattern Recognition, pp. 7132–714 (2018)
7. Xavier, G.: Shake-shake regularization (2017). Preprint arXiv:1705.07485
8. Bertinetto, L., Valmadre, J., Henriques, J.F., Vedaldi, A., Torr, P.H.S.: Fully-convolutional siamese networks for object tracking. In: European Conference on Computer Vision, pp. 850–865 (2016)
9. Liang, H.H., Xin, Z., Kai, Q.H.: GOT-10k: A large high-diversity benchmark for generic object tracking in the wild. In: IEEE Transactions on Pattern Analysis and Machine Intelligence (2019)
10. Yi, W., Jongwoo, L., Ming-Hsuan, Y.: Online object tracking: a benchmark. In: IEEE Conference on Computer Vision and Pattern Recognition, pp. 2411–2418 (2013)
11. Yi, W., Jongwoo, L., Ming-Hsuan, Y.: Object tracking benchmark. In: IEEE Transactions on Pattern Analysis and Machine Intelligence, pp. 1834–1838 (2015)
12. Li, Y., Zhu, J.: A scale adaptive kernel correlation filter tracker with feature integration. In: European Conference on Computer Vision Workshops, pp. 254–265 (2014)
13. Martin, D., Gustav, H., Fahad, S.K., Michael, F.: Accurate scale estimation for robust visual tracking. In: British Machine Vision Conference, pp. 1–5 (2014)

14. Sam, H., Stuart, G., Amir, S., Vibhav, V., MingMing, C., Stephen, L.H., Philip, H.S.T.: Struck: Structured output tracking with kernels. In: IEEE Transactions on Pattern Analysis and Machine Intelligence, pp. 2096–2109 (2016)

15. Zdenek, K., Jiri, M., Krystian, M.: P-N learning: Bootstrapping binary classifiers by structural constraints. In: IEEE Computer Society Conference on Computer Vision and Pattern Recognition, pp. 49–56 (2010)

16. Henriques, J.F., Caseiro, R., Martins, P., Batista, J.: Exploiting the circulant structure of tracking-by-detection with Kernels. In: European Conference on Computer Vision, pp. 702–715 (2012)

17. Xu, J., Hu, C.L, Ming-Hsuan, Y.: Visual tracking via adaptive structural local sparse appearance model. In: IEEE Conference on Computer Vision and Pattern Recognition, pp. 1822–1829 (2012)

18. Helmut, G., Michael, G., Horst, B.: Real-time tracking via on-line boosting. In: British Machine Vision Conference, pp. 1–6 (2012)

19. David, A.R., Jongwoo, L., Ruei-Sung, L., Ming-Hsuan, Y.: Incremental learning for robust visual tracking. In: British Machine Vision Conference, pp. 125–141 (2008)

20. Matej, K., Ales, L., Jiri, M., Michael, F., Roman, P., Luka, C.Z., Tomas, V., Gustav, H., Alan, L., Abdelrahman, E., Gustavo. F.: The sixth visual object tracking vot2018 challenge results. In: European Conference on Computer Vision (2018)

21. Deng, J., Dong, W., Socher, R., Li, L.J., Li, K., Fei-Fei, L.: Imagenet: A large-scale hierarchical image database. In: IEEE Conference on Computer Vision and Pattern Recognition, pp. 248–255 (2009)

22. Zhang, H., Cisse, M., Dauphin, Y.N., Lopez-Paz, D.: mixup: Beyond empirical risk minimization. In: International Conference on Learning Representations (2018)

23. Chen, Y., Fan, H., Xu, B., Yan, Z., Kalantidis, Y., Rohrbach, M., Feng, J.: Drop an octave: Reducing spatial redundancy in convolutional neural networks with octave convolution. In: IEEE International Conference on Computer Vision, pp. 3435–3444 (2019)

24. He, Y., Zhang, X., Savvides, M., Kitani, K.: Softer-nms: Rethinking bounding box regression for accurate object detection (2018). Preprint arXiv:1809.08545

25. Danelljan, M., Bhat, G., Khan, F.S., Felsberg, M.: Atom: Accurate tracking by overlap maximization. In: IEEE Conference on Computer Vision and Pattern Recognition, pp. 4660–4669 (2019)

26. Danelljan, M., Hager, G., Shahbaz Khan, F., Felsberg, M.: Convolutional features for correlation filter based visual tracking. In: IEEE International Conference on Computer Vision Workshops, pp. 58–66 (2015)

27. Ma, C., Huang, J.B., Yang, X., Yang, M.H.: Hierarchical convolutional features for visual tracking. In: IEEE International Conference on Computer Vision, pp. 3074–3082 (2015)

28. Qi, Y., Zhang, S., Qin, L., Yao, H., Huang, Q., Lim, J., Yang, M.H.: Hedged deep tracking. In: IEEE Conference on Computer Vision and Pattern Recognition, pp. 4303–4311 (2016)

29. Henriques, J.F., Caseiro, R., Martins, P., Batista, J.: High-speed tracking with kernelized correlation filters. IEEE Trans. Pattern Anal. Mach. Intell. **37**(3), 583–596 (2014)

30. Sun, C., Wang, D., Lu, H., Yang, M.H.: Correlation tracking via joint discrimination and reliability learning. In: IEEE Conference on Computer Vision and Pattern Recognition, pp. 489–497 (2018)

31. Xu, T., Feng, Z.H., Wu, X.J., Kittler, J.: Joint group feature selection and discriminative filter learning for robust visual object tracking. In: IEEE International Conference on Computer Vision, pp. 7950–7960 (2019)

32. Wang, N., Song, Y., Ma, C., Zhou, W., Liu, W., Li, H.: Unsupervised deep tracking. In: IEEE Conference on Computer Vision and Pattern Recognition, pp. 1308–1317 (2019)

33. Li, P., Chen, B., Ouyang, W., Wang, D., Yang, X., Lu, H.: Gradnet: Gradient-guided network for visual object tracking. In: IEEE International Conference on Computer Vision, pp. 6162–6171 (2019)

34. Wang, G., Luo, C., Xiong, Z., Zeng, W.: Spm-tracker: Series-parallel matching for real-time visual object tracking. In: IEEE Conference on Computer Vision and Pattern Recognition, pp. 3643–3652 (2019)
35. Nam, H., Han, B.: Learning multi-domain convolutional neural networks for visual tracking. In: IEEE Conference on Computer Vision and Pattern Recognition, pp. 4293–4302 (2016)
36. Song, Y.B., Ma, C., Wu, X.H., Gong, L.J., Bao, L.C., Zuo, W.M., Shen, C.H., Rynson, W.H.L., Ming-Hsuan, Y.: VITAL: Visual tracking via adversarial learning. In: IEEE Conference on Computer Vision and Pattern Recognition, pp. 8990–8999 (2018)
37. Ian, G., Jean, P., Mehdi, M., Bing, X.: Generative adversarial nets. In: Advances Inneural Information Processing Systems, pp. 2672–2680 (2014)
38. Ross,G.: Fast R-CNN. In: IEEE International Conference on Computer Vision, pp. 1440–1448 (2015)
39. Jiang, B., Luo, R., Mao, J., Xiao, T., Jiang, Y.: Acquisition of Localization confidence for accurate object detection. In: European Conference on Computer Vision, pp. 816–832 (2018)
40. Russakovsky, O., Deng, J., Su, H., Krause, J., Satheesh, S., Ma, S., Huang, Z., Karpathy, A., Khosla, A., Bernstein, M., Berg, A., Fei-Fei, L.: ImageNet large scale visual recognition challenge. Int. J. Comput. Vision, 115(3), 211–252 (2015)
41. Martin, D., Goutam, B., Fahad, S.K., Michael, F.: Eco: Efficient convolution operators for tracking. In: IEEE Conference on Computer Vision and Pattern Recognition, pp. 6931–6939 (2017)
42. Zhu, Z.,Wang, Q., Li, B., Wu, W., Yan, J., Hu, W.: Distractor-aware siamese networks for visual object tracking. In: European Conference on Computer Vision, pp. 101–117 (2018)
43. Martin, D., Gustav, H., Fahad, K., Michael, F.: Adaptive decontamination of the training set: A unified formulation for discriminative visual tracking. In: IEEE Conference on Computer Vision and Pattern Recognition. (2016)
44. Wang, Q., Gao, J., Xing, J., Zhang, M., Hu, W.: DCFNet: Discriminant Correlation Filters Network for Visual Tracking (2017). Preprint arXiv:1704.04057
45. Ran, T., Efstratios, G., Arnold, W.M.S.: Siamese instance search for tracking. In: IEEE Conference on Computer Vision and Pattern Recognition (2016)
46. Luca, B., Jack, V., Stuart, G., Ondrej, M., Philip, H.S.T.: Staple: Complementary learners for real-time tracking. In: IEEE Conference on Computer Vision and Pattern Recognition (2016)
47. Wang, N.,Yeung, D.Y.: Learning a deep compact image representation for visual tracking. In: International Conference on Neural Information Processing Systems, pp. 809–817 (2013)
48. Ning, J.F., Yang, J.M., Jiang, S.J., Zhang. L., Ming-Hsuan, Y.: Object tracking via dual linear structured svm and explicit feature map. In: IEEE Conference on Computer Vision and Pattern Recognition, pp. 4266–4274 (2016)
49. Smeulders, A.W., Chu, D.M., Cucchiara, R., Calderara, S., Dehghan, A., Shah, M.: Visual tracking: An experimental survey. IEEE Trans. Pattern Analy. Mach. Intell. 36(7), 1442–1468 (2013)
50. Johnson, R., Zhang, T.: Accelerating stochastic gradient descent using predictive variance reduction. In: Neural Information Processing Systems pp. 315–323 (2013)
51. Papini, M., Binaghi, D., Canonaco, G., Pirotta, M., Restelli, M.: Stochastic variance-reduced policy gradient. In: International Conference on Machine Learning, pp. 4026–4035 (2018)
52. Kveton, B., Wen, Z., Ashkan, A., Szepesvari, C.: Tight regret bounds for stochastic combinatorial semi-bandits. In: Artificial Intelligence and Statistics, pp. 535–543 (2015)
53. Kiani Galoogahi, H., Fagg, A., Lucey, S.: Learning background-aware correlation filters for visual tracking. In: IEEE International Conference on Computer Vision, pp. 1135–1143 (2017)
54. Wang, L., Ouyang, W., Wang, X., Lu, H.: Visual tracking with fully convolutional networks. In: IEEE International Conference on Computer Vision, pp. 3119–3127 (2017)
55. Tang, M., Yu, B., Zhang, F., Wang, J.: High-speed tracking with multi-kernel correlation filters. In: IEEE Conference on Computer Vision and Pattern Recognition, pp. 4874–4883 (2018)
56. Lu, X., Ma, C., Ni, B., Yang, X., Reid, I., Yang, M.H.: Deep regression tracking with shrinkage loss. In: European Conference on Computer Vision, pp. 353–369 (2018)

57. He, A., Luo, C., Tian, X., Zeng, W.: A twofold siamese network for real-time object tracking. In: IEEE Conference on Computer Vision and Pattern Recognition, pp. 4834–4843 (2018)
58. Park, E., Berg, A.C.: Meta-tracker: Fast and robust online adaptation for visual object trackers. In: European Conference on Computer Vision, pp. 569–585 (2018)
59. Yao, Y., Wu, X., Zhang, L., Shan, S., Zuo, W.: Joint representation and truncated inference learning for correlation filter based tracking. In: European Conference on Computer Vision, pp. 552–567 (2018)

# Chapter 6
# Summary and Future Work

In this chapter, we mainly summarized our work introduced in this book in three aspects: correlation filter based tracking methods, correlation filter trackers with deep features; deep learning based tracking methods. All these methods are also consistent with the evolution of the tracking algorithms, which show a complete improvement process of tracking algorithms. Besides, we also introduce some ideas and thoughts in the future work in the aspects of appearance model construction and update, which hope to promote the development of tracking algorithms.

## 6.1  Summary

Visual object tracking is an important part of video analysis, which is widely used in real life. With the diversification of tracking object and the complexity of video sequences. The research of visual object tracking algorithms also faces great challenges. In order to express the basic concepts and evolution of visual object tracking, this book mainly focuses on the improvements of correlation filter based trackers, correlation filters with deep feature for visual object tracking and deep learning based visual object trackers three aspects and proposed a series of improvement strategies. Some innovations and achievements are made in the following aspects.

For correlation filter based visual object tracking: we mainly proposed three improved correlation filter based trackers. All those three trackers are designed to take advantage of the fast tracking speed of KCF tracker to further improve the tracking performance when handling the challenges such as occlusion and scale variation, etc. Context aware based global background information and adaptive update model is used to enhance the use of background information and improve the tracking robustness. Two correlation filters are combined together to estimate the position and scale of the object to handle the scale variation challenge, and a

W. Xing et al., *Visual Object Tracking from Correlation Filter to Deep Learning*, https://doi.org/10.1007/978-981-16-6242-3_6

manually designed feature is used to construct the appearance model and improve the tracking robustness. Besides, in order to use the structure information of the object, the state of the object is viewed as the best combination of sub-object patches which is segmented by superpixel methods. The optimal problem can be solved through min-max criterion and GEP algorithm. Generally, context aware information and carefully designed features could improve the robustness of appearance model in correlation filter based trackers. Re-detection methods can also help correlation based trackers to cope with the occlusion challenge. Segmenting the object into several patches and using the multiple KCF trackers to use structure information of the object could improve the performance when handling scale variation challenge, but loss some tracking speed. It is a trade-off between tracking accuracy and speed.

For correlation filter with deep feature for visual object tracking: we mainly introduce three correlation filter methods using deep feature. By combining the deep feature with the correlation filter, the tracking method's ability to express the tracking target can be effectively improved. The experiment results show that through mechanisms such as long-term and short-term memory, content perception, and feature channel attention, more discriminative features can be obtained for distinguishing targets and backgrounds. At the same time, the target relocation method based on depth features can also effectively reduce the target loss caused by challenges such as occlusion. In summary, the correlation filter method based on depth features can obtain features with stronger discriminative ability, and can improve the tracking ability of tracking methods on targets in complex environments such as occlusion and rapid movement.

For deep learning based visual object tracking: we introduce four visual object tracking methods based on deep learning. The first method introduces attention shake layer into Siamese network, which helps to improve the expression power of Siamese network without increasing the depth of the network. The second method combines high-frequency features with compressed low-frequency features to reduce the network calculations and improve the method's ability to identify targets. The third method uses an improved adversarial learning strategy and precise ROI pooling to improve the performance of tracking method. The last method introduces $\epsilon$-Greedy strategy for action space exploration, which can help the method jump out of the local optimal solution and obtain better tracking results.

## 6.2  Future Work

Visual object tracking is a fundamental research in the field of video analysis. There are many kinds of visual object tracking algorithms. In some benchmarks and datasets, some trackers could achieve excellent results. However, it is difficult to design a general tracking algorithm because of the diversity and uncertainty of the objects and the tracking challenges in video sequences. Therefore, visual object tracking is still an open and challenging problem. There are still many contents and directions that is worth to study. The work proposed in this book can improve the tracking effect in some aspects and make some progress, but there are still some problems difficult to solve and need further study. Therefore, we will further focus on how to build more robust object appearance model, how to better monitor the tracking process, and how to adaptively update the appearance model and how to build a more general visual object tracking algorithm. In view of some shortcomings in the existing work, we show some possible further work below.

In the construction of appearance model: the performance of visual object tracking is directly affected by appearance model. Recently, some deep learning based tracking algorithms could track object by violent searching window without updating and motion model. These kind of trackers can also obtain comparable tracking results. However, the feature of these deep learning based appearance models is extracted and fused from the object image in single frame, which ignores the temporal relationship. This also leads to the weak performance of tracking algorithm in dealing with deformation and occlusion. Since frames in the video are continuous, object model of each frame in the video will also show a certain temporal relationship. Thus, integrating the temporal relationship of the objects into the construction of appearance model could further improve the representation ability of the appearance model and the tracking performance. Therefore, how to introduce the temporal information into the appearance model and how to construct the appearance model based on multi-scale time and multi-scale space will be the future work direction.

In the tracking process monitoring and model updating: in order to ensure real-time performance of tracking algorithms, most of the tracking algorithms are designed as an open-loop system. In the open-loop system, it is difficult to monitor the process of the object tracking, and adjust the parameters of the tracking algorithm to update the object appearance model. For the deep learning based trackers, there are many parameters to be trained and the update time is long. In order to ensure the real-time performance of tracking algorithms, deep learning based tracking algorithms often ignore the model directly, which makes the performance of deep learning based trackers weak in dealing with the challenges and deformation. Thus, how to monitor the tracking process while ensuring the tracking speed and how to guide the update of appearance model, and how to update the deep learning based tracking algorithm while ensuring the real-time tracking is the next research.

Printed in the United States
by Baker & Taylor Publisher Services